LIST OF ILLUSTRATIONS

Feeding a koala bear in Australia, 1970
Walkabout in New Zealand during the 1977 visit
Dazzling her hosts in Mexico, 1975
A tea ceremony during the visit to Japan, 1975
Carried on a golden chariot in Borneo, 1972

Between pages 144 and 145

At the start of the tour of the Gulf, Saudi Arabia, 1979
With Prince Andrew in Zambia in 1979
The 'bloody' visit to Morocco, 1980
Royal walkabout in Switzerland, 1980
With tough security in Tunisia, 1980
Visiting Pope John Paul in the Vatican, 1980
Revisiting the place where she became Queen, 1983
In San Diego, USA, 1983
With President Reagan, in San Francisco, 1983
At Qutub Shahi Tombs in India, 1983
Receiving gifts in Jordan, 1984
Welcomed by President Li Xiannian in China, 1986
The Queen with a family in Hong Kong, 1986

Picture Credits
BBC Hulton Picture Library: 2, 3, 4, 5, 8, 11, 12, 15, 18, 19, 20, 21, 22, 23, 24, 26, 27, 28, 30, 32, 33; Camera Press: 34, 35, 37, 41; Ministry of Defence: 16, 17; The Photo Source: 6, 7, 9, 10, 13, 14, 29, 31, 36, 39; The Press Association: 1; Syndication International: 25, 38, 40, 42, 43.

THE QUEEN'S TRAVELS

THE QUEEN'S TRAVELS

Graham & Heather Fisher

ROBERT HALE · LONDON

Robert Hale Limited
Clerkenwell House
Clerkenwell Green
London EC1R 0HT

British Library Cataloguing in Publication Data

Fisher, Graham
 The Queen's travels.
 1. Elizabeth II, *Queen of Great Britain*
 —Journeys   2. Visits of state—
 History—20th century
 I. Title   II. Fisher, Heather
 941.085'092'4   DA590

ISBN 0–7090–3157–2

Photoset in Linotron Bembo by
Rowland Phototypesetting Limited
Printed in Great Britain by
St Edmundsbury Press Limited, Bury St Edmunds, Suffolk
and bound by WBC Bookbinders Limited

CONTENTS

AUTHORS' NOTE

After reigning only a few years the Queen had already travelled further – and faster – than any monarch in history. Today, when she has been thirty-five years on the throne (as this book is being published), the logbook of her travels covers many times the circumference of the Earth. This book is the story of those travels. Regretfully, we have been obliged to limit it to her Commonwealth tours and state visits. To have included her travels throughout the length and breadth of Britain would have necessitated several volumes. If we have tended also to focus on the highlights of her overseas travels – the exciting, the amusing, the potentially hazardous – we make no apology. To have done otherwise would have been to turn this book into a mere catalogue, and catalogues, while they have their uses, are apt to make for dull reading. The story of the Queen's travels is the reverse of dull.

G. and H.F.

1 THE QUEEN'S TRAVELS

A royal page, summoned on one occasion to the large bay-windowed sitting-room at Buckingham Palace which also does duty as the Queen's study, was doubtless surprised to witness the unusual spectacle of the Queen, the Duke of Edinburgh and a senior official of the Queen's Household crawling about the floor on hands and knees after the manner of small children. However, this was not some childish game, nor some ancient form of royal ceremonial, but part of the advance planning for yet another royal tour.

Focus of attention was a large-scale map spread out on the floor because it was too big to be adequately accommodated on the flat top of the Queen's desk (even had she been minded to clear the desk of the many other workaday items which normally crowd its surface). It happened, on this occasion, to be a map of Canada, but it might equally well have been one of Australia or India, the islands of the Caribbean or those of the Pacific, of Brazil or – more recently – China, or indeed of some eighty other countries the Queen has visited during her years of monarchy.

Quite early in her reign she was already the most travelled monarch in Britain's history. By 1982 it was calculated that she had already travelled thirty times the circumference of the globe. Today she is arguably the world's most travelled woman. A pity no one has kept an exact record. Still, as Prince Philip has said, 'You count it in people seen rather than miles travelled.'

Some indication of the extent of the Queen's travels may be gauged from the many highlights of her life which have come and gone outside Britain. She celebrated her coming-of-age in South Africa. She was in France when a spell of dizziness revealed her first pregnancy and, years later, toured Canada while pregnant with Prince Andrew. She was in Malta on her second wedding

11

anniversary, in Ghana on her fourteenth, and arrived back from Brazil in 1968 as midnight ushered in her twentieth anniversary. She was in Kenya when word reached her that her father had died and she was now Queen Elizabeth II. She celebrated her twenty-fifth birthday in Italy, her twenty-eighth in Colombo and her forty-fourth in Australia. She was in Indonesia when she learned of the horrifying attempt to kidnap Princess Anne.

Statistics for individual royal tours are impressive. The round-the-world Commonwealth tour of 1953–4 lasted six months and totalled nearly 44,000 miles. There was an 18,000-mile tour of Canada in 1959, a 15,000-mile trek round India, Pakistan and Nepal two years later, 18,000 miles in South America in 1968, 25,000 miles to the Far East and back in 1972 and 15,000 miles of Africa in 1979. Visits to Commonwealth countries during the Queen's Silver Jubilee year of 1977 logged up another 56,000 miles.

She has travelled by plane and train, by royal yacht and royal barge, in a gondola (in Venice, of course), in native canoes and, on one occasion at least, in a rubber dinghy. In the air she has experienced everything from the bumpiness of an unpressurized Dakota (on the first leg of her journey from Kenya to London as Queen) to the supersonic smoothness of Concorde. In Portugal she once travelled in an old-fashioned open charabanc, while in Quebec it was a bullet-proof limousine and in Brunei she was hauled around in a gilded chariot towed by forty-eight hefty men.

She has experienced almost every type of climatic condition, from the deep-freeze of the Canadian Arctic to the steam-heat of Sri Lanka. She has seen deserts, rain forests, tundra; looked down on Everest from the air; taken her own photographs of the world's most famous picture-postcard views. But scenery is far from being her principal objective. 'I want to see the people, not the scenery,' she has said more than once when considering some fresh tour itinerary.

She has *seen* the people – of all colours and creeds, from kings and presidents to tribesmen in diminutive loincloths fashioned from bark, and native women in grass skirts and bras made from coconut shells. She has talked with Commonwealth leaders at length and to ordinary folk in the crowd during the course of the walkabouts which have become a common feature of royal tours in more recent years. And the people have seen her, turning out sometimes in their hundreds of thousands for no more than a passing glimpse, hailing her as everything from 'Liz-a-beth' to 'Betty Windsor'.

She has collected enough travel souvenirs to stock a museum, spears and boomerangs, fans and flywhisks, whales' teeth and sharks' teeth, cloaks made of kiwi feathers, shawls made of animal skins and drinking-cups fashioned from animal horn. There have also been more valuable gifts: mink coats, diamond and ruby necklaces, gold wrought into numerous forms.

She has been serenaded with singing and chanting, steel drums and war drums, cowhorn trumpets, nose flutes and conch shells.

She has eaten from plates of gold and plates made from palm leaves. She has eaten, once or twice, with chopsticks and even with her fingers. Menus at times have included such local delicacies as sharkfin soup, barbecued turtle, smoked reindeer, raw fish, roast bat, roast rat and coral worms. In the Seychelles she sampled *coco-de-mer*, the supposedly forbidden fruit of the Garden of Eden. Drinks have ranged all the way from the fiery *kava* of Fiji to the frothy green tea of Japan.

Royal tours and state visits are not a twentieth-century invention, of course. They can be found far back in history. Henry II, who was Duke of Normandy, Count of Anjou, Count of Touraine and Duke of Aquitaine as well as a twelfth-century King of England, spent twenty-one of his thirty-five years on the throne away from England, riding from one part of his empire to another. Henry VIII, visiting France in the sixteenth century, staged the magnificent encampment on the Field of the Cloth of Gold with a view to impressing Europe with his majesty and wealth. Coming down to more recent times, however, Queen Victoria saw little or nothing of the vast far-flung empire over which she reigned, though she did despatch her eldest son, the future King Edward VII, to India and Canada. Later, as King, he also paid state visits to France, Sweden, Norway and Italy. His 1860 visit to Canada also took in the United States. He was unmarried at the time; the world's most eligible bachelor. As a result, so many hopeful young ladies and ambitious parents crowded into a New York ball given in his honour that the floor collapsed under the strain, and dancing had to be delayed some three hours while it was repaired.

The Queen's grandfather, George V, journeyed to India for his installation as King-Emperor at the spectacular Delhi Durbar. That apart, royal travel overseas was largely deputed to his sons. Twenty years in the Navy before becoming King had left him with little enthusiasm for foreign parts. 'Abroad is awful', he was wont to say. Thus it was that the Queen's father, in the year following her birth, was despatched to Australia to open the first Parliament to be held in the new federal capital of Canberra. Her mother, then Duchess of York, went with him, but they did not take their eight-month-old daughter along as their grandson and his wife would one day take Prince William. Even had they wished to do so, Grandpapa George V would doubtless have vetoed the idea.

The Duke of Windsor, in the days when he was a boyish-looking Prince of Wales, was his father's main emissary. Throughout the 1920s and into the 1930s he was despatched here, there and everywhere on an almost non-stop succession of show-the-flag tours: to Canada and the United States, Australia and New Zealand, India and Japan, South Africa and South America. He disliked 'abroad' as much as his father did, though for a different reason. His overseas trips also meant enforced separations from his longtime mistress, Freda Dudley Ward.

King George V gave all his sons blunt advice on how to cope with the strain of a royal tour. 'Never refuse an invitation to take the weight off your feet,' he told them, 'and never miss an opportunity to relieve yourself. You never know when the chance will come again.' Years of experience have seen his granddaughter devise her own travel tricks. At every opportunity the Queen nudges off her shoes and sits with her feet up. On whistle-stop tours by train this sometimes results in her dashing shoe-less to the observation platform to wave at some small group of people as the train chugs past them. Prince Philip goes one better. Given the chance, he will stretch out full-length and take a quick cat-nap.

Given the hours of walking and standing around the Queen is required to do in the course of a royal tour, comfortable shoes are important. So while she invariably takes several dozen pairs of shoes with her, she usually ends up wearing the few pairs she finds easiest on her feet. Sharp-eyed journalistic eyes in Australia on one occasion resulted in the headline: 'Does The Queen Have Only One Pair of Shoes?'

Waving to people from the window of her car or train compartment, the Queen eases the strain by perching her elbow on an arm-rest. Similarly, she always wears gloves to protect her hand from scratches during handshake sessions. To reduce the risk of having her fingers crushed, she employs a special, rather limp handshake, a technique developed by her father after a session of some three hundred handshakes had left him with a badly swollen hand. Even this technique has been known to fail. There was an occasion, again in Australia, when a man gripped the Queen's hand so heartily and pumped it so enthusiastically that she was still feeling the after-effect two days later. Royal males, of course, can hardly follow the Queen's practice of wearing gloves – neither does the Princess of Wales, come to that – and Prince Charles once ended a walkabout in Chicago with a scratched and bleeding hand caused by the beringed fingers of a score of American matrons. Charles has devised his own remedy for 'handshake hand' – a good long soak in cold water.

That the Queen has travelled so far and so often owes much to the development of air transport. Without it, her travels would have been fewer, with many of her tours taking considerably longer. Her parents, for instance, took nearly two months to reach Australia on the battleship *Renown* in the 1920s. It was the Duke of Windsor who first pointed the way ahead. Both he and the Queen's father learned to fly in the 1920s. From then on, Windsor in particular made growing use of air travel. In 1930, in a succession of short hops, he flew from Malakal to Khartoum in the Sudan, from there to Cairo, then to Marseilles, to Lyons, to Le Bourget, finishing with a hop across the Channel to a touchdown at Windsor. The following year, during his tour of South America, he made a number of similar flights, short by present-day standards but signposting the future of royal travel.

The Queen's father, when he visited the United States in 1939 and South Africa eight years later, made the journeys each way by sea. But in between, to visit British troops overseas during World War II, he took to the air, sometimes in extremely hazardous conditions. Years later, in 1958, his widow, the Queen Mother, would fly right round the world.

The present Duke of Kent's father was the first of the Royal Family to fly the Atlantic. That was in 1941, flying in a war-time Liberator to visit aircrews training in Canada. The following year, sadly, he was killed on his way to visit British troops in Iceland

15

when his Sunderland flying boat lost its way in thick cloud and ploughed into a Scottish hillside.

The Queen had her first experience of flying during her 1947 visit to South Africa with her parents. She was married later that year and, as a young wife, flew several times to Malta when Prince Philip was based there as a naval officer. It was in Philip's company that she first flew the Atlantic in 1951. Their flight to Canada, in that pre-jet era, took a tedious seventeen hours.

Since then, flying has become almost a way of life for her. If monarchs were still known by nicknames, as in the days of Edward the Confessor and Richard the Lionheart, she would surely go down in history as Elizabeth the Airborne. She jets annually to different parts of the world with more ease and in greater comfort than the first Elizabeth progressed around England on horseback and by coach. On balance, she would rather fly somewhere than go by sea, though helicopters still make her nervous. Even so, she will use a chopper if she has to and did so on her Silver Jubilee visit to Northern Ireland, when the risk of helicopter travel was deemed less hazardous than the dangers posed by the IRA on the ground.

Why does the Queen take it upon herself to travel so far and so often? Certainly not for pleasure. Royal tours are no holiday jaunts. 'Showing the flag' is the continuing reason for many of the Queen's tours; bolstering Britain's prestige and creating goodwill, making friends and influencing people on Britain's behalf. With the bolstering of prestige goes the boosting of exports. While the Queen is ashore in foreign parts, the royal yacht *Britannia* has several times served as the venue for a get-together between British businessmen and those of the country the Queen is visiting. How far royal visits serve to boost British exports long-term it is, of course, impossible to know. What is known is that a visit to a particular country has not infrequently been followed by an increase in exports to that country over the next few years. There are one or two specific instances of the royal touch at work. The Queen's visit to Morocco helped Britain land a big engineering contract. A speech by Prince Philip in Chile undoubtedly swung Britain's way a nuclear reactor contract which France was also after. And the establishment of a Japanese-financed factory in Wales was almost certainly due to a suggestion Prince Charles made during his visit to Expo 70 in Osaka.

But 'showing the flag' in the old royal tradition, though with contemporary motives, applies to only some of the Queen's tours. Others are undertaken for a different reason: the Queen's love for the Commonwealth. She is proud to be Head of the Common- wealth, a title devised rather hurriedly at the time of her accession, principally as a sop to India and Pakistan, desirous of maintaining their links with Britain and Britain's monarch while not recogniz- ing that monarch as their own Queen. The Commonwealth at that time consisted of only seven countries in addition to Britain, three of which would later withdraw. Despite those withdrawals, the Commonwealth has since grown out of all recognition as former British colonies and dependencies have achieved independence until (as this book is written) it has a membership of forty-nine countries, including Britain. They range from such vast land-masses as Australia and Canada to tiny dots on the map like Nauru and Tuvalu, an estimated total of 1.25 billion people spread over more than 10 million square miles of the Earth's surface.

Elizabeth II is Queen of some Commonwealth countries – Queen of Canada, Queen of Australia and of New Zealand, 'Misis Kwin' to the pidgin-speaking inhabitants of Papua New Guinea – just as she is Queen of the United Kingdom. Other countries of the Commonwealth, a few with their own monarchs, most because they prefer to be republics, while not accepting her as Queen, still look upon her as Head of the Commonwealth. It is a role she finds both rewarding and fulfilling, a concept which touches something emotional deep within her. She was visibly moved to tears when a former Australian Prime Minister welcomed her to that country with the words: 'We are all yours – all parties, all creeds.' By the same token, she is said to have reacted with indignation when news reached her that American marines had invaded the tiny Common- wealth island of Grenada. Over her years of monarchy, moved by a desire to maintain and reinforce the sometimes fragile links which bind the Commonwealth, she has visited every country, some of them many times, though, with new countries gaining indepen- dence all the time, it took her more than thirty years to get round them all.

The Commonwealth has been dear to her heart since she first pledged herself to serve it 'my whole life'. That was in 1947, when she celebrated her twenty-first birthday in South Africa, ironically a country which is no longer a member of the Commonwealth. The concept of Commonwealth took on a yet deeper meaning for her when Pierre Trudeau, then Prime Minister of Canada, invited her to open the 1973 Commonwealth Conference in Ottawa, the first time she had played a part in any Commonwealth Conference outside Britain. Other Commonwealth countries were quick to follow Trudeau's lead, and she has been to every Commonwealth Conference since.

Though the Queen takes no part in the actual debates, the role she plays is nevertheless an important one. Between debates she has off-the-record talks with the leader of each country, in a native bungalow in Zambia, in a cabin aboard *Britannia* in Australia, according each leader, regardless of the size of their country, as nearly as possible the same amount of time, on average twenty to thirty minutes each. As with the question of Britain's export trade, it is impossible to know how much such talks have achieved in maintaining links, cementing relationships, smoothing out differences, but the Queen's influence has undoubtedly been considerable. She is rather like 'a grandmother toning down family squabbles', it has been said.

Where overseas travel is concerned, the Queen draws a distinction between her roles as Queen of the United Kingdom and Head of the Commonwealth. As Queen, she visits only those foreign countries of which the British Government of the day approves. It was for this reason that it was not until twenty years after VE Day that she first visited West Germany; even longer before she went to Japan. She has never been to South Africa since becoming Queen. Nor yet to Soviet Russia, though she has visited that other colossus of the Communist world, China. As Queen of the United Kingdom, she is constitutionally obliged to accept the 'advice' of the prime minister of the day, but this does not necessarily apply, she feels, to her role as Head of the Commonwealth. It was this which caused her to jib against Margaret Thatcher's initial advice that it was perhaps unwise for her to attend the 1979 Commonwealth Conference in Lusaka at a time when there was fighting on the Zambia–Zimbabwe border. It was her 'firm intention' to go, she is said to have told Mrs Thatcher. In the event, Queen and Prime Minister both went.

The Queen regards her worldwide travels as part and parcel of royal duty and has never permitted threats, implied or actual, to keep her from going where she has planned to go. Examples spring readily to mind. A theatre visit in New Zealand despite a threat that a bomb had been hidden in the building. Her insistence, against the pleas of at least one of her personal staff, on driving through Quebec at a time when there was rioting in the streets. Similar insistence on visiting Northern Ireland in her Silver Jubilee year in the face of IRA threats. In Japan, when, fearing a possible assassination attempt, she was supplied with a closed and bullet-proof car, she asked that it be changed to an open vehicle so that people could see her better. She declined to cancel a visit to Jordan simply because a bomb had exploded in Amman, the country's capital.

Her attitude to the possibility of personal danger was never better illustrated than when another Prime Minister, Harold Macmillan,★ suggested that perhaps she should not go to Ghana at a time when there were threats against the life of Kwame Nkrumah, the country's president. 'Danger,' the Queen is said to have replied, 'is part of the job.'

Of necessity the Queen's travels have to be planned a long way ahead, with each fresh invitation having to take its turn in an engagements diary booked solid for the next eighteen months and with occasional entries pencilled in even further ahead. It was some eight years after she was first invited to visit China before she actually went there in 1986. Delicate negotiations between Britain and China over the future of Hong Kong had to be concluded first.

The job of planning a state visit or royal tour takes a long time. A state visit, though it lasts only a few days, will take anything up to six months to plan and arrange, while a Commonwealth tour of any magnitude can take as long as eighteen months or even longer. Arrangements start with a proposed itinerary and the large-scale map around which the Queen and Prince Philip crawled at the beginning of this chapter. After that the map goes down to one of the offices on the ground floor of Buckingham Palace where it is displayed on a wall for ease of reference. Coloured pins are stuck in to indicate the cities and towns the Queen will visit, while coloured tapes show the form of transport to be used between one place and another, red for air travel, blue for sea, green for train and black for car.

★ Later Earl of Stockton

A document is sent to the country which will be hosting the Queen setting out the ground rules and royal preferences. It says, for instance, that engagements should preferably not start before ten in the morning, though they sometimes do. This preference for a seemingly late start is not so that the Queen can lie in bed but so that she can first deal with the state papers from London which pursue her wherever she goes. Flowers presented to her, the host country is informed, should be in simple bunches rather than wired bouquets. This is so that they can be later placed in vases either for the Queen's personal pleasure or to brighten the hospitals to which she often passes them on. Personal gifts, it is emphasized, should preferably be small and of sentimental value, though this guideline was certainly not observed by the Arab rulers of the Gulf States who heaped her with gold and precious stones. Presentation of gifts should be notified in advance and, to avoid any possibility of subsequent exploitation, the products of commercial firms are not acceptable as gifts. It was this prohibition which saw the Queen declining to accept a number of unexpected gifts which were thrust at her during a visit to the Chicago Trade Fair. Nor are animals welcomed as royal gifts, though this is another guideline which has been disregarded at times.

It was ignored at Windsor, Ontario, during one of the royal tours of Canada, though the gift on that occasion was not actually a personal one. It took the form of an Appaloosa pony, a breed with which the Queen at that time – 1959 – was apparently unfamiliar. 'I've never seen one like this before,' she reportedly said. She was asked to pass the pony on to some deserving child in Britain. As a result, children in that other Windsor, in Berkshire, were invited to write to the local mayor saying why they felt they most deserved the pony. It went to a ten-year-old girl who wrote that she would share the pony with her brother and sister and also 'let it help out at local fêtes for good causes'.

To arrange that particular tour of Canada, which lasted forty-five days during which the Queen travelled 16,000 miles, the Canadian Government called in a retired Chief of Staff and gave him the services of four assistants, eight secretaries, and seventy-four other people grouped into seven committees. Advance planning included laying on jet aircraft to ensure that state papers from Britain and elsewhere would reach the Queen promptly, and other aircraft to leapfrog three cars across the country to be ready for the royal party at each fresh stopping-place. Schedules and maps were shuttled continuously between Ottawa, the Canadian High Commissioner's office in London, the Commonwealth Office and Buckingham Palace. Canada's Under-Secretary for External Affairs flew twice to London for on-the-spot consultation. A party of royal aides flew the other way to undertake a dummy run, as they do in advance of every royal tour.

This advance guard includes an Assistant Private Secretary who travels the route the Queen will take and times the arrangements; a senior royal detective who consults with local police chiefs on matters of security; and usually the Master of the Household or his deputy, who advises those who will be hosting the Queen on her likes and dislikes. He tells them that she does not like laying foundation stones (though she has done so upon occasion) but is happy enough to plant a tree. Prince Philip is equally happy to read the lesson at church services. Luncheons should not last more than an hour; evening functions up to 1¾ hours, including speeches. Shellfish should not be included in menus because of health risk. Favourite dishes include saddle of lamb, Dover sole, chicken Maryland. A single glass of wine, white or red, will suffice the Queen at mealtimes. Prince Philip's drink preferences are champagne, lager and gin-and-tonic.

It is inevitable that members of the advance party should be bombarded with questions, some practical, some odd in the extreme. An elderly chieftain in Botswana wanted to know if it was Queen Victoria he would be entertaining. No, he was told, her great-great-granddaughter. Those who ask what sort of pillows the Queen prefers are told not to worry; she will be bringing her own.

Preparations for a royal tour necessarily add to the Queen's work-load. While the actual itinerary is a matter for the host country, she is consulted at each step of the way and not infrequently comes up with an improving suggestion. Ahead of one visit to the United States, for instance, she noticed that it would be after dark when her aircraft touched down in Washington. 'Can't we land in daylight?' she asked. 'People will be disappointed if they can't see me.' The point was a good one, and her itinerary was revised accordingly.

Itineraries for royal tours are meticulous in the extreme. The itinerary for one Canadian tour ran to 400 printed pages. Studying the proposed itinerary for another tour, of Australia, the Queen noticed that lunch on a certain day was due to end at two o'clock and that she was scheduled to leave the building at 2.17. The oddness of the timing caused her to ask why it couldn't be 2.15. It had been rehearsed and timed, she was told, and this had shown that it would take her exactly seventeen minutes to walk to the door, shake a number of hands and get into her car. 'What happens if I spill my coffee?' she joked. 'Will there be time for a second cup?'

Before each royal tour she does her 'homework'. Notes on the places she will be visiting and the people she will be meeting are sent to her in advance. Prince Philip, who has frequently been already to the same places on his own individual tours, sometimes helps out with background information. If the country is new to both of them, as China was in 1986, the Queen will read books about it or talk to someone who knows that country well.

There is also the question of injections. Over her years of travel the Queen has been immunized against poliomyelitis, smallpox, typhoid, yellow fever and Asian flu.

Getting together a suitable wardrobe is a time-consuming task. Suggested outfits are first sketched for the Queen's consideration. Each sketch is a miniature full-length portrait enabling her to judge how she will look in the proposed outfit. Swatches of the materials to be used are attached. As the work of making the wardrobe progresses, fittings can take up hours of the Queen's time. Making the gown she will wear for the traditional state banquet is a particularly lengthy task. With its elaborate hand-worked embroidery, it can take months to make and involve hours of fittings.

Royal fashion designers take the Queen's known, if unwritten, rules into account. Because quick changes are often involved, clothes must be easy to slip on and off. Materials must suit the climatic conditions of the country she is visiting. There must be nothing that will snag or catch if she inspects a factory or building site. Colours must be such that she is clearly distinguishable at a distance. Shoes should give her an inch or so of additional height (again so that she can be clearly seen). Hats should not shade her face.

The extent of the task can be gauged from her state visit to Japan. Comparatively short though the visit was, a mere six days, her wardrobe included thirty dresses, forty pairs of shoes, fifteen hats and four tiaras. As well as clothes, there are cosmetics to be considered and decided on. Different climatic conditions, different lighting conditions, in particular the bright lights required if an opening of Parliament in some Commonwealth country, say, is to be televised, require different shades of powder and lipstick.

No matter how important a particular overseas visit, the Queen never takes the Crown Jewels with her. These belong to the state rather than the monarch and are not permitted to leave the country, as her grandfather, King George V, found out at the time of the Delhi Durbar. Prohibited from taking either the Crown of St Edward or the Imperial State Crown with him to India, he had a new one specially made for the ceremony in Delhi, at a cost of £60,000. However, the Queen does take with her a selection from her personal jewel collection, tiaras and necklaces, brooches and bracelets, rings and ear-rings, each in its individual case, the cases packed in turn into a well-worn and inconspicuous suitcase.

There are the gifts she will distribute in the course of a tour to be selected and stockpiled, cufflinks and brooches, powder compacts and silver pencils, photographs to be signed, something for everyone from the maids who make her bed and the chauffeurs who drive her around to presidents and their ladies. If the selection of less important gifts can be delegated to others, the Queen always ensures that gifts for important people, such as heads of state, are carefully selected to suit and please the recipients.

The amount of luggage that has to be manhandled around in the course of a royal tour has to be seen to be believed. For a state visit to France the advance luggage alone weighed nearly a ton. Included in it was a dinner service handed down from Queen Victoria and a collection of gold Georgian cutlery which were used when the Queen hosted the French President at the British Embassy. A visit to Mexico saw six tons of luggage air-lifted ashore by helicopter, while the amount of luggage involved in the Queen's 1953–4 Commonwealth tour is said to have been double that – a staggering twelve tons of it.

When the Queen travels anywhere, it is not simply a matter of tossing a few outfits into a couple of suitcases. To keep dresses, suits and coats uncreased, she has two large travelling wardrobes which are mounted on wheels to make for ease of handling. Items such as lingerie, gloves and handkerchiefs are neatly layered into a portable chest-of-drawers which she had specially designed and made for her worldwide travels. There is a further selection of leather trunks, including a specially large one for the state gown, along with hat-boxes and shoe-boxes. A crocodile-skin dressing-case holds a thirty-two piece set of silver-gilt brushes, combs, hand mirror and cosmetic containers. Umbrellas and sunshades fit neatly into a long, slender case of unusual design which the Queen inherited from her grandmother, Queen Mary.

Substantial though it is, the Queen's own luggage represents only a fraction of what goes along on a royal tour. There is also the luggage of all those who go with her, a considerable entourage. For her state visit to Japan, for instance, she was accompanied not only by Prince Philip but also by the Lord Privy Seal, two ladies-in-waiting, an equerry, her private secretary, an assistant private secretary, a Press secretary, the Captain of the Queen's Flight, a physician, a hairdresser, two detectives, two dressers to supervise her wardrobe, six footmen, two maids and four clerks. And that was a modest total. There were nearly twice that number for her 1981 tour of Australia. Prince Philip, more modestly, is usually content to take only an equerry, a detective and a valet.

Taking along her own pillows helps to ensure the Queen of a sound night's sleep. She also takes a hot-water bottle in case the nights turn chilly, her own bathsalts and pine-scented soap, a cannister of her favourite tea. Crates and crates of bottled water go with her as a precaution against upsets through drinking the local water, and a supply of barley sugar as an antidote to travel sickness (though she seldom suffers from that these days). Royal travel stores have also been known to include shortbread, fruitcake, jam, mint sauce and even sausages, though it is possible that some of these items were for members of her retinue rather than for the Queen herself.

What she does take along for herself is a batch of crossword puzzles. Tackling them in odd moments between engagements, she has found, helps her to relax. She also takes a supply of her scarlet-crested notepaper and includes some which is black-edged against the possibility that a letter of condolence may have to be written while she is on her travels. Interestingly, she does not take a passport; she does not have one. As United Kingdom passports are issued in her name, it would be absurd to issue one to herself. But Prince Philip, like any other of his wife's subjects, has a passport. Whether he ever has to show it is another matter.

Wherever she goes, the Queen also takes at least two cameras, one of them a movie camera. She is a keen photographer, even if her expertise does not quite match that of her husband, and one of the rare occasions when she was late for a public engagement was due to her enthusiasm in this direction. She was on her way to a tree-planting ceremony in Canada when she came across a magnificent maple, its leaves tinted with the reds and golds of the Canadian fall. Nothing would satisfy her but she must take a photograph of it, and the tree-planting ceremony in which she was due to participate suffered a slight delay while she went back for her camera.

The Queen's worldwide travels have given her a unique opportunity to indulge her passion for photography, and her collection of home movies and still photographs is perhaps the modern equivalent of the journals her great-great-grandmother, Queen Victoria, kept so assiduously. She has filmed Everest from the air and the spectacular ceremony of Buddha's Tooth in Sri Lanka. She has taken photographs of the Taj Mahal in India and the hot springs at Rotorua in New Zealand. At varying times she has filmed the apes on Gibraltar and elephants hauling logs in Thailand, a tiger hunt and a crocodile shoot, shark fishing and porpoises undulating in the wake of the royal yacht. She had been photographing wild game in Kenya the day word reached her that the King, her father, was dead and she was now Queen Elizabeth II.

2 TRAVELS AS A PRINCESS

To find the roots of the Queen's deep devotion to the Commonwealth you have to go back to her first-ever royal tour, that 1947 visit to South Africa during which she celebrated her twenty-first birthday (at that time the legal coming-of-age).

It was a tour she viewed with divided emotions. It was planned by her father, King George VI, partly as a royal thank-you to General Smuts for overturning General Hertzog's policy of neutrality and rallying to Britain's cause during World War II and partly because the King hoped that his personal presence might reinforce loyalty to the monarchy in a country where Boer nationalism was again making itself felt. Strong family man that he was, the King was eager for his wife and daughters to accompany him. Close to him as she was, his elder daughter could not disappoint him in this, but she was distressed at being separated from the man to whom she was already secretly engaged (though the formal announcement of her betrothal to Prince Philip would not be made until she was back in Britain).

It was 1 February when the Royal Family, all four of them, sailed for South Africa on *Vanguard*, the battleship the then Princess Elizabeth had herself launched during the war years. Behind them they left the hardest winter Britain had known for nearly seventy years, the bitter cold compounded by shortage of coal and continued food rationing. Royal father and daughter alike felt 'guilty at being away from it all', as the Princess said in one letter written during the course of the voyage. Rough weather in the Bay of Biscay may have done something to assuage her sense of guilt. She found it 'exhausting', she wrote, and was 'so miserable'.

The tour itself, lasting nine weeks and encompassing 6,000 miles, was to prove a resounding success on the surface, but among the

26

four principals there were stresses and tensions of which the public was unaware. There were times during the tour when the Princess pined for Philip. There were times when the Queen (as the Queen Mother then was) was concerned for her husband. It had been hoped that exposure to South African sunshine might benefit his always uncertain health, but such was the strain of the many public engagements he was required to undertake that, far from benefiting from the trip, he had lost seventeen pounds in weight by the time it was over. The youngest of the party, Princess Margaret, then in her seventeenth year, was often at a loose end. A royal ADC named Peter Townsend was assigned the task of keeping her amused, and the friendship which grew between them would create yet further stress for the Royal Family in the years ahead.

Despite missing Philip, there was much about the tour which Princess Elizabeth found exciting and enjoyable. She saw sights as varied as Table Mountain and the Victoria Falls. She was fitted out with a white dustcoat so that she could ride on the footplate of the luxurious White Train which had been specially built for the tour. It was during that stay in South Africa that she flew for the first time, a bush-hopping trip to a game reserve in the Orange Free State and a longer flight from Johannesburg to what was then Rhodesia.

Though mostly in the company of her parents, the Princess also carried out a few small engagements of her own, deftly fending off questions about Philip. In East London, for instance, she opened a new graving dock. Elsewhere she inspected a parade of Basuto Girl Guides. During the course of her inspection she spotted a small group sitting some small distance away in a bus. Her curiosity aroused, she asked about them. Told that they were lepers, she nevertheless insisted on going over to talk to them. So touched was she by their plight that, in the years ahead, she and Prince Philip would each 'adopt' a succession of small children afflicted with the disease.

It being the year of her twenty-first birthday, many of the gifts presented to her during the course of the tour were lavish in the extreme. The De Beer Corporation gave her two large blue-white diamonds, with a similar gift to Princess Margaret. In East London she was given a casket of diamonds, and another in Cape Town.

It was in Cape Town that she celebrated her twenty-first birthday. The public functions arranged for that day were very much in

27

her honour. In the morning there was a military parade at which she took the salute. In the afternoon a rally of youth organizations was staged for her benefit. In the evening she made the memorable broadcast which has echoed down the years.

The words of the broadcast were not actually her own. They were written for her by her father's private secretary, 'Tommy' (Sir Alan) Lascelles. But they came so close to her own thoughts and feelings that, reading them through before the broadcast, it is said that she was moved to tears.

Keystone of the broadcast was her personal pledge: 'I declare before you all that my whole life, whether it be long or short, shall be devoted to your service and the service of the great Imperial Commonwealth to which we all belong.'

The Commonwealth has changed much in the years since she made that pledge. It is certainly no longer 'Imperial'. Some people in more than one Commonwealth country now see it as an anachronism which has outlived its purpose. But the Queen's devotion to it remains as strong as ever. She still believes, as she said in that 1947 broadcast, that: 'If we all go forward together with an unwavering faith, a high courage and a quiet heart, we shall be able to make of this ancient Commonwealth which we all love so dearly an even grander thing – more free, more prosperous and a more powerful influence for good.'

Over a year passed after the South African tour before the Princess next travelled abroad. By that time she was not only married to Prince Philip but pregnant with her first child, though no one outside the family yet knew the newlyweds' secret. It was pregnancy which caused her to feel faint while laying a wreath at the Arc de Triomphe in Paris. Philip, who was with her, noticed her sway slightly and stepped forward quickly to steady her.

The Princess had gone to France primarily to open an exhibition depicting 'Eight Centuries of British Life in Paris'. A number of other engagements were added on, including an afternoon at the races (where Philip backed a winner) and a visit that evening to a smart Parisian nightspot. It happened to be a Sunday and it was perhaps inevitable that such royal goings-on on the Sabbath in a wicked city like Paris should arouse a degree of criticism back home. One Scottish prelate over-reacted to the extent of labelling it 'a dark day in our history'. It was the first time the Princess had been the focal point of public criticism, and she was naturally upset.

With Prince Philip's resumption of his active naval career, the Princess flew back and forth between London and Malta, where he was based, to be with him. From Malta, at different times, the two of them travelled to Greece and Italy. Philip at that time was in command of the frigate *Magpie*. Because the ship lacked accommodation suitable for a princess, Elizabeth sailed for Greece in the frigate *Surprise*, with Philip in *Magpie* and a destroyer completing the flotilla. Light-hearted radio banter between the two frigates enlivened the voyage.

'How is the Princess?' Philip inquired from aboard *Magpie* as the flotilla ran into some heavy weather.

'Full of beans,' *Surprise* radioed back.

'Is that the best you can give her for breakfast?' Philip demanded, jokingly.

While the trip was ostensibly a private one, to visit Philip's Greek relatives, King Paul and Queen Frederika, it was inevitable that the private and the public should overlap. Guns boomed a welcome as the Princess sailed into Phaleron Bay, and there was a state drive through Athens before she and Philip were free to become tourists sightseeing their way round such splendours as the Parthenon, the Palace of Agamemnon and the Temple of Apollo.

Similarly on the visit to Italy there was an official luncheon with the Italian President and members of the Cabinet as a prelude to sightseeing in Rome and Florence. There was also a call on Pope Pius XII – the cause of more criticism back home. There would certainly have been more had the couple gone ahead with a plan to visit Prince Philip's sisters in Germany. Even in a private capacity, Britain's future Queen could not be seen to visit the old enemy so soon after the end of World War II. So the idea was stillborn and it would be another fourteen years before she could call upon her sisters-in-law in their own homes.

With the exception of South Africa, the countries of the Commonwealth (as it was constituted at that time) had never seen the Princess who would one day be their Queen, and none had seen the young naval officer who was now her husband. Canada was to be the first. The plan started modestly as a visit to three main cities during a trip lasting only a few days, but all Canada, once the news leaked out, was eager to get in on the act. So was the United States. As a result, the itinerary grew and grew until it became a five-week tour covering 16,000 miles with no fewer than seventy stops in ten Canadian provinces plus a two-day side-trip to Washington, DC.

The original plan had also included a sea-crossing to Canada in the liner *Empress of France*. But this too was to be changed. As the day of departure drew near, the King's failing health necessitated further drastic surgery, and the Princess flatly refused to leave until she knew her father was out of danger. So sailing was postponed and it began to look, indeed, as if the tour might not take place at all. Then, with the operation over successfully and the King showing signs of improvement, it was on again, though their whole schedule would have to be changed through their late arrival in Canada. It was Prince Philip who suggested that they could still make it on time if they flew instead of going by sea. Clement Attlee, the Prime Minister, did not like the idea at all. A return flight from Malta had necessitated an emergency touchdown at Nice when the Princess's aircraft ran into bad weather, and there could be no such touch-down in mid-Atlantic. But eventually he was talked round and the Princess made her first Atlantic crossing in a BOAC airliner. The flight, in that pre-jet era, took seventeen hours.

The tour did not get off to a good start. The Princess was worried about her father, and the necessity for taking with her a sealed package 'to be opened in the event of the King's death' can have done nothing to ease her fears. If she was often unsmiling, as the newspapers reported at the time, this was the reason. And if Philip was 'tetchy', as the newspapers also said, it was because he was worried for her. 'Tetchiness', however, was sometimes justified. 'A waste of time,' he grumbled at one reception where the two of them, for some inexplicable reason, found themselves shaking hands with the same people all over again. 'What are they belly-aching about now?' he demanded at Niagara Falls when photographers who had missed out on a shot of the couple in waterproof clothing urged that they should don them over again.

Each day the Princess telephoned London to find out how her father was progressing. News of improvement buoyed her spirits. In the course of one telephone conversation, her mother, who had read the newspaper reports, urged her, 'Try to smile more.'

She was all smiles during a lively square dance at Government

House. The dance was arranged at short notice and she found herself with nothing suitable to wear, though she had taken a wardrobe of thirty different outfits with her. Her personal maid, the indispensable Margaret Macdonald, investigated the offerings of a nearby department store and came back with a blouse and skirt. Prince Philip, similarly, was obliged to invest in a pair of jeans at such short notice that he took to the dance floor with the price tag still on display.

The dance came at the end of a day in Ottawa during which the Princess had attended an official luncheon, a state dinner and thirteen other engagements. Yet she enjoyed the dancing so much and stayed so late that there was no time to change before driving to the station, and the couple boarded the waiting train still in their square-dance rig.

More and more, as the tour progressed, it took on something of the air of a national carnival. In town after city the streets were choked with Canadians eager to glimpse the Princess and her husband. Again and again she ordered her chauffeur to slow to a tortoise-like crawl so that people could see her better. When bad weather in Toronto necessitated the use of a closed car, the ingenious Philip came up with the idea of a plexiglass top so that the Princess could still be clearly seen. Workers in a local aircraft plant turned it out in double-quick time. Again and again, too, the Princess displayed the same human touch she had shown with the lepers in South Africa. In one hospital she visited, a small crippled boy was all poised to take her picture when she stopped at his bed, then found his camera wouldn't work. 'See if you can get it mended and I'll come back,' said the Princess. The camera was mended, the Princess kept her promise and the small boy got his picture.

A whistle-stop tour of the Prairie Provinces was enlivened, in private, with purchases made in a joke store in Toronto. At varying times the Princess found herself biting into a bread roll that squeaked, opening a tin labelled 'Nuts' from which a rubber snake shot out and receiving a mild electric shock when she pressed a bell-push. Philip, of course, was the culprit. During the course of the tour she met the Dionne quins, saw her first game of ice hockey, watched the Calgary Stampede while warmly swaddled in an electric blanket, made a speech in French in Quebec and visited Montreal's McGill University where 7,000 boisterous students greeted her with a raucous yell of 'Yea Yea Betty Windsor Rah Rah Rah'.

If she was 'Betty Windsor' to the students of McGill, she was the even more plebeian 'Liz' to the citizens of Washington. An estimated half-million lined her route from the station. Prince Philip, by the same token, was plain 'Phil'. Her host in the American capital, President Truman, was more picturesque: 'a fairytale Princess', he called her.

The White House being in the process of redecoration at the time, the royal couple were entertained in the more homely atmosphere of the annexe, Blair House – so homely that the President even took them upstairs to call upon his ageing mother-in-law. 'I've brought Princess Elizabeth to see you,' he said by way of introduction. The old lady either did not hear properly or was confused by the excitement of the occasion. Somehow linking the Princess with Winston Churchill, who had just won Britain's 1951 General Election, she said to her, 'I'm so glad your father's been re-elected.'

During a hectic two days in Washington the Princess visited the Capitol, the Supreme Court and George Washington's old home at nearby Mount Vernon. During a reception at the British Embassy she shook hands with 1,600 guests, though even this total had been surpassed in Toronto, where she was clocked as shaking hands a staggering 3,000 times in a single day.

'A stimulating visit,' the British Ambassador, Sir Oliver Franks, said of those two days in Washington. 'As one father to another, we can be very proud of our daughters,' President Truman wrote to King George VI.

Canada having been visited, it was the turn of Australia and New Zealand. As far back as 1948 the King himself had planned a tour 'down under', but failing health had necessitated postponement. Now, delighted with the success of his elder daughter's tour of Canada, he decided that she should go in his place.

Like the Canadian tour, that proposed for Australia and New Zealand grew in the planning. On the way out, it was decided that the Princess and her husband should also visit what was then Ceylon. But first, at her own wish, she would go to Kenya. She wanted very much to see the country where her parents had spent a happy holiday in their early days of marriage and about which they had told her so much. She was also eager to see the stone-and-cedar-built hunting lodge on the slopes of Mount Kenya which had been among her many wedding presents. In consequence, it was arranged that she should fly to Kenya and spend a week there before boarding the liner *Gothic* at Mombasa on 7 February for the onward journey to Ceylon, Australia and New Zealand.

Looking the desperately sick man he was, her father journeyed from Sandringham to London to see her off. With her on the flight she again took the sealed package 'to be opened in the event of the King's death'. This time it would be opened.

Private though her visit to Kenya supposedly was, there were the inevitable public engagements. The Princess attended a civic reception and a state banquet, inspected a new maternity hospital, officially opened the headquarters of the Kenya Regiment and visited the Nairobi National Park, where she filmed a lion devouring its kill. Then, public consumption satisfied, it was off to the peace and quiet of the Sagana royal lodge. It is history now that the peace and quiet were abruptly shattered, on the last day but one of her stay there, by the news of her father's death. The sealed package was opened and Princess Elizabeth became Queen Elizabeth II. The royal tour of Australia and New Zealand was unavoidably postponed yet again, and the new twenty-five-year-old Queen returned to London instead.

3 ROUND THE WORLD

Over thirty years later, the round-the-world tour which the Queen undertook shortly after her coronation still ranks as the longest royal tour ever, certainly in terms of time. It lasted from 23 November 1953 (when she flew from London to Bermuda in a BOAC Stratocruiser) until 15 May 1954 (when she returned to London aboard the new royal yacht *Britannia*), a total of 173 days.

In the course of the tour the Queen opened seven Commonwealth parliaments, held eleven investitures, made four broadcasts, attended 223 receptions, banquets, balls, garden parties, exhibitions, displays and sports meetings, made 157 speeches and sat through nearly twice that number delivered by other people. The printed schedule of her many engagements ran to 130 pages of small print. Distances travelled are logged at 18,850 miles by sea, 19,650 by air, 9,900 by road and 1,600 by rail. She took along an entourage of forty, from ladies-in-waiting and private secretaries to maids and footmen, and the accompanying luggage is said to have weighed twelve tons. Certainly the Noel Coles, who hosted the Queen and Prince Philip for a weekend at Lake Rotoiti in New Zealand, were rather taken aback when two truckloads of royal luggage turned up at their door. It filled the billiards room and effectively put paid to Mr Coles' hope that he and Prince Philip might enjoy the odd game.

Interestingly, among those who accompanied the Queen on that tour was a certain Viscount Althorp,★ at that time Acting Master of the Royal Household. Before the tour was over he would request leave of absence to fly home to make arrangements for his wedding to Frances Roche.★★ One of their daughters is now the Princess of Wales.

★ Later the 8th Earl Spencer
★★ Now the Hon. Mrs Frances Shand-Kydd

The very first day of the tour gave clear indication of what lay ahead. It was just before 4 a.m. when the royal Stratocruiser made a refuelling stop at Gander in Newfoundland. Word of the Queen's arrival had travelled ahead of her, and the airport was crowded with people who had stayed up through the night in the hope of seeing her. Rather than disappoint them, the Queen dressed and left the aircraft while refuelling was in progress. By 10 a.m., when her aircraft reached Bermuda, she was up and dressed again, starting a day of engagements which would go on until midnight, sacrificing even her scheduled rest periods so that everything could be squeezed in. Despite such a long and tiring day, and broken rest the night before, she was up again just after 4 a.m., on her way to the airfield by 5.30, airborne at 6.10 and landing in Jamaica at 9.54. She ate her breakfast in flight.

Her three days in Jamaica were like Bermuda three times over, crowded with inspections and visits, presentations and speeches, though she also managed to squeeze in a briefly refreshing swim at the Silver Sands Beach Club. Even so, she was not altogether unhappy when a polo game in which Prince Philip was to have taken part and which she should have watched was called off because of bad weather. The game had been scheduled to start at 7.30 a.m. 'I think I'll go back to bed,' the Queen sighed with relief when she heard it was off.

With *Britannia* not yet completed, the liner *Gothic*, its holds filled with a curiously mixed cargo of wallpaper and pianos, cars, fire pumps and brandy, became a royal yacht for the long sea voyage ahead. First leg of the voyage was through the Panama Canal, where the Queen went ashore to lunch with the US Governor, attend a reception at the British Legation and be guest-of-honour at a presidential banquet. So thick and excitable were the crowds that it took baton charges by the local police to prevent people from clambering onto the Queen's car. Indeed, Prince Philip became so alarmed for the Queen's safety at one point that he left his own car and forced his way through the crowd to join her in hers. And not all the efforts of the police could prevent people invading the grounds of the Legation. So crowded did the place become with gatecrashers that at one stage the Queen was temporarily cut off from her accompanying entourage and they could keep track of her movements only through the bobbing of her tiara.

Two and a half restful, though by no means dull, weeks at sea followed before the next spate of public engagements. The Queen took advantage of the lull to speak to her children by radio-telephone. (Charles was five at the time and Anne three.) Prince Philip broke the monotony of long days at sea by joining in games of deck hockey which became so frenetic on at least one occasion that the Queen, filming the game with her movie camera, became concerned that someone could be seriously hurt. In those games of deck hockey 'anything went except downright murderous assault,' recalls one who took part in them. The game over, the players would take a cooling dip in the ship's pool. Prince Philip, on one occasion, was quick to spot that two Royal Marines who had taken part in the game were not among those who were splashing about in the pool. When he asked where they were, the answer was that they were only non-commissioned officers doing duty as orderlies. It was not put that bluntly, of course, but Prince Philip got the drift. 'Of course they can use the pool,' he ordered.

The ship's pool became the focal point of a hectic and hilarious crossing-the-line ceremony the day *Gothic* sailed over the Equator. Prince Philip's detective, Inspector Frank Kelley, became King Neptune for the occasion, with Michael Parker, Philip's private secretary, as the traditional barber and Philip himself, his nose reddened with lipstick, a borrowed blue and white apron flapping about his legs, a more than enthusiastic barber's assistant. Whitewash (representing lather) and cochineal (for blood) flew in all directions as victim after victim was hauled before Neptune, charged, pronounced guilty, daubed, shaved with an outsize wooden razor and tossed unceremoniously into the pool. The Queen herself went scot-free, thanks to having crossed the Equator earlier, on her 1947 trip to South Africa. Even then she was given no more than a genteel dusting with an outsize powder puff. Other ladies aboard the *Gothic* did not get off so lightly. Even the Queen's two ladies-in-waiting, Lady Pamela Mountbatten★ and Lady Alice Egerton, ended up in the ship's pool. 'I think you're all quite mad,' said the Queen, laughing, as the proceedings ended with everyone throwing everyone else into the pool.

The Queen's arrival in Fiji was greeted with ceremonies which

★ Later Lady Pamela Hicks

would not have been out of place in the days of her great-great-grandmother, Queen Victoria, in whose reign the island first became part of the old British Empire. Outrigger canoes brought a deputation of chiefs out to the *Gothic* where they knelt in obeisance before the Queen and presented her with a whale's tooth as a symbol of friendship. Ashore, later, there was a welcoming ceremony at which the Queen was handed a coconut cup filled with *kava*, a traditional island drink made from the root and stem of the pepper plant. To her credit, she drank it without flinching. 'You have to drink it straight down,' she has recalled since. 'Quite sharp.' A former royal servant who also sampled *kava* on that visit to Fiji puts it more vividly: 'It's terrible stuff; tastes like soap and numbs your whole mouth.' But if the Queen drank *kava* without flinching, she was momentarily less composed during a war dance staged in her honour, nearly jumping out of her chair as the dancers rushed menacingly towards her brandishing vicious-looking clubs.

Next port of call was the island of Tonga, where the Queen renewed her friendship with Queen Salote, whose beaming smile had enchanted Londoners as she drove to and from Westminster Abbey in an open carriage while the rain poured down on Coronation Day. There was a spatter of rain too on Tonga, causing both Queens to unfurl their umbrellas momentarily as they climbed into their carriage, but it stopped almost as quickly as it had started. The visiting Queen was shown, among other things, a tortoise which legend said had been brought to the island by Captain Cook in the days of her great-great-great-great-grandfather, George III, while Prince Philip had the privilege of riding in a London taxi which Queen Salote had brought back from Britain as a coronation souvenir. High-spot of the day was an open-air feast of roast pig, roast chicken, raw fish, yams, water melon, bananas and coconuts. Wisely perhaps, the Queen did not sample the raw fish, though Prince Philip did.

It wanted only two days to Christmas when *Gothic* berthed at Auckland and the Queen became the first reigning monarch ever to visit New Zealand. She has been back many times over the years since. It was raining that first day as she made a speech (the first of twenty-nine speeches she would make in New Zealand) outside the town hall in Auckland, and the Deputy Mayor gallantly took off his raincoat and draped it about her shoulders. 'Thank you, Sir Walter Raleigh,' said the Queen, smiling.

Over the course of the next thirty-eight days she would visit fifty-six different places and see many different aspects of New Zealand life, dairy herds and Maori dancing, sheep-shearing and sulky racing; many varied sights, among them the glow-worm grotto at Waitomo – 'I don't think I've ever seen such a wonderful sight,' she said – and the spouting hot springs at Rotorua. Enthused by what she saw, she was constantly using her cameras. At Rotorua she particularly hoped to film the famous triple geyser known as the Prince of Wales Feathers, but though she waited patiently for some time, camera poised, the geyser remained quiescent. Then, just as she was leaving, an excited shout of 'It's spouting' arrested her. Regal dignity forgotten, she turned hurriedly and raced back to film the spectacle for the benefit of her children back home.

The Queen had been in New Zealand less than forty-eight hours when the unexpected happened, as it has happened many times since in the course of royal tours, though not often so tragically. On Christmas Eve a bridge collapsed into a flooded river, taking with it a train which was crossing at the time. With 166 people dead, it was the worst railway disaster in New Zealand's history. At the Queen's request, her schedule was hastily revised so that she could call upon a bereaved family in Auckland. Prince Philip, despite the fact that he had been at a civic dinner until nearly midnight the night before, got up at 5 a.m. to fly to Wellington to attend the mass funeral of those who had died. After the service he flew straight back to Auckland, cat-napping on the aircraft. All in all, he carried out thirty-six hours of public engagements with only five hours proper sleep.

It was Philip too who, later, at Waikato, soothed the hurt feelings of local Maoris. The Maoris very much wanted the royal visitors to visit their meeting-house, but this was not included in the day's itinerary. Philip decided to ignore the itinerary and, to the delight of the Maoris, took the Queen to see the meeting-house.

The Queen made her Christmas broadcast that year from Auckland. As always at Christmas, the Commonwealth was the keynote of her speech. 'The Commonwealth bears no resemblance to the empires of the past,' she said. 'It is an entirely new conception built on the highest qualities of the spirit of man – friendship, loyalty and the desire for freedom and peace.' Mother-like, she also mentioned her children. 'Of course we all want our children at Christmas time – for that is the season above all others when each family gathers at its own hearth. I hope that perhaps mine are listening to me now.'

They were. They spent that Christmas with 'Granny' – the Queen Mother – at Sandringham, excitedly opening the gift parcels Mummy and Papa had left for them a month beforehand. Later that day the Queen spoke to them by telephone, telling them of her own Christmas in New Zealand sunshine: children singing carols to her on the lawn of Government House, Father Christmas arriving in a coach drawn by four ponies, a diamond brooch from the women of Auckland among her gifts, a walkie-talkie doll for Anne and an electric train-set for Charles.

The Queen missed being with her children and kept their photographs constantly in view beside her bed. 'We're really looking forward to seeing them again,' she said at one point. 'Let's hope they recognize us,' joked her husband.

As on most royal tours, there were occasional snags and hitches along the way, though such minor difficulties were usually ironed out without the Queen herself even being aware of them. At one small hotel in which she was due to stay overnight, the manager, not realizing the considerable amount of paperwork which pursues her wherever she goes, had furnished her suite with only a small, dainty writing bureau. The situation was explained and the manager's own large, flat-topped desk was quickly substituted. Elsewhere the lack of provision of a full-length mirror presented a small problem. The Queen likes to inspect herself from head to toe before appearing in public, and the mirror with which her suite was equipped was woefully inadequate for such a purpose. It was the indispensable Margaret Macdonald who eventually located a suitably large mirror fixed to the wall of the ladies' powder room. Between them, a royal page and a footman took down the mirror and carried it to the Queen's room, where it was propped into an upright position with the aid of some heavy books.

It was in New Plymouth that the biggest hiatus of the tour occurred. The Queen and Prince Philip had already left their hotel to start a round of engagements which would end at Government House in Wellington. Royal servants were busy packing, with a squad of soldiers to manhandle the royal luggage and with two army trucks to convey it to the local airport. The task of packing and loading was almost complete when it was realized that the suitcase containing the Queen's jewels, normally conveyed from place to place by a member of her personal staff, was nowhere to be seen. In it, wherever it was, were jewels worth a Queen's ransom – half-a-dozen tiaras, the jewelled Order of the Garter, necklaces, bracelets and brooches, including a favourite brooch fashioned from the famous rose-pink Williamson diamond which had been among the Queen's wedding gifts. The hotel manageress was sent for and the hotel searched, without success. Then someone suggested that perhaps the case had been loaded onto one of the army trucks in error. But by that time the trucks had left for the airport. Members of the Queen's staff piled into a car and set off in pursuit, arriving at the airport only to find that the baggage plane had already taken off. They boarded another plane and flew to Wellington in pursuit. It was there that they finally caught up with the missing jewel case, heaped casually among all the other luggage on the steps of Government House.

The tour had its more light-hearted moments too – and one of tremendous regality. This was when the Queen opened a special session of the New Zealand Parliament clad in all the splendour of her coronation gown. Among the light-hearted moments was her arrival in Dunedin where surplus naval flags had been used for bunting. The signal they spelled out brought a chuckle from Philip, and from the Queen when he translated it to her: 'Danger – Am Loading High Explosives.' Another such moment was when the Queen found herself walking through a closed and deserted department store on her way to a banquet. The irrepressible Michael Parker promptly popped behind one of the counters and inquired after the fashion of a solicitous shop assistant: 'Is there anything I can show modom?' The Queen laughed delightedly.

It is often said that the Queen's first walkabout was in New Zealand in 1970. The country is right, the year wrong. It was in January 1954, during that first-ever royal visit to New Zealand, that the Queen dispensed with her car for the first time and took a walk along the crowded main street of Nelson.

It was from an hotel in Invercargill, as the tour came to an end, that the Queen broadcast her thanks to the New Zealand people for the warmth of their welcome. But what was perhaps the most touching moment of that New Zealand visit was still to come: when the crowd outside the hotel joined spontaneously in singing 'Will ye no come back again?'

Three days at sea rested and refreshed the Queen for the more strenuous tour still to come, eight weeks in Australia, during which time she would travel 14,000 miles by train, plane and car to visit sixty-eight towns and cities. Over those eight weeks she opened three Parliaments, attended twenty-six receptions, four state banquets, six balls and the same number of garden parties, and made fifty-eight speeches. She saw the Blue Mountains and the Barrier Reef, the Woomera rocket range, surf-riding at Bondi Beach and the flying doctor base in Adelaide. At Flemington, a day at the races resulted in a panic call: 'For Pete's sake get someone to the royal box who really knows the form. Her Majesty knows bloodlines right back to Eclipse.'* At Kalgoorlie she also saw something of the flies for which the area is notorious. The town itself had been liberally drenched with insecticide ahead of the Queen's arrival, but the air strip had been overlooked. As a result, the clothes of several of those in the royal party and the reception committee turned almost black under the swarm of flies which homed in on them.

Compared with New Zealand, the Australian tour was rumbustious in the extreme. Much has been written in more recent times of the enormous crowds which turned out in Australia to see the Princess of Wales, but a generation ago the arrival there of a new young monarch aroused even greater fervour. In Sydney the crowd which turned out to see her on one occasion was estimated at a million plus. Nine times sections of the crowd broke through the police cordon. So intense was the excitement that the Queen herself confessed to feeling 'nervous' and so great the delay that she was, very unusually for her, fifty-three minutes late arriving at a hospital she was due to visit. Time and again she returned to her car to find that the miniature royal standard mounted on it had disappeared into the pocket of some souvenir-hunter. Indeed, this happened so frequently that a fresh batch had to be flown out from Britain.

As usual, the Queen displayed those human touches which, over her years of travel, have endeared her to people around the world. At the Military College in Canberra, when she spotted a small

* A celebrated racehorse bred by George II's son, the Duke of Cumberland.

41

drummer-boy seemingly on the verge of collapse, she had a quiet word with the College Commander and an ambulance was summoned. In Hobart, when she saw a small girl burst into tears because she could not get near enough to present a posy, the Queen left her car, walked over to the child and took the flowers from her. In Melbourne, among all the thousands who turned out to see her, she recognized the face of a man who had been a footman at Buckingham Palace before emigrating to Australia. She asked for him to be traced so that she could meet him and his family.

There was a degree of concern for the Queen's health when a woman with whom she was known to have shaken hands in Canberra was admitted to hospital and found to be suffering from poliomyelitis. She was immediately given an anti-polio injection and in Perth, where there were several cases of the disease, more stringent precautions were taken. A display by schoolchildren was cancelled. People presented to the Queen were told not to approach closer than six feet and not to shake hands. The Queen herself seemed to know nothing of these precautions or, if she did, to consider them unnecessary. There were many occasions when she herself bridged the supposed gap of six feet, and others on which she continued to shake hands.

However, she did not take up residence at Government House, as planned. Instead, she lived aboard the *Gothic*, with the ship's crew banned from going ashore and mixing with the locals. When the Queen went ashore, everything needed for meals, from food and wine to cutlery and table napkins, was landed from the *Gothic* and ferried around in a refrigerated van normally used for the conveyance of ice-cream. There was one occasion, after the van had been loaded, when it was realized that the Queen's favourite cheese had been overlooked. To save opening the van again, the cheese was handed to the driver. Asked later what he had done with 'the Queen's cheese', the Aussie driver looked considerably embarrassed. 'I thought that was my tucker,' he said. 'I ate it.'

Having off-loaded its cargo of wallpaper, pianos and what-have-you, the *Gothic* took on a load of frozen meat for the return voyage. The traditional Australian cry of 'Coo-ee' from Sir Eric Harrison, minister in charge of the royal visit, echoed across the harbour at Fremantle as the Queen set sail again.

Eight days at sea gave the Queen an opportunity to relax,

interrupted only by a half-day stop at the Cocos Islands where she went ashore to meet John Clunies-Ross, whose family were granted a perpetual lease of the islands back in Victorian times (though they now come under Australian jurisdiction). There being no vehicles on Home Island, where John Clunies-Ross lived with his wife, a Land Rover had been flown in from West Island to serve as royal transport. Unaccustomed to seeing such a conveyance – indeed, to seeing conveyances of any sort – ducks and chickens picked their leisurely way across the road as the Queen was driven to the Clunie-Ross home to watch a display of native dancing.

Next stopping-place was Ceylon (now Sri Lanka), where a small hiccup in the welcome proceedings resulted in one of the ladies-in-waiting being accorded the artillery salute intended for the Queen. Despite the intense heat and high humidity, the Queen again donned the thirty pounds of her lavishly embroidered coronation gown to open Parliament in Colombo. It was slightly cooler at Kandy, where a *Perahera*, a procession of musicians, dancers and ornamented elephants, was staged in her honour and became another rich memory captured by her movie camera.

Then it was on to Aden, where, before she bade farewell to the *Gothic*, she sent for the ship's captain, David Aitchison, and knighted him on deck. There were awards and gifts too for members of the ship's crew. From Aden the Queen flew to Tobruk by way of Entebbe, from where, two years before, she had taken off for her return flight to London following the death of her father. But this time she was returning to her capital by a different route and in a new form of royal transport.

Awaiting her in the harbour at Tobruk was her new royal yacht, *Britannia*, which would take her home via Malta and Gibraltar. 'It's beautiful,' she exclaimed, delightedly, when she first glimpsed its bluebottle hull and snowy-white superstructure from a balcony of the palace of King Idris. And awaiting her on board *Britannia* were the two small children she had not seen for five months. 'I don't think they knew who we were at all,' the Queen has recalled since. 'They were extremely polite.' Politeness on the part of five-year-old Prince Charles included an attempt to shake hands with his mother. 'Oh, no – not you,' the Queen sighed as she took both children in her arms.

The homecoming, in mid-May, was like Coronation Day all

over again and on a grander scale. Britain's south coast became a huge natural grandstand for the crowds of people eager to witness the Queen's return. Prime Minister Winston Churchill, ever the man for a great occasion, journeyed south from London to join the Queen aboard *Britannia* for the last leg of a tour which had taken her round the world. A flotilla of small ships set sail to greet her and escort her to the mouth of the Thames. As the first of these dipped its ensign in salute, the Queen ordered that *Britannia*'s ensign be dipped in acknowledgement. Then it was up the Thames, to the accompaniment of cheering crowds, hooting sirens and pealing bells, to a final landfall at Tower Bridge.

4 NUMBAWAN FELLA

Throughout that long round-the-world tour Prince Philip was constantly at the Queen's side, bolstering her with whispered asides, bridging the gap if she dried up in conversation, easing nervous tension with the occasional joke. 'No, thanks. I might nick it and we've had enough mutton,' he responded when asked if he would like to try his hand at sheep-shearing. A considerate and protective husband, he was sometimes angered by the demands made on his wife. 'You can't expect the Queen to suffer this glare,' he snapped when he saw the mass of lighting which had been installed for the opening of the Australian Parliament.

In Papua New Guinea, where the Queen is known as 'Misis Kwin' in the local pidgin, Philip has been accorded the title of 'Numbawan Fella Blong Misis Kwin'. The title is surely an apt one. Lacking his help, she would have achieved much less. On the Queen's tours, it is often Philip who takes the extra strain when the unexpected crops up. Just as he went without sleep to attend the mass funeral of those who died in the New Zealand train disaster, so, years later in Algeria, it was Philip who piloted his own aircraft to an earthquake disaster area. In 1959, when the Queen was obliged to cancel a planned visit to Ghana because she was pregnant with Prince Andrew, Philip went there on his own. In Australia in 1974, when an unexpected General Election compelled the Queen's return to London, he carried on alone until she was free to rejoin him. If the Queen is the most travelled monarch in British history, Prince Philip, over the years, has travelled a great deal further – perhaps three times as far. Not only does he accompany the Queen on her frequent tours but in between he frequently takes off on his own.

His own travels, in part, are also designed to ease the strain on the

Queen. As her personal representative, he has attended independence celebrations in several Commonwealth countries, Malta and Malawi, Tanganyika and Zanzibar (since united as Tanzania) and Kenya. It was in Kenya, as the old flag came down and the new one was hoisted, that he remarked slyly to Jomo Kenyatta, 'I suppose you don't want to change your mind?' He has represented the Royal Family at state funerals (including that of America's assassinated president, John Kennedy), memorial services, royal weddings and the accession of King Juan Carlos of Spain.

His own long list of presidencies, patronages and other appointments has also caused the Prince to travel widely. He has visited British regiments serving in Germany, and Royal Air Force units overseas, attended naval exercises and dropped in on Royal Marines training amidst the snow and ice of Norway. There have been travels in connection with his Duke of Edinburgh Award scheme (now operating in some fifty countries, even if not all give him the credit by naming it after him); more travels through his presidency of such organizations as the World Wildlife Fund, the International Equestrian Federation, the English-Speaking Union and the Royal Agricultural Society of the Commonwealth. It was as President of the FEI that he visited the Soviet Union, one of the few countries his wife has not yet been to.

A restless man, easily bored by routine, Prince Philip loves travelling. If there is such a thing as a 'born traveller', he is surely it – conceived in Switzerland, born in Corfu, voyaging into exile with his parents at the tender age of eighteen months, shuttling between schools in France, England, Germany and Scotland in boyhood, travelling as far afield as South Africa and the United States, Canada, Australia and the Far East as a young naval officer in World War II. On that round-the-world royal tour of 1953–4 he took time out to look up old friends of his wartime days in Sydney and Tasmania.

Far from tiring him, that tour would seem only to have whetted his appetite for travel. Within a few months he was off again, this time without the Queen. Invited to Vancouver to open what were then still known as the Empire Games, he saw the invitation also as an opportunity to see something of the Canadian wilds. The result was an entirely new style of royal tour during the course of which he bush-hopped to such old pioneer outposts as Whitehorse,

Yellowknife, Coppermine and Fort Simpson, the original head-quarters of the Hudson Bay Company. He met trappers and prospectors, Eskimos and Indians and sampled such un-royal delicacies as bison, moose and caribou. For crossing the Arctic Circle, an exploit Prince Charles and Prince Andrew would later emulate, the Royal Canadian Air Force awarded him the certificate of an 'Airborne Iceworm'. In Vancouver he was presented with a commemorative Empire Games medal . . . and thereby hangs a tale.

Philip was in the royal box at the Games the day Jim Peters, leading by a full mile in the marathon but physically and mentally exhausted, crossed the wrong finishing line and was disqualified. On his return to Britain the Prince had his own commemorative medal suitably mounted, inscribed 'For A Very Gallant Marathon Runner' and sent it to Peters.

Just as the invitation to Open the Empire Games had sparked the idea of venturing into the Canadian wilds, so an invitation to open the 1956 Olympic Games in Melbourne gave Philip the idea for what perhaps still ranks as the most adventurous royal tour ever, and the most informal. From the outset, the Prince made it clear that he wanted a minimum of 'pomping up'. In consequence, his own speech at the Melbourne Games was limited to a mere seventeen words. The rest of his time in Australia was spent visiting sheep farms, cattle stations and timber mills, talking with the uranium miners of Rum Jungle and roustabouts working on the giant new hydro-electric project in the Snowy Mountains. And even that was only a small part of a 39,000-mile tour – 'expedition' would perhaps be nearer the mark – during which Philip dropped in on not a few lonely islands and isolated outposts which could not normally hope to receive a royal visitor: Deception Island and the South Shetlands, Tristan da Cunha, St Helena, Ascension Island, survey teams in the Falklands and even the Trans-Antarctic Expedition. It took him four months and ended up costing him £8,000 out of his own pocket despite the fact that he had the use of the new royal yacht.

The Prince was accompanied by a number of like-minded souls, including the irrepressible Michael Parker and the artist Edward Seago. During their days at sea Seago taught Philip to paint, and by the end of the trip he had turned out some commendable, if amateur, works in oils, portraits and landscapes. A keen photographer, he was also active with his camera, taking shots of seal colonies and whale-catching, penguin rookeries and sea-birds in flight which would later form the basis for his book *Birds from Britannia*.

The whaling photographs were taken the day *Britannia* came up with a whaler. Going aboard the whaler involved being slung across in a wicker basket. 'He stunk to high heaven when he got back,' recalls someone who was aboard *Britannia* at the time.

On Christmas Day, with the royal yacht heading south-east towards the Antarctic, the Prince broadcast an introduction to the Queen's message to the Commonwealth. Later he spoke to her by radio-telephone, as he had from Australia on 20 November, their seventh wedding anniversary.

With the temperature dropping as *Britannia* headed further and further south, the crew were given permission to wear beards, with prizes of razor blades and after-shave on offer for the best – and worst – efforts. Though declining to be considered for a prize, Philip himself grew a beard . . . and the story has an amusing sequel.

At the end of the trip the Prince was due to join the Queen in Portugal for her state visit to that country. His new beard, he felt, was not quite the thing for a state visit, and he shaved it off. Clean-shaven again, he bounded aboard his wife's aircraft when she landed at Montijo airport – to be confronted by a mass of bearded faces. The Queen, having heard what had gone on aboard *Britannia*, had hired a selection of false beards for herself and her entourage from a London theatrical costumier.

There had been similar jokey moments aboard *Britannia* as Philip's tour ran its course. The 'Airborne Iceworm' certificate he had been awarded in Canada gave him the idea of presenting a similar certificate, 'The Order of the Red Nose', to members of the ship's crew the day they crossed the Antarctic Circle. Edward Seago helped him design it. But the long voyage also had its serious side and set purpose. Of the eleven British bases on the Falkland Islands, Philip visited seven. Getting ashore at Tristan da Cunha involved a tricky trip in a canvas-skinned longboat. To visit the survey team on Deception Island, he went ashore in thick fog, later entertaining members of the team to a meal and film show aboard *Britannia*.

It was the first of a number of new-style royal tours which Philip would make and which the Queen would eventually copy. (Her 1974 tour of Pacific islands, for instance, seems to have been modelled on a similar tour her husband had undertaken three years before.) Successive British Governments have not been slow to see the advantage of such tours. It was the Government of the day in 1959, when Prince Philip was scheduled to attend scientific conferences in Delhi and Karachi and afterwards go on to Bermuda for its 350th anniversary as a Crown colony, which suggested that he should turn these visits into another island-hopping expedition. Sorry, said Philip, but he couldn't afford another £8,000 out of his own pocket. So the Government agreed to meet the cost, and the tour itinerary was extended to take in Singapore, Sarawak, Brunei, North Borneo (now Sabah), Hong Kong, the Solomon Islands, the Gilbert and Ellice group, Christmas Island and the Bahamas.

The Prince's solo tours are usually very different in character from those on which he is simply along in support of the Queen, less stereotyped, more informal. He is at his best while travelling from place to place, airborne or at sea, thoroughly at home in the masculine world of a ship's bridge or an aircraft flight deck. Airborne, he will often take over the controls, but he has also been known to take his turn at making the coffee and sandwiches. At sea, aboard *Britannia*, he is frequently to be found on the bridge and has sometimes taken charge of the docking procedure. During the 1970 royal tour of Australia and New Zealand, the royal yacht ran into weather so bad that three men aboard an escorting frigate were swept overboard. Aboard *Britannia* the Queen retired white-faced to her cabin, but Philip climbed into oilskins and went onto the bridge. 'He was there during the worst of the storm and actually seemed to be enjoying it,' one of the yacht's officers said afterwards.

Official engagements ashore, which are the point of all this travelling, sometimes seem to irritate him with their pomp and circumstance, with the result that he has achieved a reputation around the world of being a prickly prince upon occasion.

In particular, the pressmen who accompany royal tours not infrequently seem to upset him. 'Hope he breaks his bloody neck,' he was quoted as saying in Pakistan when a photographer who had scaled a pole in the hope of a better picture lost his grip and fell backwards. In Gibraltar, taken to see the famous apes, he looked from apes to the accompanying pressmen and asked, 'Which are the monkeys?' Probably he intended it as a joke, but the pressmen did not think it funny. Certainly he maintained that a somewhat similar remark in Dominica was intended as a joke. When a hospital matron lamented being 'plagued by mosquitoes', quipped Philip, 'You've got mosquitoes. We've got the Press.' Accompanying pressmen took umbrage to the extent that one, at least, threatened to quit the tour, and Philip found himself having to soothe ruffled feelings. It had been a joke, he said. 'I hope you haven't lost your sense of humour, but if you are offended, I most sincerely apologize.'

Prince Philip is a man who speaks his mind and does not suffer fools gladly, a tricky combination. Visiting a San Francisco art museum in 1962, he was not slow to voice his opinion of some of the more modernistic exhibits. 'Something to hang your bath towel on,' he said of a piece of three-dimensional artwork by Victor Passmore. A bronze sculpture by Lynn Chadwick looked like 'a coffin for a beatnik'. A painting by William Scott found him asking, 'Are you sure this is right side up?' While many people might be inclined to agree with all this, he could hardly expect the museum's director to do so. 'I think these works have some permanent value,' he told the Prince.

At a World Wildlife Fund dinner in New York the Prince made an outspoken speech which some people saw as a curious contradiction in terms, given the great amount of game-shooting he himself has done over the years. He roundly denounced the shooting of elephants 'because people want chessmen or a new set of billiard balls', rhinoceros 'to get its horn for export to China, where for some incomprehensible reason they think it acts as a sex stimulant', the American golden eagle for their 'feathers and claws' and the Arabian oryx 'to inherit its legendary courage and virility'.

A man who shoots often from the verbal hip must sometimes expect a bullet in return, and Prince Philip has stopped his share. His condemnation of kangaroo-shooting found an Australian politician retorting, 'Perhaps he will likewise denounce the organized and cruel slaughtering of animals in the United Kingdom; children taught to shoot stags and pheasants flying over hidden sportsmen to their deaths by the bagful.' Teasing a Brazilian general about his elaborate display of medals – 'I didn't know Brazil was in the war that long' – is said to have elicited the pointed retort, 'At least, sir, I didn't get them for marrying my wife.'

It is not all quips and ripostes, of course. Prince Philip's world-wide travels have their more serious, less controversial side. While the Queen is the central figure holding the Commonwealth together, her consort, through his travels, has played – and still plays – an important part. 'There are some things for which it is worthwhile making personal sacrifices,' he has said. 'I believe the Commonwealth is one of those things and I, for one, am prepared to sacrifice a great deal if by doing so I can advance its well-being by even a small degree.' By the same token, Britain's economy has also benefited. 'Foreign tours by the Duke of Edinburgh do a tremendous amount of good from the commercial point of view,' an official of Britain's National Export Council said in 1964. 'Since his tour of South America two years ago, trade has increased with Peru, Venezuela, Ecuador, Colombia and Brazil.'

On that particular tour he travelled a total of 36,000 miles, visited ten South American countries, paid sixty-eight visits to mines, factories and plantations, attended eighty-four receptions, dinners and luncheons and made thirty speeches. As always, he wrote most of the speeches himself, losing no opportunity of recalling Britain's historic ties with the country he was in at the time. With few exceptions, the people of Latin America enthused over him from the moment he made his first speech in slow but creditably accented Spanish. Among the few exceptions were two youthful extremists in Argentina who pelted his car with eggs and a tomato. Philip intervened to secure their release after they had been arrested, and sent them a joking message: 'Don't do any more throwing, because I have only a limited supply of suits.'

Because Prince Philip does not take actual contracts and samples of merchandise along on his travels, because (as he has said himself) he can only 'create the right atmosphere', specific examples of the way Britain has benefited from his efforts are difficult to pinpoint. But one at least stands out crystal clear, when in 1968 he was back in South America, this time with the Queen. In Chile at a time when Britain was competing with France for the contract to build a new nuclear reactor, it was Philip who tipped the scale in Britain's favour with a speech to the Santiago Chamber of Commerce. 'There can be no doubt whatever that British industry has a very great deal to offer Chile,' he said. 'Every kind of advanced technological equipment is available, but someone has to make it his business to convince potential customers in the teeth of efficient and ruthless competition.' Philip, on that occasion, was definitely that 'someone', and the £630,000 contract with Chile was signed a month later.

There have been non-commercial benefits too. His 1966 tour of the United States was calculated to have raised more than a million dollars for Variety Club charities, including $100,000 from a wealthy American who offered to stump up that amount if the Prince would take a dip in his pool. Philip accepted the challenge, and the charities got the money. His own reward came on his return to Britain, when the Institute of Public Relations presented him with a medal for his 'magnificent service to public relations and mutual understanding'.

You win some and you lose some. On a visit to Canada to see how his Duke of Edinburgh Award Scheme was coming along there he was perhaps a shade too outspoken on the subject of the monarchy. Previous visits by the Queen, in 1964 and 1967, had had their critics, Canadians who thought the country should have a Canadian head of state. Now, in 1969, Philip declared: 'If people don't want it, they should change it. But let us end it on amicable terms and not have a row. The monarchy exists not for its own benefit but for that of the country. We don't come here for our health. We can think of better ways of enjoying ourselves.' Not unnaturally, such comments upset a lot of Canadians at the time.

Prince Philip's diary for any year is indicative of his restless nature, his need to be up and doing, his desire to do his share and more than his share. In 1970, for instance, between accompanying the Queen on a nine-week tour of Australia and New Zealand and a ten-day visit to Canada, he sandwiched in a trip to Strasbourg for the European Conservation Conference, visits to Cape Kennedy, the Helsinki International Trade Fair, the World Wildlife's International Park in Italy and British troops in Germany, and a session of the FEI in Brussels. And also, of course, quite a lot back home in Britain.

It was in his capacity as President of the FEI that Prince Philip went to the Soviet Union in 1979. Object of the exercise was to inspect the equestrian facilities for the following year's Olympic Games. Wearing gumboots and a protective helmet with 'Labour' written on it in Cyrillic script, he strode around the frozen mud site of what would eventually become an £18 million equestrian complex, asking questions, throwing out suggestions. What about getting rid of the horse dung? More seats would be needed over there. How about security? Told that identity cards with photographs would be issued for security purposes, he retorted, 'Quite useless. Much better to have plastic wristbands.' Shown the stabling for competitors' mounts, he thought they lacked sufficient drainage. 'Have to hope all the horses don't pee at the same time,' he said in his forthright fashion. 'A great expert,' one Soviet official commented after listening to Philip expound on the best composition for the stadium floor.

Sadly, the 'great expert' never made it to the actual Olympics to see how far his ideas had been carried out. Britain's voluntary boycott of the Games following the Russian invasion of Afghanistan, though ignored by many athletes, could hardly be similarly disregarded by the Queen's husband.

Prince Philip's years of travel by everything from Dakota to Concorde, from royal yacht to canvas-skinned longboat, have been remarkably free of accident. Those with him in the longboat were worried that he might poke the point of his shooting stick through the canvas hull, but it did not happen.

There has, inevitably, been the occasional near miss. One such, more inconvenient than dangerous, occurred when he was returning from the 1978 Commonwealth Games, when take-off from Calgary in an Air Canada jumbo jet had to be aborted when a cabin door was found not to be securely shut. A second attempt at take-off ended similarly in failure when four tyres fractured and a small fire developed in the under-carriage of the aircraft. The fire was quickly extinguished and the aircraft evacuated. The royal VIP was immediately offered the use of a Royal Canadian Air Force plane to get him to Edmonton so that he could connect with another flight to London. He shook his head. It speaks volumes that, rather than be the subject of special privilege, he hung around with the other passengers until they could all board another flight nearly nine hours later.

5 ROYAL *BRITANNIA*

The voyage home from Libya in 1954 had given the Queen ample opportunity to explore the new royal yacht. She was delighted with everything about it, though the fact that it was not yet fitted with stabilizers would cause problems later. Certainly it was fitted with about everything else to make sea voyages comfortable and even luxurious.

Indeed, *Britannia*'s official designation as 'Her Majesty's Yacht' is something of an understatement. It bears about as much resemblance to an ordinary yacht as Buckingham Palace does to a semi-detached villa in the London suburbs. For a start, at 412 feet 3 inches (125.65 metres) from stem to stern it is half as long as an ocean-going liner. The accommodation aboard includes state apartments which can host a reception of 200 guests and a dining-room which seats fifty-six people. It has a maximum speed of 22.5 knots and a range of 2,800 miles (4,506 kilometres) at 20 knots. A reduction in speed to 14 knots can extend its cruising range to 3,765 miles (5,914 kilometres). It has a crew of twenty-one officers and 256 ratings. It goes almost without saying that there is keen competition in the Royal Navy to serve on *Britannia*, its crew members distinguished by white (instead of the customary red) badges and by caps bearing the title 'Royal Yacht'.

The Queen herself, as she said at the launching, sees a royal yacht as 'a necessity' for the monarch of a seafaring nation, 'not a luxury', and all these inflationary years later the original £2.1 million cost of construction fades into insignificance. But at the time it aroused a degree of criticism of which Prince Philip found himself bearing the brunt. 'Philip's Folly' one Labour politician dubbed the new yacht.

In fact, Prince Philip had little to do with it. He was still a schoolboy at Gordonstoun when the idea was mooted of a new royal yacht to replace the old *Victoria & Albert*, always unstable because of confusion over the metric measurements in plans borrowed from the Tsar of Russia and fast becoming unseaworthy into the bargain. That was during the brief reign of Edward VIII, but before anything could be done he had abdicated, to become Duke of Windsor. The idea was revived again once the Queen's father had settled on the throne but had gone no further than the planning stage when the outbreak of World War II brought another halt. It was 1951 before the plans for the new yacht were again taken out of their pigeonhole and dusted off and February 1952, the month of the King's death, before construction started. Building at John Brown's shipyard on the Clyde took two years.

Given a clipper (instead of the traditional swan) bow and a modified cruiser stern, *Britannia* was designed with the idea that it could be converted to serve as a hospital ship in time of war, and it has occasionally practised its wartime role since in NATO exercises. The nearest it has come to the real thing was when it was on its way to Australia in January 1986 and was hastily diverted to rescue several hundred British and other foreign nationals during the civil war in South Yemen. Told of the rescue at the time, the Queen expressed herself delighted that the royal yacht had been so opportunely placed to render assistance. In recent years she has also allowed the yacht to be used several times as a floating conference centre for British businessmen and their opposite numbers from whatever country she is visiting at the time.

While Prince Philip had nothing to do with the original planning, he took a keen interest, both as the Queen's husband and as a naval officer, in the construction of the royal yacht. When it was being fitted out at Portsmouth, he travelled there with a party of royal aides and palace servants to test its suitability. Among other things he discovered that the dining-room, as fitted, would seat only thirty-two people. Not enough, he said. In consequence, removable wings were designed which could be added to the dining-table to increase the number to fifty-six, with extra chairs also made to supplement and match the genuine Hepplewhite products being transferred from the old *Victoria & Albert*. Other items from the *Victoria & Albert* were, and still are, also to be found aboard *Britannia*, among them a satinwood desk once used by Queen

Victoria and a gimbal table designed by her husband, Prince Albert.

If the Royal Navy is known as 'the silent service', *Britannia* is easily the most silent ship in that service, at least when members of the Royal Family are aboard. Instead of the shouted commands customary aboard ship, orders on the upper deck are given as far as possible by a system of silent signals. Crew members wear soft-soled pumps on their feet as they go about their duties. They also work bare-headed. Technically, they are thus out of uniform and not required to salute, which avoids the necessity for the Royals constantly to acknowledge or return salutes. In addition, to ensure royal privacy, the windows of the royal bedrooms on the upper-most deck of the superstructure – they can hardly be classed merely as cabins – are set considerably higher than usual, against the possibility of anyone peeping in.

Like a child with a new bicycle or an older person with a new car, the Queen was naturally eager to show off her new yacht. King Haakon VII of Norway, her great-uncle through his marriage to King George V's sister Maud, was perhaps an obvious first choice. When he had visited Britain for the Coronation in his own yacht, *Norge*, the Queen, at that time, had no royal yacht, nor even a barge. A police launch was the best she could manage to greet her Norwegian great-uncle. Now, in June 1955, it was in her own royal yacht that she sailed to Norway on the first of a series of European state visits. Norway in 1955 was to be followed by Sweden in 1956, Portugal, France and Denmark in 1957, the Netherlands in 1958, with many more – Italy, Austria, Finland, Luxembourg – to come in the years ahead.

A state visit is more or less what the name implies, a courtesy call paid by one head of state on another. 'A waste of time, money and energy,' the Duke of Windsor termed them. Clearly the Queen does not share that view. The itinerary is fairly stereotyped, including usually an official welcome, a state drive through the streets of the capital, a visit to the opera or ballet, some sightseeing on a cultural or historical level, the laying of a wreath on a war memorial, the planting of a commemorative tree, a state banquet given by the Queen's host and a reciprocal banquet held aboard *Britannia* if it can be suitably berthed or at the British Embassy if it cannot. The visit may last anything from one or two to ten days, though three or four days is usually considered about right. If the Queen stays on longer, as she sometimes does, it is usually in a private capacity and often due to her interest in horses, as was the case in 1956 when her state visit to Sweden was deftly arranged so that she could stay on to watch the equestrian events of the Olympic Games at which Britain won the gold for the three-day event.

The crossing to Sweden pointed up the need for the royal yacht to be fitted with stabilizers (which would be added in the future). The North Sea was in a rough mood, and *Britannia* rolled and pitched so much that the Queen found herself eating her dinner with one hand while holding her plate in place with the other. Elsewhere aboard the vessel, chinaware was thrown about so that it shattered, and some of Prince Philip's collection of gramophone records suffered the same fate. Later, when the Queen was in bed, she was awakened by a tremendous thud. She switched on her bedside lamp to find that her dressing-table had broken free from its fixings and was careering back and forth with every roll of the yacht. Her silver-backed brushes and mirrors, along with their matching scent bottles and cosmetic jars, were on the floor, though fortunately nothing was broken. The Queen promptly summoned help and sat on the side of her bed in her dressing-gown while members of the crew manhandled the dressing-table back into place and, as an emergency measure, secured it with rope. Briefly disturbing though the incident was, the Queen fared rather better than her great-grandmother on an earlier North Sea crossing, when Queen Alexandra was having tea aboard the *Victoria & Albert* and a sudden lurch sent her, her chair and her tea-things flying.

Once in Sweden, *Britannia* served as a floating palace from which the Queen went ashore in the blue and gold royal barge. Sightseeing included both the city hall in Stockholm and new apartment blocks in the city suburbs. Entertainment included an evening at the quaintly old-fashioned Court Theatre in Drottningholm with its candle footlights and eighteenth-century scenery. Breakfast included eggs in abundance. The Swedish chef in charge of culinary arrangements for the Queen had asked a member of her staff what she preferred for breakfast. 'Eggs,' he was told. 'The Queen loves eggs.' Too late he realized he had not asked how the royal eggs should be prepared. As a result, the Queen found herself confronted with eggs in every conceivable guise – boiled, fried, scrambled, poached, plus an omelette or two.

Lengthy though the Queen's round-the-world tour had been, many Commonwealth countries had inevitably been omitted. It would have been impossible to include them all. So between those state visits to Norway and Sweden came a three-week tour of Nigeria, at that time Britain's largest colony and destined to achieve independence in 1960. With her when she flew out to Lagos in the same stratocruiser – *Atalanta* – which four years before had brought her back from Entebbe as Queen, she took a crown-topped canopy of gilded aluminium draped with velvet, which could be toted round Nigeria to protect her from the scorching heat of the sun. Like the bubble top fitted to her car in Canada when she went there as a princess, the canopy was Prince Philip's idea, though royal dress-designer Norman Hartnell sketched the actual design. It was Philip's idea too to include two Nigerian equerries in the royal entourage.

It was the first time Nigeria had been visited by a reigning sovereign, and those hosting the Queen were eager to display the country's more westernized aspects, carefully sterilizing the Lagos rubbish-tips prior to her arrival and installing a commercial air-conditioning plant in the royal bedroom at Government House. Fortunately, the Governor General's wife decided to test the efficiency of the new air-conditioning by sleeping in the room beforehand. She awoke in the night with teeth chattering and limbs shivering. The newly installed plant had plunged the room temperature to zero, and some hurried adjustments had to be made.

The Queen was welcomed by crowds who jigged so enthusiastically that her clothes were quickly filmed by the red dust which billowed up. During her three-week tour she saw both sides of the Nigerian coin, a spectacular pageant staged by 10,000 masked and painted dancers, jugglers and musicians, a race between war canoes manned by ninety paddlers apiece – and the distressing sight of the many patients at a leper settlement on the Opi River. During their visit to the leper settlement the Queen and Prince Philip both shook hands with a number of the patients, a royal act which the supervisor said would 'do more to conquer man's fear and hate of the disease' than any other single act he could think of.

In the Muslim region of the country, when the Queen went north, only men lined the processional route, their womenfolk being obliged by custom to keep out of sight. It was Prince Philip, of course, who tapped on the door of a hut and asked the woman inside if he could come in and look round.

Spectacular even among so much spectacle staged in the Queen's honour was the Durbar at Kaduna. It started with drumbeats at four in the morning. By nine o'clock, when the Queen appeared magnificently clad in full royal regalia, the crowd was estimated at 50,000, with the procession numbering perhaps 8,000 more, chiefs and warriors, horsemen and archers, jugglers and acrobats, a scene of colourful, noisy pageantry straight out of the unwritten pages of African history. As always, the Queen was showered with gifts, shawls and turbans and a paperweight fashioned from a tiger's paw. Nor was spectacle to end with the Durbar. A touchdown at Kano on the journey home saw the Queen welcomed by the Emir, a resplendent figure in ceremonial robes of green and gold, accompanied by a mounted escort clad in armour dating back to the days of the Crusades.

Britannia had been in service a mere three years when the Queen paid her state visit to Portugal. Considerable sprucing up was nevertheless required due to the buffeting the yacht had received during Prince Philip's Antarctic venture (as related in the previous chapter). To this end, *Britannia* put in at Gibraltar before proceeding to Portugal, with Philip staying there while the overhaul was carried out. He did so because of the type of man he is – one who considered it unfair to fly home to his wife and children if the crew of the royal yacht, who had shared the Antarctic venture with him, could not equally be with their families. Unfortunately, his stay in Gibraltar added fuel to the fire of gossip, which made big headlines at the time, that all was not well with the royal marriage. In consequence, there were more reporters and photographers even than usual when the couple were reunited at Montijo airport in Portugal. However, their obvious happiness as they left the Queen's aircraft together gave a firm denial to the rift rumours, with one eagle-eyed reporter even claiming to have spotted a smudge of royal lipstick on Prince Philip's face.

Reunion with her husband made the state visit doubly enjoyable for the Queen – and it showed in everything she did and said. In Oporto, so that people could see her better, she commandeered an open charabanc intended for the accompanying photographers, leaving them to follow on in style in the Cadillac intended for her. Elsewhere, she was both intrigued and amused by the local custom of hanging out coloured bedspreads to supplement the bunting and flags. 'It must be washing day,' she joked.

As that early series of state visits proceeded, it was as though each country in turn sought to better the others. To welcome the Queen to France, the airport was adorned with Aubusson carpets, Gobelins tapestries and paintings from the national collection. She slept in a satin-draped bed dating from the days of Louis XVI, while nearby, on her dressing-table, as a gift from France, stood a queen-sized bottle of perfume, half a litre of specially blended jasmine fragrance in an elegant container of Baccarat glass.

Nor was that the only gift with which she was presented. There was, in addition, a gold inkwell, a Renault car, French dolls for Anne and a working model of the Paris Metro for Charles. 'It will amuse his father very much,' the Queen joked. But the gift which delighted her most was a gold and platinum watch, said to be the smallest in the world, its dial measuring barely three-eights of an inch across. The watch was, in fact, the second of its kind. Her parents, visiting France in 1938, had been given a similar watch to take back to her, and she had worn it almost continuously for nearly seventeen years until she lost it one day when out walking her dogs at Sandringham. Despite extensive searches conducted by the police, Royal Engineers equipped with mine-detectors, Boy Scouts, estate workers and loyal members of the public, it was never found. The theory is that it vanished into the innards of a threshing machine being operated near where the Queen thought she had lost it. 'One of the loveliest gifts I have ever had,' she exclaimed with genuine delight when the French, in 1957, presented her with an exact replica.

Over a period of three days in Paris, the Queen spent twenty-eight hours at official functions, including making a speech in French at a state banquet in the Elysée Palace, and a further eleven hours travelling from one function to another. For the first time television cameras relayed the various royal engagements to a wider audience. Even so, an estimated 150,000 excited sightseers almost fought to catch a glimpse of her as she drove to the opera, climbing lamp-posts for a better view, scaling roofs and clambering on parked cars, one of which collapsed under the weight of the many people on it. Visiting Versailles, the Queen heard that she would be passing the famous Marcel Boussac stud and asked for her car to stop there so that she could look at the horses. During the course of the visit Prince Philip was decorated with the Grand Sash of the Legion of Honour. 'It is for you, Madame, to bestow the accolade,' said President Coty. Laughing, the Queen did so, embracing her husband and kissing him on both cheeks in the French fashion.

Highspot of the visit was a night trip by river boat along the Seine, five miles of its length given over to illuminated tableaux of French history. Behind the scenes, ahead of the trip, there was considerable debate as to what the Queen should wear. For the river boat trip, Norman Hartnell had created a dress like nothing the Queen had worn before, a figure-hugging design of silver lace over silver tissue with a low, square-cut neckline. At almost the last moment, however, she shied away from something so spectacular and opted to wear one of her traditional crinolines instead. It was her dresser, the loyal Margaret Macdonald, who finally prevailed upon her to wear Hartnell's latest creation, hinting that she might have difficulty negotiating the narrow gangplank of a river boat in a bulky crinoline. The Queen took the point, wore the new dress and was to be delighted that she had done so. Her appearance that night was such as to stun even the fashion-conscious Parisiennes. She was 'ravissante,' they said.

France was followed almost immediately by Denmark, and later that year came yet another state visit, this time to the United States. The following year came a visit to the Netherlands.

The itinerary for Denmark, perhaps predictably, included a visit to the Royal Copenhagen porcelain works. Less predictable was a tour of the Carlsberg brewery, where the Queen found herself being conveyed from floor to floor in a goods lift and was obliged to shout in order to make herself heard above the rattle and roar of the lager-making process.

Her visit to the Netherlands the following year, 1958, included an inspection of the diamond-cutting premises of the Asscher brothers, where the huge Cullinan diamond, 3,025 carats in the rough, had been split half a century before. The four largest stones which resulted are now part of the Crown Jewels, but Queen Mary had two of the lesser gems, a diamond of 92 carats and another of 62 carats, made into a brooch which the Queen has inherited and which she wore on the day of her visit, much to the delight of the firm's surviving partner who, though he had not done the actual cutting, had witnessed a task so delicate that the man who did it promptly fainted from strain once the job was done.

The Queen's visit to the United States was ostensibly to celebrate the 350th anniversary of the founding of the first British colony in Virginia, at Jamestown. In reality, and more importantly, it was designed to heal the rift in Anglo-American relations caused by the Suez adventure. However, news that the Queen was visiting the United States aroused hurt feelings in Canada, a Commonwealth country which had not yet enjoyed a visit from its new Queen (though she had been there as a princess). 'You can't visit a friend and ignore a daughter who lives next door' was the theme of indignant editorials in Canadian newspapers. In consequence, arrangements were hurriedly changed so that the Queen should go first to Canada and then cross the border into the United States as Queen of Canada.

Because it was tacked on somewhat belatedly, the royal visit to Canada was necessarily a brief one. With Prince Philip, the Queen arrived in Ottawa on a Saturday morning and flew out again for the United States mid-morning the following Wednesday. A lot was crowded into a few days: a Press reception at which she is said to have shaken hands with 500 people in something under an hour, two other receptions, a Press conference, a wreath-laying ceremony and an inspection of army veterans, a state dinner (noteworthy for its lack of speeches), the opening of the Canadian Parliament (for which the Queen again wore her coronation gown), a Sunday morning service at Christ Church Cathedral and her first-ever telecast.

The Press conference was also her first ever, and she handled it with skill. Would she send the Queen Mother to Canada to serve as Governor General? she was asked, among other things. 'Oh, no,' she replied, smiling. 'We couldn't possibly spare her.'

The telecast was to prove a bigger ordeal. In Britain previously, she had turned down a BBC suggestion that her Christmas Day message to the Commonwealth should be televised. The idea of appearing on television unnerved her. However, a subsequent approach by Canadian television elicited a different response. Encouraged by Prince Philip, who had himself appeared on television to give a witty account of his Antarctic sortie, she agreed, though still extremely nervous about the whole business. Before leaving Britain for Canada, there was a dummy run at Buckingham Palace. It was hardly a success. Indeed, viewing the tele-recording, both the Queen and Prince Philip castigated it as 'a flop'. Another run-through in Ottawa was hardly any better and, as the minutes ticked away towards transmission time, the Queen wore what the Canadian producer later described as a look of 'congealed terror'.

It was Prince Philip who saved the situation. Watching on a monitor screen, he saw how tense and nervous his wife was. He called over one of the production team. 'Please give the Queen a message from me,' he said. 'Tell her to remember the wailing and gnashing of teeth.' The messenger may not have understood the meaning of so cryptic a message, but he delivered it accurately enough. It was, in fact, a reminder that Philip himself had boobed when reading the lesson at the service in Christ Church Cathedral, skipping a line. The Queen gave a big smile and was still smiling a few seconds later when the transmission went live and her face appeared on television screens across Canada. She was also relaxed as she went on to speak in both English and French and, if she did not enjoy the experience, ended sufficiently acclimatized to television to accede to a further request from the BBC that her traditional Christmas Day broadcast should be televised in future.

'A fairytale princess', President Truman had styled her when she visited the United States in 1951. Now, six years later, she was in the full bloom of regal womanhood, and her appearance at a dinner in Williamsburg, for which she wore a jewel-encrusted gown, moved one US columnist to write that it was 'as if Marilyn Monroe walked into a roomful of adolescent girls in gym bloomers'.

Her visit to Williamsburg, the first capital of Virginia, which American ingenuity has cleverly reconstructed to its original seventeenth-century design, was marked by the presentation to her of a painting of Colonel Augustine Warner, who emigrated from England to Virginia around 1628 and who is numbered among the Queen's ancestors on her mother's side. Earlier she had been shown the Jamestown site of the first British settlement in America with its

63

reconstructed fort and full-scale replicas of the three small ships which carried the first British settlers across the Atlantic. 'The settlement at Jamestown was the beginning of a series of overseas settlements made throughout the world by British pioneers,' the Queen said in her after-dinner speech at Williamsburg. 'Jamestown grew and became the United States. Those other settlements grew also and became nations now united in our great Commonwealth.'

Dwight D. Eisenhower was now President, and it was in his personal aircraft that the Queen flew to Washington. (This, incidentally, was the flight changed on the Queen's suggestion so that she should arrive in Washington in daylight.) She and Prince Philip stayed this time at the White House. Philip prefers a bed in which he can stretch out full-length, and in Washington he certainly got it, the massive eight-footer which Mrs Lincoln bought for husband Abe. The Queen's bed was an eighteenth-century four-poster.

Even by America's go-go-go standards her first day in Washington was a busy one. She was welcomed by the President, was presented with the keys of the city by the City Commissioners, visited Arlington National Cemetery and made a speech at a state banquet. There was also a Press conference during which she was asked how she managed to survive such a 'terrific skedjule'. 'By enjoying myself every minute of the day,' she replied.

While the Queen undoubtedly meant what she said, it did not escape observers that she was looking jaded when she arrived back at the White House from Arlington. Once in the privacy of her apartment, she nudged off her shoes to ease aching feet and asked for that traditional British reviver, a cup of tea. However, there was a snag. In all the unpacking and re-packing which had gone on in Canada and Virginia, the cannister containing her favourite blend, which always travels with her, had somehow gone astray. Members of her staff investigated the White House kitchen, but all they could find there were tea-bags. These were tried, but the resulting brew, it was felt, was hardly to the Queen's taste. Fortunately, the presidential housekeeper arrived on the scene. 'I like a good strong brew myself,' she said when the situation was explained. 'I always keep a packet of tea in my room. You can have that.'

If the Queen's pace was hectic, members of her personal staff were no less busy, and none more so than Margaret Macdonald. Working from a schedule jotted down by the Queen herself, it was her task to ensure that the correct change of clothes was laid out, bandbox fresh, for each engagement: 'green silk' for Jamestown, 'dartboard blue and white' for Williamsburg, 'blue satin' for the White House dinner, 'gold lamé' for a reception, 'white satin' for another state dinner, 'Portuguese green' for a reciprocal dinner given by the Queen at the Australian Embassy, 'nut velvet with ermine collar' for her arrival in New York later, 'lace and tulle' for a farewell ball, and eight more besides.

Back home in London there was a degree of hurt pride when the newspapers reported that at the White House banquet the Queen had worn the Hartnell-designed dress she had worn at the state dinner in Ottawa. In fact, as her own notes made clear, this was not so. In Ottawa it had been 'green satin', Hartnell designed and with a motif of maple leaves. For the White House banquet it was 'white satin', designed by Hardy Amies and with a motif of autumn leaves.

Concurrent with the Queen's arrival in the United States, though surely not simply a matter of coincidence, the *Saturday Evening Post*, at that time perhaps America's most prestigious magazine, published an article provocatively entitled 'Does Britain Really Need A Queen?' Written by Malcolm Muggeridge, formerly editor of *Punch*, it questioned whether the monarchy was really anything more than 'a sort of royal soap opera . . . a substitute or ersatz religion . . . a generator of snobbishness and a focus of sycophancy'. Prince Philip, when the article was drawn to his attention, was furious. 'If they must print such things, does it have to be while we are here?' he demanded. But that, of course, was surely the object of the exercise. In Britain national newspapers reprinted the juicier portions of the article, and as a result the author was spat upon in the street and had his contract with a Sunday newspaper abruptly terminated.

While in Washington the Queen went to a 'ballgame' between the Universities of Maryland and North Carolina. At her own request, she was also taken to see round a supermarket, a style of retailing which at that time had not yet crossed the Atlantic to Britain. Or if it had, the Queen had never seen it. The American visit was so hurriedly arranged that the manager, told the Queen was coming to see his supermarket, decided he was the intended victim of some sort of legpull and went home, so one of his assistants had the unexpected privilege of showing the Queen round. Horses had to be included in her itinerary, of course, and there was a trip to Middleburgh to visit the training centre run by Paul Mellons.

To visit New York, the Queen travelled by overnight train from Washington to Staten Island, where she arrived at ten o'clock in the morning. From then on until one o'clock the following morning it was all go. In order to view New York's skyscraper skyline from the best vantage point, the Queen crossed from Staten Island to the Battery in an army ferry. Guns boomed, bands played and fire floats welcomed her with criss-crossing jets. The Queen thought it 'fabulous', a word she has seldom used. There was a ticker-tape parade along Broadway in a bubble-topped limousine similar to the one specially and hurriedly devised during her 1951 visit to Canada. Two hundred tons of ticker tape had to be swept up later. The Queen had lunch with New York's mayor, addressed the United Nations, was taken to the top of the Empire State Building for a bird's-eye view of the city, attended a march-past of Veterans and a dinner given jointly by the Pilgrims and the English-Speaking Union, and went on to a Commonwealth Ball. She had only two 'rest' periods – a break of twenty-five minutes before lunch and a full two hours between her ascent of the Empire State Building and dinner in the evening. Part of the pre-lunch break was spent telephoning home to speak to Princess Anne (Prince Charles was away at school), and later most of the two hours was taken up in changing outfits and dealing with a pile of official documents which had pursued her from London.

The VIP suite at the Waldorf Towers Hotel was made available to the Queen. In the lobby of the suite was a commemorative plaque listing others who had occupied it before her, among them TRH* The Duke and Duchess of Windsor. As the Queen well knew, the Duchess of Windsor had never been accorded the style of Royal Highness, and at least one of those in her entourage thought to detect a disapproving frown as she studied the wording.

If the Queen had little rest during those hectic fifteen hours in New York, Prince Philip had even less. While she was enjoying two hours' privacy, if not rest exactly, in her suite at the Waldorf Towers, he was being shown round the American Institute of Physics on East 45th Street. That done, he decided he would like to

* Abbreviated form of Their Royal Highnesses

see something of New York from the viewpoint of the ordinary New Yorker. So instead of being driven to the hotel, he walked – along Lexington Avenue and 42nd Street, then through Grand Central Station. Arriving at the Waldorf Towers, he found the main entrance blocked by a large crowd which had gathered in hope of seeing the royal visitors. A side door offered a possible alternative. Philip elbowed his way in that direction only to find the door guarded by a burly New York cop. 'All right – it's only me,' he said affably to the surprised cop as he slipped past him into the hotel.

The Queen's schedule for that day had been drawn up to allow her and Philip forty-five minutes at the Commonwealth Ball before leaving to board their aircraft at what was then Idlewild (now Kennedy) Airport. But they enjoyed themselves so much that, despite their long and tiring day, they stayed on nearly an hour longer.

At the airport, meanwhile, their staff were already loading the royal luggage, increased now by many gifts, among them a mink coat, a gold-plated model of the Empire State Building, a replica of George Washington's riding crop, a doll for Anne, a football for Charles, a ceramic model of Philip playing polo, a pair of eighteenth-century spurs and a portrait of Prince Charles which President Eisenhower had painted himself. For the President, the Queen had brought a pair of porcelain birds (American parula warblers) and a walnut table on which was depicted the D-Day battle plan.

Among the items being loaded onto the royal aircraft was the zip-fastened case containing the Queen's cameras. The zip-fastener had broken and, as a temporary measure, a piece of string had been tied round. The case was just being carried aboard the aircraft when a sharp-eyed American security man intervened. 'Hold it there,' he said. 'What's that?'

'The Queen's cameras,' he was told.

'Tied with string?' the security man queried, disbelievingly. 'Don't give me that. Put it on the ground. Gently now.'

While he guarded the royal footman who had been carrying the camera case, another security man carefully untied the string and inspected the contents.

'OK,' he said. 'It's like he said – cameras.'

'Well, it could have been a bomb,' said his partner.

6 A PREGNANT PAUSE

A flying four-day visit from a monarch who had already been Queen of Canada for five years could hardly be expected to satisfy Canadian loyalists, and the Queen was scarcely back in Britain from her 1957 trip than she was planning a longer stay there, a period of six weeks, during which time she would tour the country from coast to coast. Highspot of the visit would be the opening of the St Lawrence Seaway.

Planning so long and complex a tour took the best part of eighteen months. Some idea of the complexities involved can be gauged from glancing at a single day in the Queen's schedule.

Take the day she was to visit Port Arthur, Fort William and Calgary. Between ten in the morning, when she would disembark from the royal barge at Port Arthur, and an unspecified time in late evening, when she would board the royal train, there were thirty-two entries in the schedule. They included drives through Port Arthur and Fort William, the presentation of leading citizens, two hospital visits, an official luncheon, a baseball game, an exhibition of square dancing, a flight to Calgary, another drive through the streets and more presentations, a children's entertainment, a visit to an Indian village, chuck-wagon races and a barbecue, with everything except the departure from the barbecue timed to the minute. For instance, the Queen was scheduled to arrive at St Joseph's Hospital in Port Arthur at 10.08 a.m., leave again at 10.13, arrive at the General Hospital at 10.23 and leave again at 10.28. And so on throughout the day.

Planning was complete when the unexpected happened. Almost on the eve of departure the Queen discovered that, at the age of thirty-three, she was pregnant again after a gap of nine years. Joyful though the news may have been to her personally, the pregnancy

68

could hardly have happened at a worse time. Esmond Butler, her Canadian Press Secretary, though knowing nothing of the Queen's personal circumstances, had already suggested that the planned itinerary was far too arduous and should be modified. 'I am going to work – not on holiday,' the Queen told him. Prince Philip, who did know of his wife's condition, equally suggested that the Canadian tour should be abridged or even postponed, but the Queen would hear of neither. The only small concession she made to changed circumstances was to add a seamstress to her entourage so that her clothes could be altered, if necessary, during the time she was in Canada.

However, while she might dutifully insist on going ahead with the Canadian tour, there was clearly now no question of making a planned trip to Ghana later in the year. Prince Philip offered to go there on his own, and one of the Queen's private secretaries accordingly flew to Ghana to announce the change in plan. Explanation was required, of course, and so President Nkrumah became privy to the Queen's personal secret. But she was adamant that the Canadian authorities should not be told. She wanted no more arguments about curtailing the Canadian tour.

She and Prince Philip flew to Canada in a Comet which had been specially adapted as a royal aircraft. Ordinary seating was removed so as to provide a dining-room for eight people, a sitting-room with divans which could double as beds, and two mini-dressing-rooms with built-in wardrobes. Newspapers in Canada recorded that the Queen seemed to be 'in high spirits' over the course of the next few days as she visited a paper-mill, an aluminium works and an iron-ore mine in temperatures which soared as high as 82°F. Prince Philip, in contrast, was said to be 'subdued', which was hardly to be wondered at. He was worried about the Queen. And with good cause. High-spirited though she may have been initially, the combined effects of pregnancy and the arduous nature of the tour itself were not long in making themselves felt. The Queen was seen more than once by Surgeon-Captain D. D. Steele-Perkins, the doctor travelling with her, and this fact somehow leaked to the accompanying pressmen. Rumours that the Queen was pregnant began to circulate amongst them.

Speaking in good faith, doubtless repeating what he himself had been told, Esmond Butler firmly denied the rumours. As the tour progressed, with the Queen sometimes in high spirits but some-times looking exhausted, a variety of excuses was trotted out to account for exhaustion. It was something she had eaten, it was said; an upset stomach; sinus trouble; something to do with her teeth. The last was true enough, and a one-day side-trip across the border into the United States saw her visiting a Chicago dentist to have a tooth filled. She gave the dentist a pair of cufflinks to remember her by.

By the time she reached Toronto, the temperature was into the nineties, and this too had its effect. But doggedly the Queen insisted upon clinging to her schedule over a non-stop day of fourteen hours. There were times that day when Philip was visibly beaded with sweat. By contrast, in Port Arthur, later, they were both drenched by a sudden rain squall while riding in an open car.

Though the Queen was in the United States only one day, the Americans did her proud. Twenty-four US warships formed a guard of honour for the royal yacht while five squadrons of jet aircraft flew overhead in salute. Guns, bells and ships' sirens sounded a raucous welcome. A 200-foot barge filled with flowers was moored to the landing-stage. Trumpeters blared 'Rule Britannia'. Mayor Dick Daley greeted the Queen with the words: 'Chicago is yours', a striking contrast to that earlier mayor, Bill Thompson, who threatened 'to bust King George [V] on the snoot' if he visited the city. One among many banners epitomized the enthusiasm of the estimated 1½ million people who crowded the city's streets; 'Welcome to the Windy City, Liz and Phil'.

Over the course of thirteen hours the Queen watched a display of fire floats, visited the International Trade Fair (where 2,300 feet of red carpet had been specially laid for her to walk on) and the city's Art Institute and the Museum of Science, ate lunch with seven state governors, forty mayors and 300 other guests and attended a dinner for which the tablecloths had been dyed gold in her honour. America does nothing by halves. Even the hotel where she changed for dinner had re-carpeted the rooms in which she was accom-modated, issued its staff with new uniforms and sprayed its elevators with perfume – though she was to be in the building no more than forty-five minutes.

For the opening of the St Lawrence Seaway the Queen was joined aboard *Britannia* by the American President, Dwight D.

Eisenhower, and his wife Mamie. (Incidentally, the 139-foot main-mast of the royal yacht had been found to be too tall to pass under the bridges of the Seaway. The problem was overcome by inserting a hinge some twenty feet down.)

'My, I've never seen you look so beautiful,' the exuberant Mamie Eisenhower exclaimed as the Queen welcomed her on board. Beauty was the bloom of approaching motherhood. The Queen was dying to tell someone her secret, and she told Mrs Eisenhower. John F. Diefenbaker, Canada's Premier, was also let in on the secret and immediately suggested that the tour should be abridged. The Queen, in high good spirits that day, would not hear of it, but later events would compel a change of mind.

For five hours the royal party cruised the Seaway, *Britannia* coming so close to the concrete of one lock that there was risk of collision. 'It was as close as that,' the Queen said to John Diefenbaker, stretching her fingers. The day ended with a ball in Montreal which came close to chaos. Elegantly gowned women stood on chairs and even on tables in their efforts to glimpse the Queen; couples so crowded the dance floor that dancing was impossible. The Queen and Prince Philip tried twice to dance, then gave up in despair and left.

The trip continued with a train tour of Ontario, a cruise of Lake Superior, the Wild West spectacle of the Calgary Stampede and another train tour, the Rocky Mountains this time. The train had an observation platform from which the Queen made good use of her movie camera.

If that part of the visit had its relaxing moments, Vancouver was something else. During a succession of engagements totalling ten hours, the Queen managed only three brief periods of rest, no more than forty minutes in all. It was enough to exhaust any woman in normal health, let alone one who was pregnant. And the Queen, by the time she reached Nanaimo, where she was ceremonially installed as an Indian princess, was certainly exhausted, with the most arduous part of the tour, a trek through the Yukon and North-West Territory, still ahead. It was a part of Canada the Queen was particularly eager to see, having heard much about it from Prince Philip, who had been there five years before. But the onset of morning sickness was to compel the abridgement she was so reluctant to make. Such was her condition when she arrived in

71

Whitehorse that Steele-Perkins insisted on her spending a day in bed. So Prince Philip, looking worried, went alone to Whitehorse and subsequently to Yellowknife and Uranium City.

Anxious that her mother should not be worried by anything she might read in the newspapers, the Queen called London to speak to her. John Diefenbaker suggested abandoning the remainder of the tour, but again the Queen would not hear of it. She was 'better, but not fully recovered', said an official bulletin when she resumed her itinerary with a flight to Edmonton. Engagements there were followed by a four-day whistle-stop tour of the Prairie Provinces, though it was in fact a bell rather than a whistle which alerted the Queen wherever a crowd had gathered ahead so that she could appear on the observation platform. Sometimes the alert came at such short notice that the Queen, who frequently nudges off her shoes to ease her feet, had to make a dash for the observation platform in her stockinged feet. She visited Saskatoon, Regina, Winnipeg and fifteen smaller places. In Sudbury she went down a nickel mine. Then it was on to the three Eastern Maritime Provinces. In Halifax she sat in on a meeting of the Cabinet, something she has never done in Britain.

Throughout those six weeks in Canada, as on every royal tour, the Queen was showered with gifts. She herself had suggested that she would prefer money to be used to set up scholarships in her name rather than spent on expensive personal gifts. The Canadian Government promptly established a million-dollar scholarship fund. Ontario set up its own half-million-dollar fund, the Hudson's Bay Company funded bursaries at the University of Manitoba, the International Nickel Company endowed a two-year research fund, and Newfoundland launched the Queen Elizabeth Assistance Grant for Retarded Children. But even the Queen's own expressed wishes could not completely overcome the desire to make personal gifts. London, Ontario, for instance, observed her wish by setting up two scholarships in her name but also gave her a pair of bookends. Altogether, by the time the tour was over, she had been given a total of 120 gifts, ranging from a gold and silver desk set to an Indian totem pole, from a statuette of herself carved in green serpentine to the fossilized bone of a dinosaur.

By the end of the tour the Queen was so worn out that a plan to sail home in *Britannia*, stopping off for visits to the Shetlands and

Orkneys, had to be abandoned. Instead, she flew straight to London to be checked over by royal physicians. Fortunately, they found nothing wrong that a well-earned and much-needed rest would not put right.

The following year, 1960, the year of Prince Andrew's birth, is the only one in which the Queen has permitted herself a sabbatical from overseas travel. But in January 1961, cutting short her customary winter holiday at Sandringham, she was off again, to India, Pakistan and Nepal by way of Cyprus. Again she was away some six weeks.

It was almost exactly half a century since King George V, wearing a new crown specially made at a cost of £60,000 (because the two true crowns were not permitted to leave Britain) had been installed as Emperor of India amidst all the magnificence of the Delhi Durbar. Now it was his granddaughter who was in Delhi, not as Empress, not even as Queen, but witnessing the Republic Day parade in her capacity as Head of the Commonwealth. Times change, as the Queen noted in more than one of the several speeches she made in the course of her tour. 'A triumphant vindication,' she called it on one occasion, 'of the vision of the statesmen who changed the old Empire into a free association of equals.'

From Delhi she went on to Karachi, Peshawar, Calcutta and Madras. She was in Madras on Prince Andrew's first birthday and cut a birthday cake to mark the occasion. Then it was on to Bangalore, Benares and the Nepalese capital, Kathmandu. Back in Britain, Winston Churchill was surprised and delighted to receive a telegram from the royal couple, sent from Malakand, where the old war-horse had seen action as a young officer some sixty years before.

As always, throughout the tour the Queen was constantly busy with her cameras. She took photographs of the Taj Mahal in sunshine and went back to see it again by moonlight. She filmed Everest from the air as she flew over, the painted elephants at Jaipur and a crocodile hunt at Udaipur in which Prince Philip took part. He also participated in a tiger shoot, an excursion which aroused so much controversy that when another such shoot was later arranged in his honour he excused himself on the grounds that he had a whitlow on his trigger finger.

Advantage was taken of the return flight to make brief stop-over visits to Iran and Turkey. As always, the Queen had done her homework, which enabled her to call out 'Merhaba asker' to the guard of honour lined up for her inspection in Turkey. These are the traditional words, meaning 'Hello, soldiers', with which Turkish officers greet their men, and the Queen was rewarded with the equally traditional shouted reply of 'Sagol', which roughly translates as 'May you live long.'

Travel-wise, that year was an unusually busy one for the Queen. There was a deal of catching up to do. She had been back only two months when she was off again, this time on a state visit to Italy and the Vatican. There was a stay in Rome (which she had visited before) and a trip to Venice (her first visit), though she saw comparatively little of either, so crowded was her itinerary with receptions, luncheons and banquets.

In Rome the Queen was accommodated in the suite at the Quirinale Palace originally designed for the first Napoleon and traditionally occupied by visiting heads of state. Heads of state usually being male, she was probably amused to find her bathroom fitted with a shaving mirror and to learn that Philip's dressing-room was conversely equipped to accommodate one hundred ball-gowns.

There was a meeting with Pope John XXIII for which the Queen wore a long-sleeved dress of black lace over black satin with a headdress and veil of lace and tulle. She had taken an ebony walking-stick as a gift for the Pope and he gave her, in exchange, twenty gold coins found in the Catacombs. There was also a day at the races. Knowing of the Queen's enthusiasm for horse-racing, Italy obligingly changed the date of its Derby so that she could be there.

In Venice, there was of course a ride in a gondola. Prince Philip was familiar with Venice as a result of school holidays spent there with his Aunt Aspasia, and he very much wanted his wife to see the *taverna* which was the scene of a youthful escapade when he sought to liven up a party by swinging from a pergola and it collapsed on top of him. Like many another sentimental journey, the outing proved rather disappointing. Since Philip was last in Venice the humble *taverna* of his youth had become a fashionable restaurant, more elegant but lacking the old associations.

Also crammed into that year of 1961 was the visit to Ghana which had had to be called off two years before when the Queen found herself pregnant with Prince Andrew. And as she was going to the west coast of Africa, it was as though the Queen felt that she might as well kill four birds with one stone, adding Liberia, Sierra Leone and the Gambia to a tour which lasted from 10 November to 5 December. This was the tour Harold Macmillan, Prime Minister of the day, sought to dissuade the Queen from undertaking. With Ghana in a state of unrest at the time and threats against the life of its Marxist president, Kwame Nkrumah, there was the possibility that a bullet or bomb intended for him might find another target. The Queen, however, was more concerned with prestige than possible danger. Her view, as expressed to her Prime Minister, was that both she and Britain would look foolish if she cancelled her visit and Russia's Nikita Khrushchev went instead. 'And you wouldn't like that,' she reportedly said.

So to Ghana she went, with the Nigerian *Morning Post* commenting: 'A less courageous woman would have asked for special dispensation to put off until some other time a rather hazardous and dangerous undertaking such as the visit to Ghana looked.'

It was cold enough the morning the Queen flew out for her to wear a sable coat for the drive to London Airport. But once aboard her aircraft she took it off and had it returned to Buckingham Palace. 'I don't think I shall need that in Ghana,' she said. Her arrival in Accra was greeted by an improvised song from a group of the city's famous 'market mammies', echoing in more down-to-earth words the article in the *Morning Post*:

> Dey say she mustn't come
> But she come here today.

Only six days before her arrival the statue of Nkrumah which graced the capital had been damaged by an explosion. The President himself pointed it out to her as they drove together in an open Rolls Royce. However, the nearest the Queen came to anything like violence was a small group of demonstrators chanting 'Freedom! Freedom!' For ten days she toured around, seeing the old and the new, tribal dancing and a modern nursery named after her, often in the company of Nkrumah and his wife. They were with her the day she walked round one of the local markets, with the 'market mammies' again serenading her. This time it was a rousing chorus of 'Onward, Christian soldiers'. During the period of her stay seven members of her entourage were taken ill with what was styled 'Accra tummy', but the Queen herself did not succumb.

There was more tribal dancing in Sierra Leone, including a puberty rites dance performed by wiggling maidens of the Bundu tribe. In the Gambia insecticide had to be employed to exterminate the mosquitoes infesting the area around the old fort on Tames Island before the Queen went ashore from the royal yacht to gaze upon the historic site where Britain first secured a toehold on the African continent. Gifts took unusual forms, among them lion skins and leopard skins, a tomtom for Prince Andrew, elephant tusks and a gold model of a chief's palanquin (a cross between a throne and a sedan chair). For Prince Philip, in Sierra Leone, there was a live boa constrictor. For the Queen, in the Gambia, there was a silver box with a pierced lid. Told that it contained a baby crocodile, she quickly handed it to someone else.

7 CALLING ON
IN-LAWS

Old enmities die hard. In consequence, and because the Queen's foreign visits (as distinct from Commonwealth tours) tend to be a reflection of Britain's foreign policy, it was to be some twenty years after the end of World War II before she could visit her husband's sisters in their own homes. During that time she had entertained them often enough, along with their sons and daughters, on their visits to Britain, at Balmoral and elsewhere. But not until 1965, with Britain needing German support for its application to join the European Economic Community, could there be a reciprocal visit to Germany.

The two years before that brought further tours of Australia, New Zealand and Canada along with state visits to Ethiopia and the Sudan.

Despite official denials in Australia and elsewhere, there were those who thought that the Queen's 1963 visits to that country and New Zealand – the first time she had visited either since her round-the-world tour nearly ten years before – were also linked to the Common Market, designed to lessen the impact of Britain's entry and the effect it would have on the Commonwealth.★ The expectations of the time were reflected by the Speech from the Throne which the Queen made when opening the New Zealand Parliament. 'The movement among the countries of Western Europe towards closer economic and political association,' she said (or *read*), 'has important implications for New Zealand and other Commonwealth countries. The broader developments of today

★ Britain's application to join the EEC was twice vetoed by France, and it was not until 1969, when Georges Pompidou succeeded the ageing de Gaulle as President of France, that the way would be cleared for Britain's entry.

require a close and searching appraisal of additional measures to provide New Zealand and other developing countries with the wider opportunities they need for international trade.'

The Queen travelled to New Zealand by way of Canada, Honolulu and Fiji. The flight to Fiji, where she was to board *Britannia* for the remainder of the journey, was not without incident. It was February and a planned touchdown at Vancouver had to be aborted because of a snowstorm. Instead, the royal Boeing 707 landed at Nisku Airport, near Edmonton, after snowploughs had been used to clear the runway there. The aircraft was refuelled and set off for Honolulu, but some 900 miles out it ran into bad weather and was forced to turn back, As a result, the Queen spent the night in a Vancouver hotel and was twenty-three hours behind schedule when she took off again the following day.

However, the possibility of delay had been allowed for and, despite further bad weather and rough seas between Fiji and New Zealand, the royal yacht landed her at Waitangi as planned on 6 February, Waitangi Day, the anniversary of the controversial treaty with Britain which New Zealand's Maoris feel has deprived them of land and rights. Their long-felt grievance did not prevent some 20,000 Maoris gathering at Waitangi to greet the Queen's arrival with the traditional grimacing challenge, songs of welcome and a foot-stamping *haka* dance, and later bidding farewell to her with the haunting strains of '*Poatarau*' – 'Now is the Hour'. But in between greeting and farewell, Sir Turi Carroll, President of the Maori Council, in a speech which foreshadowed the less polite protests which would be staged during future royal visits, urged that the provisions of the 1840 treaty should be embodied in the country's statutes. That, of course, was a matter for the New Zealand Parliament, but the Queen, for her part, renewed the pledge of her great-great-grandmother, Queen Victoria, to protect the Maori people.

Twelve days in New Zealand followed the same pattern as for most royal tours. There were, among other things, visits to a farm and an agricultural research station, to the theatre and a surf carnival, a horse show and a horse-trotting meeting. Prince Philip, on his own, went to watch boys paddling kayaks and rigging a whaler at the Outward Bound School on Queen Charlotte Sound.

That tour 'down under' had been arranged to coincide not

only with Waitangi Day in New Zealand but with the golden jubilee celebrations of the Australian capital, Canberra. The Queen arrived there to be greeted by Robert Menzies, the Australian Prime Minister, with a turn of phrase Winston Churchill might have envied: 'You are the living, loving centre of our enduring allegiance.' Before the Queen left Australia he had become Sir Robert Menzies, the accolade being bestowed at an investiture ceremony held privately during the city's jubilee celebrations. For its part, the Australian Government marked the occasion of the golden jubilee by establishing the Queen Elizabeth II Fellowships, ten post-graduate fellowships in physical and biological science.

The Queen spent five weeks in Australia, during which time she travelled a total of 9,000 miles, 5,600 by air and the remaining 3,400 aboard the royal yacht. Back home in Britain, she had already embarked upon the new-style informal royal luncheon parties designed to enable her to converse at some length with people from varying walks of life. Now, in Australia, her guest list was similarly sprinkled with people of different types. Swimmer Dawn Fraser, cricketer Bill Lawry and Louis Kahan, the artist, for instance, were among the guests invited to one luncheon aboard *Britannia*.

While the majority of the Queen's public engagements were predictable, some were less so or had a slightly unusual twist. Among the places visited was a new town near Adelaide built to house 30,000 factory workers and named Elizabeth after her. While there, she performed the small ceremony of turning on the fountain in the town's park. That too was appropriately named – Windsor Park. In Melbourne she attended the annual Moomba festival, a typically Australian occasion, an exuberant razzmatazz of bands, decorated floats and marching girls.

In Tasmania there was a drive to the top of Mount Wellington for a bird's-eye view of Hobart and its deep-water harbour. In Sydney the Queen saw how work was coming along on the spectacular new opera house which she would open ten years later. In Darwin, at her own request, she visited the home of Philip Roberts, a full-blood Aboriginal working as a laboratory assistant in both the local hospital and the Outback. Her visit took Mrs Roberts by surprise, it appears, for while her husband had known the Queen was calling, he had deemed it wiser not to tell his wife, an extremely shy woman, in case she took fright and absented herself.

As on so many royal tours, there were the inevitable unscheduled incidents, some serious, others amusing. Perhaps the most serious was a telephone call threatening to 'throw acid' over the Queen as she drove in an open car through the gate of the Royal Agricultural Society's showground where she was due to attend a Pageant of Nationhood forming part of the jubilee celebrations. Extra police were at once rushed to the showground entrance, but the threat turned out to be a hoax. Among the more amusing incidents was one at the University of New South Wales where a group of high-spirited students let out a hail of 'Taxi' as the Queen's car cruised past them.

As on so many royal tours too, the Queen's deep love for the Commonwealth was reflected in at least one speech. It was a time when the Commonwealth was in the process of change. South Africa had quit two years before. Newly independent countries elsewhere in Africa and in the Caribbean had become members or were expected to do so in the near future. Some people, said the Queen in a speech in Brisbane, saw this changing pattern as 'the beginning of the end'. Those who thought that forgot that the Commonwealth was not bound by any rigid treaty or rules but was an organic association of like-minded people. 'It is like a plough which is quite useless standing in a shed but in the right hands can cultivate soil into productive farmland. Properly used, the Commonwealth can help cultivate a prosperous, enlightened civilization for all its members; neglected, it will rust into scrap.'

Prince Philip, during the visit to Australia which formed part of his 1956–7 Antarctic expedition, had seen something of the giant new hydro-electric scheme in the Snowy Mountains. Now it was the Queen's turn to venture into those mountains, in her husband's company. A drive beyond the winter snowline brought them to Cabramurra, at 4,880 feet the highest point in Australia. A launch took them for a cruise on the lake held back by the giant new dam, 381 feet high and half a mile thick at its base. Kangaroos, wallabies and emus could be glimpsed on the island sanctuaries as they cruised past. There were visits to three other dams, to two power stations and to the work-face of what would one day be a nine-mile tunnel. That visit involved the Queen's travelling two miles underground, wearing a protective coat and helmet.

The royal couple spent that weekend in a small white-boarded

Thousands cheered the Royal Family in Maritzburg, Natal during their South
African tour in 1947

Australia's Queen stepping ashore in Sydney, Australia, 1954

The State Opening of Parliament by Her Majesty the Queen in New Zealand,
1954

Leaving a banquet with the Australian
Prime Minister Mr (later Sir) Robert
Menzies, 1954

The Queen and Prince Philip get their first
view of Hobart as the 'Gothic' enters the
harbour, 1954

Cheered by Girl Guides and Brownies in Bermuda, 1953

The royal visitors accompanied by Mr Clunies-Ross (left), leaseholder of the Cocos Islands

Queen Salote of Tonga seated between Her Majesty and the Duke of Edinburgh during a sumptuous feast, 1953

Inspecting school kitchens in Copenhagen during her State visit to Denmark, 1957

With Queen Juliana of the Netherlands at a reception in The Hague, 1958

The Queen conquers France, 1957

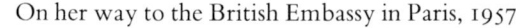

On her way to the British Embassy in Paris, 1957

Leaving Ottawa for Virginia at the end of her Canadian tour, 1957

(*Overleaf*) Chief Oba Adeniji-Adele II escorts the Queen to her car, Nigeria, 1956

Floating down the Ganges to view the Balua Ghat during the tour of India, Pakistan and Nepal, 1961

cottage sited some 4,300 feet above sea-level, and on the Sunday they attended morning service in a timber-built church with a roof of corrugated iron. Visiting Alice Springs, the Queen stayed in a similarly unregal residence, a bungalow with a roof of unpainted galvanized iron, the home of District Officer Dan Conway and his wife. The bungalow, they told her, had been built in 1927 with materials humped across-country on camels.

The Queen flew from Darwin to see the Ord River irrigation project in the Kimberley Mountains. She also visited the iron-mining community at Yampi Sound and the pearl-fishers of Broome (where prisoners in the local gaol were allowed out for the day in order to see her). Royal tours, it seemed, were becoming more adventurous, perhaps due to Prince Philip's influence. Certainly the Queen was again retracing her husband's earlier footsteps when she went with him to the Hamilton Downs cattle station – another place he had visited during his 1956 visit – to witness the spectacle of shorthorn cattle being rounded up by Aborigine stockmen with cracking whips. Despite getting herself liberally covered in the red dust of the area, it was a day out which she thoroughly enjoyed, and she was clearly amused rather than offended when Colonel Lionel Rose, a member of the Legislative Council, sitting a few feet away from her during lunch at the Stuart Arms, silenced conversation with a bellow of 'Shut up!' when it was time to propose the loyal toast.

The birth of Prince Edward in March 1964 involved a gap of eighteen months in the Queen's travel programme, but the fourth of the royal children was only some seven months old when she was off yet again, this time to Canada. It was a visit some people thought it unwise, even unsafe, for her to make. A Canadian expatriate, Sir Campbell Stuart, wrote to *The Times* urging Britain's Prime Minister, Sir Alec Douglas-Home, to advise her against going. If Sir Alec did, then presumably he received much the same sort of reply Harold Macmillan had received over her earlier visit to Ghana. The matter was also raised in the Canadian Parliament, but Canada's Prime Minister, Lester Pearson, said he saw no reason to advise against the visit. And it was, after all, more a matter for him than for Britain's Prime Minister.

The Queen's eight-day visit was to mark the centenary of those gatherings of the Fathers of the Confederation which had led to the British North American Act and the birth of Canada as a nation. One of the places visited by the Fathers of the Confederation, and which the Queen would now visit, was Charlottetown on Prince Edward Island. The other was Quebec, a city seething at that time with French nationalism and at the heart of a separatist movement dedicated to achieving secession from the rest of Canada 'by force if need be', extremists in the movement muttered ominously. Rubbing salt in the wound of French-Canadian feeling, as it were, was the fact that the royal visit to Quebec would start with a landing at Wolfe's Cove, where two centuries before General Wolfe had also landed, with the small British force which was to rout the French on the Plains of Abraham. If the visit went ahead, extremists threatened, Quebec would be turned into 'a second Dallas', a threat which echoed the assassination there of America's President Kennedy less than a year before.

Given the situation in Canada at the time, it was not a threat to be treated lightly. Raids on armouries and army barracks had brought the extremists a supply of weapons. A counter-raid by the police resulted in the recovery of fifteen machine-guns, shotguns, handguns. Fifty people had been arrested and three killed. In Montreal two extremists died in a shoot-out with the police. Elsewhere, a janitor was killed when a bomb exploded in a dustbin. Other bombs were planted in mailboxes, and an army bomb expert lost an arm trying to defuse one. The leader of Quebec's largest separatist party voiced the opinion that the Queen would not be in danger, but added, 'Of course, you can never be sure. It takes only one person with a gun to do it.'

None of this deterred the Queen from carrying out what she conceived to be part of her duty as Queen of Canada.

Security was on a massive scale, of course. Armed airmen and members of the Royal Canadian Mounted Police were everywhere when the Queen's aircraft landed on Prince Edward Island. Four hand-picked Mounties were assigned as her personal bodyguards. One of them rode in the bullet-proof car which conveyed the Queen from the airport. The driver was armed too. Banners in the crowd bore the message 'Liz Go Home.' The message was repeated on walls in French: 'Elizabeth *Chez-Vous.*' None of this seemed to unnerve the Queen in the slightest. On the contrary, at one point she and Prince Philip even lowered the windows of their bullet-proof car so that they could be better seen.

At a concert in Charlottetown the Queen joined enthusiastically in the singing of the tongue-twisting 'Susannah's A Funniful Man'. She had learned the words of the song from her father in childhood. 'He loved funny songs like that,' she told comedienne Anna Russell after the concert.

In her first speech, televised across Canada, the Queen not only spoke in French but took the opportunity to point out that it was a Frenchman, Georges Etienne Cartier, who first promulgated the idea of a Canadian Federation. 'This great act of political states-manship,' the Queen termed it.

Ahead of her arrival in Quebec, frogmen searched the cove in which *Britannia* would anchor. Troops were brought in to reinforce the police, and cars entering the city were stopped and searched. An estimated 5,000 people turned out to witness her arrival and she drove through the streets to the accompaniment of cheers and jeers. Later the jeering would turn to rioting, with riot police in action against the demonstrators. Margaret Macdonald, at least, became sufficiently alarmed for the Queen's safety to urge her to remain indoors. But the Queen herself remained relatively unperturbed. 'Don't worry about me,' she said at one point. 'No one's going to harm me.'

Nevertheless, police marksmen continued to keep watch from rooftops against the possibility of a Dallas-style assassination attempt as she drove to the Provincial Legislature. There were more jeers as well as cheers, more scuffles between police and demon-strators, and thirty-five people were arrested. At the Provincial Legislature the Queen again spoke in French. 'The role of the constitutional monarchy,' she said, 'is to personify the democratic state, to sanction legitimate authority, to assure the legality of means and to guarantee the execution of the popular will. My ardent desire is that nobody among my peoples is subject to coercion. . . . But a dynamic state should not fear to rethink its political philosophy.'

Then it was on to Ottawa where, as though seeking to apologize for what had happened elsewhere, an estimated 35,000 people turned out in the dark and in a biting wind to welcome the Queen to the Canadian capital. It had been arranged that Prince Philip would leave her to attend a reception and state dinner in Ottawa while he went off shooting duck, but all she had been through had not been entirely without effect, even if she betrayed no sign of this in public. She needed her husband's company and support. So the duck shoot was postponed until the Queen had boarded her aircraft for the journey home.

Less than four months after that turbulent visit to Canada the Queen was airborne again, this time flying eastwards. Among the items included in her baggage for the 3,700-mile non-stop flight to Addis Ababa was the baton which would enable Haile Selassie, Emperor of Ethiopia, to add 'Honorary Field Marshal of the British Army' to his several other high-sounding titles, King of Kings, Lion of Judah, Elect of God. Another gift for the ill-fated Emperor, a stallion sired by the Derby winner Nimbus, had been shipped out ahead. For the Queen, in return, there was a pearl necklace and a gold tray; for Prince Philip, a gold sword and a gold and silver fruit bowl. There were also gifts for the royal couple to take back to their children: a gold bracelet and ear-rings for Anne, a gold watch for Charles, and gold medallions for the two latecomers to the family, five-year-old Andrew and baby Edward.

A little doubtfully the Queen went on from Ethiopia to the Sudan. An invitation to visit the former Anglo-Egyptian condo-minium had been extended by General Ibraham Abboud, military ruler of the country since shortly after the Sudan became an independent sovereign state. But Abboud himself had been over-thrown since the invitation was issued. Indeed, there was some doubt as to whether his invitation still stood. It seemed that it did, but there were also fears that the royal visit could become a focus for political demonstration. The Queen decided to take a chance – with surprising results.

Her arrival in Khartoum was greeted with enthusiasm by vast crowds of excitable Sudanese. If the schoolchildren among them had been specially organized for the occasion, as seemed probable, the same could not be said of their elders. And they turned out in their hundreds of thousands. Members of the Presidential Council, which now ran the country, all wanted the honour of being the first to greet the Queen. In the end they drew lots, and the winner was Dr Tigani Almahi, a psychiatrist. There was only one solitary demonstration during the five days of the royal stay, a small affair involving no more than a handful of schoolboys. The only other untoward incident of note was a tomato thrown at the Queen's car when she visited Omdurman, scene of Kitchener's 1898 victory over the Khalifa, when a young Winston Churchill took part in a cavalry charge by the 21st Lancers.

And so to Germany, the Federal Republic thereof, in the late spring of 1965 – and the first opportunity the Queen had had in nearly eighteen years of marriage to visit her sisters-in-law in their own homes.

Of Prince Philip's four sisters, three were still alive. All three (and the dead Cecilie) had married Germans during the family's years of exile in Paris in the 1920s. Sophie, the youngest, had lost her husband during World War II but had re-married shortly after, to become Princess George of Hanover. The other two, Princess Margarita of Hohenlohe-Langenburg and Princess Theodora of Baden, had both been widowed more recently. It was to Sophie's home at Salem that the Queen and Prince Philip went on a free weekend during the state visit to Germany.

All three sisters were waiting on the platform to greet them when their train pulled in, by special arrangement the first passenger train to stop at Salem for some ten years. Others of the family were there too in force: Prince Philip's ageing mother, the widowed Princess Andrew (née Alice) of Greece; Theodora's two grown-up sons, Max, Margrave of Baden, and Prince Ludwig; Margarita's eldest son, Prince Kraft; and three of Sophie's eight children by her two marriages. Prince Philip and others of the family gave the Queen a conducted tour of the castle and the famous Salem school where he had passed a year of his boyhood, and doubtless someone pointed out the desk at which he had sat and on which he had cut his initial with a penknife. Philip's old headmaster, Dr Kurt Hahn, was among those invited to a state dinner in Bonn in the Queen's honour.

Then there was a descent to the castle cellars to sample the local wine, and a leisurely stroll through the village, which had to be cut short when word of the Queen's presence spread and a crowd began to gather, but there was no crowd to impede a drive through the surrounding countryside in a horse-drawn carriage. It was all very private, very much a family affair, as was a subsequent evening visit to Langenburg Castle to enjoy the coming-of-age party of Margarita's twin sons, Princes Rupprecht and Albrecht.

Pleasant though these family occasions were, they were but brief interludes in a busy programme of public engagements. Over the course of eleven days the Queen visited ten major cities during what was more of a royal tour than merely a state visit, and one which eighty-nine per cent of Germans, according to a local poll, saw as being of 'great political significance'.

Everywhere she went she was greeted by scenes of the wildest enthusiasm. In Stuttgart the citizens even went to the length of spraying the grass green for her. In Bonn the whole of the Petersberg Hotel was reserved for the Queen, with the word 'hotel' temporarily removed from the frontage so that technically it became a state residence. In Berlin, with an election in the offing, there was rivalry between Ludwig Erhard, the Chancellor, and Willy Brandt, leader of the Social Democrats as well as mayor of Berlin, as to who had the best right to escort the Queen. In the end both men rode with her in the royal car, sitting side by side facing her on jump seats.

For some reason, Berlin had not been included in the Queen's original programme. It was added at a late stage because Harold Wilson's Government thought it would be 'a good idea' for her to go there. She flew from Hanover along the aerial corridor which links Berlin with West Germany, landing at Gatow military airfield. There was a tour of the city with a brief halt at the Brandenburg Gate. The Queen did not get out of her car, but Prince Philip took photographs. An estimated 200,000 people thronged one of the city squares to hear her speak.

'Nowhere is the tragedy of a divided world more evident than in this city,' she said. 'The courage and persistence of the people and your tremendous achievements in spite of every difficulty are a glowing inspiration to the whole free world. My countrymen, whether at home or stationed with our American and French allies here in Berlin, are proud to have helped to create and maintain the conditions of freedom and security which are so essential to the full expression of the human spirit.' Thirteen years later, on a second visit to Berlin, she would make another speech which was politically even more pointed.

At Cologne the Queen reviewed units of Britain's Army of the

Rhine. While in Düsseldorf she paid a call on Canadian troops stationed nearby. In Munich she attended a gala performance of *Der Rosenkavalier*. There was a river-boat trip along the Rhine covering much the same stretch that her great-great-grandmother, Queen Victoria cruised over a century before. A crowd of 100,000 people turned out to see her when she drove through Bonn in an open car. This being Germany, the car was a Mercedes, not a Rolls Royce. There was the traditional exchange of gifts with President Lubke. For the President the Queen had brought an eighteenth-century coffee-pot designed by Charles Woodward; for his wife a pair of Adam cut-glass candlesticks. In return, the Queen was given a porcelain grandfather clock, while Prince Philip was doubtless pleased to be the recipient of a combination camera and telescope.

President Lubke, in his speech after a state dinner expressed Germany's 'hope and desire to see Britain included in the European Union'. However, it was to be a few more years yet before that would come about. Replying, the Queen referred to World War II as a 'tragic period in our relations happily over'. As in Berlin, her speech had an unusually political content. 'The rising generations in Europe, and indeed the whole Western world,' she said, 'are now united by common interests as well as by a common civilization. It is our task to defend this civilization in freedom and in peace together. That is why we stand together in NATO; why so many of our armed forces are serving in Germany. It is why we wholeheartedly support your natural wish for peaceful re-unification.'

Silver cutlery and candelabra were flown to Bonn from Buckingham Palace for a reciprocal dinner the Queen gave at the Petersberg the following night with President Lubke, Chancellor Erhard and Berlin's mayor, Willy Brandt, among the guests. It was the night of the West Ham *v* Munich football match at London's Wembley Stadium, and a television set was installed in an ante-room so that Chancellor Erhard, a keen football fan, could be updated on the progress of the game during dinner. Unfortunately for him, the German team lost.

8 A FAMILY AFFAIR

By the mid-1960s the Commonwealth was growing apace, becoming steadily larger and more complex as more and more colonial outposts of the old British Empire achieved independence. Between 1960 and a tail-end of 1965 a baker's dozen of Britain's former colonies had become a round dozen of independent states, the islands of Trinidad and Tobago being welded into a single unit. The Queen remained Queen of some. To others, who seized independence as an opportunity to turn themselves into republics, she became Head of the Commonwealth. Both roles required royal visits from time to time, and more and more such visits were to have political overtones.

There had, of course, been the occasional political connotation before, notably in New Zealand, where the Maoris had taken advantage of the Queen's presence to press their rights, and in Canada, where French-Canadians had made their separatist feelings felt in no uncertain fashion. But from now on there would be many more as both governments and those opposed to existing government seized upon the Queen's arrival in a particular country to make a political point. There were instances of both on her 1966 tour of the Caribbean.

It was a time of upheaval in Rhodesia (now Zimbabwe), where Ian Smith had made his Unilateral Declaration of Independence the previous November. The British Government had declared the Smith regime illegal and had imposed sanctions, but it was already apparent when the Queen flew out to the Caribbean in early February that these were going to have little or no effect.

A telephone call to London Airport delayed the departure of the Queen's VC10 by some thirty minutes. There was a bomb on board, said the anonymous woman caller. The aircraft had already undergone a security check, but in view of the telephone call a further check was deemed advisable. Nothing was found. It was yet another hoax. There was to be another bomb scare during the course of the tour, this time in what was then still British Guiana (though it would be independent Guyana soon after). What was thought to be a bomb was found beside a stretch of track over which the royal train was due to pass. Fortunately it turned out to be nothing more lethal than a plastic bag containing a few shotgun cartridges.

It was in British Guiana that the problem of Rhodesia first surfaced. In protest against the situation there, members of the People's Progressive Party boycotted the legislature on the day of the Queen's speech. In Jamaica, later, the Queen's arrival was greeted with protesting banners bearing such slogans as 'Rhodesia Sold Out By Britain'. It was in Jamaica too – an independent country since 1962 – that the Queen, opening Parliament as Queen of Jamaica, found herself reading a speech which said, in part: 'My Government in Jamaica deplore the actions of governments which deny the fundamental principles of human rights. It supports all measures which may be used to put an end to the illegal government in Rhodesia.' And in the Bahamas, a country for which independence still lay some seven years in the future, she found herself briefly caught up in a small degree of political crossfire when Leonard Pindling, the Opposition leader, presented a petition which accused the Government of gerrymandering and corruption.

Despite such political interludes, the five-week tour was an enjoyable one, with everything possible being done to entertain and impress the royal visitor. In Trinidad, where she opened the Trinidad and Tobago Parliament for the first time, she was welcomed by steel bands. She also went ashore on Tobago, the setting for Daniel Defoe's *Robinson Crusoe* adventures. On the spice island of Grenada (which would see an invasion by American marines many years later) she was amused to note that the local buses, rather like fishing boats back home in Britain, rejoiced in such exotic names as *Western Hope* and *London Pride*. In the Virgin Islands she landed on the former pirate stronghold of Tortola to open a new bridge while Prince Philip went off to look over a cable-laying ship. On Barbados local schoolchildren greeted her with a song which began:

From Big to Little England
Our Gracious Queen You Come.

The island of St Lucia staged an historical pageant for her benefit, while Antigua sought to go one better with a *son et lumière* display. There was an amusing moment during the pageant on St Lucia when a replica man-of-war passed the Queen with its mainmast listing at a perilous angle. While other children in the 'crew' hurriedly scrambled to safety, the young look-out in the crow's nest clung stoutly to his post.

In Nassau, capital of the Bahamas, there was an entertainment which brought loud cheers from the watching crowd, though for all the wrong reasons. Almost everything that could conceivably go wrong did go wrong. Mysterious yells and giggles came over the amplifying system, the flag hoisted in the Queen's honour obstinately declined to unfurl, one of six motor-cyclists in a display team came an unexpected cropper, and the conductor of the police band sent his baton flying while indulging in a particularly extravagant flourish. But it all added to the fun, and the Queen enjoyed it as much as anyone.

It was on the tiny island of Nevis that the Queen was accorded perhaps the most rousing reception of the whole tour. Originally it had not been intended that she should visit the island, presumably because it was so small, a mere thirty-six square miles, and insignificant. The omission was promptly noted when the tour schedule was published and resulted in letters of protest to *The Times*, including one from Esmond Pelham Warner, to whose ancestor, Sir Thomas Warner, King Charles I gave the island in 1625. In consequence, the royal itinerary was amended to include Nevis, and more than half the island's 12,700 population turned out to welcome the Queen during the sixty minutes she spent ashore.

Despite the fourteen years the Queen had now been on the throne, there were still European countries to which she had not yet paid a state visit. Later that year it was to be Belgium's turn and the opportunity was taken, in a speech at the state banquet, to express her hope that Britain would help to build 'a wider Europe', an indication (at least it was taken as such) that, despite the earlier French veto, Britain was still wishful of joining the European Economic Community.

Four miles of crowds greeted the Queen's arrival in Antwerp. During her four-day stay she was taken to see those scenes of slaughter in World War I, the Flanders battlefields – Passchendaele, St Julian, Langemarck. She visited Talbot House, where she was greeted by a now frail Tubby Clayton, and the Menin Gate at Ypres where the Last Post was sounded followed by Reveille. Her host in Belgium was King Baudouin, but there was also what was termed 'a private visit' to his father, ex-King Leopold, living in retirement in a *château* not far from Brussels. That visit was no doubt a gesture of reconciliation following the strained relations existing between the Queen's father, King George VI, and the former Belgian monarch which had resulted from Leopold's decision to remain in Belgium, a hostage of the Germans, following his surrender to them in World War II.

The Queen's two elder children were now of an age – Prince Charles was seventeen, Princess Anne rising sixteen – to be introduced to the royal 'roadshow'. Such travelling as they had done so far had been in a private capacity. Charles had flown out to Australia to continue his schooling at Timbertop, an educational outpost of the Geelong Church of England Grammar School, and Anne had been to Liechtenstein for skiing holidays. Both had also been to Germany to visit relatives there. Now it was time for the sterner realities of public travel.

The Commonwealth Games in Jamaica that August, the month of Anne's sixteenth birthday, afforded a suitably gentle starting point. The Queen herself did not go to Jamaica for the Games, but Anne flew there with her father to join Prince Charles. He arrived by way of a short visit to Mexico where, shy as he was at the time, he studiously avoided the choice group of dark-eyed beauties his Mexican hosts paraded for his benefit.

Over the next few years there would be further official jaunts for both children, sometimes in the company of their parents, sometimes on their own. Charles would re-visit Australia to represent his mother at the funeral of Prime Minister Harold Holt and go to Malta for the bicentenary celebrations of the university there. Anne, in 1967, would go to France for the International Horse Trials, a trip which doubtless delighted her, given her enthusiasm for things equine.

However, neither youngster was with the Queen that same year of 1967 when she again took off for Canada, a flying visit during which she would attend the Ottawa centenary celebrations of the Canadian Confederation and see something of Expo 67 in Montreal. Following upon the tension and violence which had marked her visit to Canada some three years previous, her itinerary this time was devised with a view to upsetting the country's French population as little as possible. Notre Dame Isle, the site of Expo 67, was deemed 'international territory', with arrangements made for the Queen to arrive there and leave again by what was, in effect, a back door, to avoid the necessity for her setting foot on what might be construed by separatists as being 'French soil'. For security reasons it was also decided that ordinary members of the public should not be allowed on Notre Dame Isle until the Queen was safely inside the exhibition buildings and that they should be admitted to the Canadian and British pavilions only after she had left again. John Diefenbaker, at that time Leader of the Opposition, complained in Parliament that this could mean the Canadian pavilion being closed to the public until the afternoon. In the event, torrential rain on the day of the Queen's visit to the exhibition helped to ensure that few people saw anything of her.

In Ottawa, speaking in both English and French in an open-air address to both Houses of Parliament on Parliament Hill, the Queen seized the opportunity to make a plea for unity between Canada's founding races. A nation could be sustained and would flourish, she said, only if national unity prospered. She also took the opportunity to atone for a small oversight, the failure to despatch some member of the Royal Family to attend the funeral of General Vanier, a former Governor-General who had done much for the cause of monarchy in Canada. 'I can think of no more valiant or fitting representative of the people,' she said by way of public tribute to him. She reiterated her plea for national unity during her visit to the Montreal exhibition. At a luncheon in the Canadian pavilion, again speaking in both languages, she said that a fruitful dialogue between British and French cultures was a condition for Canada's survival.

Despite the restrictions imposed both on the Queen and members of the public, her visit was deemed 'a tremendous success' by Paul Martin, Canada's acting Prime Minister. Prior to her arrival there had been a degree of speculation in the Canadian Press that it might be her last visit as Queen of Canada. The success of the visit should see an end to such speculation, said Mr Martin.

Less than a fortnight after her return from Canada the Queen was again in Germany, this time reviewing the Royal Tank Regiment on the occasion of its fiftieth anniversary in her role as the regiment's Colonel-in-Chief, and later that year there was a visit to Malta.

The last time she had been on Malta, in 1954, the island to which her father had awarded the George Cross in World War II had been a British possession. Now, like so many other former British territories, it was an independent state, its economy threatened by the rundown in Britain's defence commitments. Much had changed since the Queen's last visit, on her way back from her round-the-world tour. The National Anthem had given way to the Maltese National Hymn. The Maltese national flag now flew in place of the Union flag, though there were still a few of these to be seen, loyally flown by expatriate Britons. The Queen was no longer Queen of Malta – it was now a republic – and it was in her capacity as Head of the Commonwealth that she opened the island's Parliament. But the regiment to which she presented colours was still known as the 1st Battalion King's Own Malta Regiment. Following the presentation, the Queen dismissed her car and walked through the crowd to her next engagement, a visit to St John's Cathedral.

When the Queen visited South America in 1968, she was the first reigning monarch to do so, but not the first member of the Royal Family. Prince Philip had been there six years previously, making a 36,000-mile tour which took him to ten countries, and her uncle, the Duke of Windsor, long before that, way back in 1925, when he was a young and handsome Prince of Wales. The Duke of Windsor went by sea, a lengthy journey made in one of the famous dreadnoughts of the period. The Queen, over forty years later, went by air, flying to Recife in a Royal Air Force VC10 which had been specially adapted to provide her with a lounge, dining-room, bedroom and dressing-room as well as seats for the more important members of her accompanying entourage.

The royal yacht *Britannia* had preceded her to serve as a floating palace once she was in Brazil. And not only as a floating palace. If Commonwealth tours were more and more involving the Queen in politics, so foreign tours were more and more involving her commercially. As much as anything else, the Brazilian visit was by way of being a royal trade mission which hopefully would increase British exports, and *Britannia*, when not required by the Queen, would also serve as a short-stay cruise liner for Brazilian business-men and naval officers, hospitality for the latter being due to the British hope of a contract to supply submarines to the Brazilian Navy.

Prince Philip was already in Recife, waiting to greet his wife when her aircraft touched down at the end of an eleven-hour flight, having flown there from Mexico City where he had been attending the Olympic Games. Like so many other countries visited by the Queen before and since, Brazil was in a state of political unrest at the time. To ensure the safety of their royal visitor, the Brazilian authorities ringed the airport with police carrying sub-machine guns, lined the eight-mile route into Recife with 4,000 more and had a police helicopter hovering watchfully overhead. The worst that happened was a short-lived electrical black-out which necessitated part of the official reception ceremony being conducted by candlelight.

In Brazil, as everywhere else she has ever been, it seemed that everyone wanted to see the Queen. In São Paulo, where she opened a new art museum, 2,000 people were invited to a reception in her honour. Four thousand turned up. No trip to Brazil could be complete, of course, without a visit to Brasilia, the modernistic new capital and an architectural dream come true, built 750 miles inland and 3,000 feet above sea-level on the country's Central Plateau, and the Queen flew there for a state banquet. But imposing though the city was, the length of red carpet laid down for her arrival proved too short for its purpose. 'The man who invented the red carpet needed his head examined,' Prince Philip observed, drily, as a further length was whistled up and laid in position.

Nor was he best pleased, one imagines, on the occasion when the car allotted to him declined to start (this in São Paulo) and had to be pushed to get it going. Judging from reports, there were times too during that South American trip when he did not suffer gladly those he thought foolish. In Brasilia there was the much-publicized exchange of barbed pleasantries with a Brazilian general concerning the latter's 'war medals'. (See p. 51.) In Chile, later, there would be a similar exchange when the President of the Senate, Dr Salvadore Allende, appeared at the state banquet in a lounge suit. He had been asked not to go to the expense of hiring evening dress, he explained, to which Prince Philip reportedly retorted to the effect that it was a good job he had not been advised to come in a bathing suit. However, it was equally Prince Philip's speech to the Santiago Chamber of Commerce (as related on pp. 51–2) which succeeded in gaining Britain a contract to build a nuclear reactor.

For the state banquet in Brasilia the Queen wore the diamond and aquamarine necklace with matching ear-rings which Brazil had sent her as a Coronation gift. Her speech paid tribute to this 'splendid and unique city, visionary in concept, pure in its lines and an inspiration to the nation'. It was a city, she added, 'with which, as it so happens, I share a birthday'. There followed a small misunderstanding, perhaps caused by the translation of what she had said. The Brazilian President, Artur da Costa e Silva, thought she had said that that day was her birthday and quickly rose to propose a birthday toast to his royal guest. It was hurriedly explained to him that the Queen's birthday is on 21 April, the date on which Brasilia was formally inaugurated in 1960.

Because of the prolonged dispute over the Falkland Islands (which would later erupt briefly into armed conflict), the Queen could hardly include Argentina in her South American tour, though Prince Philip had been there two years earlier. Nor did she visit the Falklands themselves. Instead, she went to Chile, returning a state visit which President Eduardo Frei Montalva had paid to Britain in 1965. The guest-house in Santiago in which she was to have stayed had already been redecorated and refurbished for her when it was destroyed by fire. Four floors of the Carrera Hilton Hotel were promptly done up at a cost of several thousand pounds – even new doors with appropriate royal emblems were made specially – so that she could be accommodated there instead.

Brief though the visit to Chile was, it was a notable success, with large and excitable crowds flocking to see the Queen wherever she went. Five thousand people turned up for a royal luncheon at the Prince of Wales Club, so named after the Duke of Windsor's visit in the 1920s, though only 2,000 had actually been invited, and in Valparaiso, when the Queen went there, police were forced to draw truncheons to prevent her being mobbed by the huge crowd.

Austria, six months later, was relatively quiet by comparison, with the Queen greeted with curtseys on her arrival in Vienna though the country's President had democratically decreed that there should be no curtseying. The programme included the customary opera – *Die Fledermaus* this time – and a visit to Salzburg. Perhaps more to the Queen's taste was a visit to the famous Spanish Riding School and a special gala performance by its Lippizaner stallions. After the performance she was presented with two Haflinger ponies to be taken home for Andrew and Edward, then aged nine and five respectively.

It had been planned that Princess Anne, as part of her induction into the royal travel round, should accompany her parents on the state visit to Austria, but an attack of influenza kept her in bed. However, she was sufficiently recovered to fly out and join them before the visit ended – too late to see the Lippizaner stallions, but she did accompany the Queen on a visit to the Federal Stud near Graz. At Innsbruck she was also offered the opportunity to sample schnapps, which, at eighteen, she cheerfully accepted, though her mother declined with thanks.

Princess Anne again accompanied her parents the following March, when the Queen set off on another 'down under' tour which, over a period of nine weeks, would take her again to Fiji, Tonga, New Zealand and Australia. Prince Charles was not in the royal party when it left London – he was concurrently studying at Trinity College, Cambridge, and edging towards his private pilot's licence – but would join it later.

So far, both youngsters' entry into the royal travel round had gone remarkably well. Anne, in particular, had emerged with a burst of youthful vitality which was like a refreshing breeze blowing across the dull surface of traditional royal engagements. At her age she could do things which might have seemed unregal for the Queen. In Germany, for instance, visiting the 14/20th Hussars the previous year, she had taken the controls of a 52-ton tank and fired a burst from the hip with a sub-machine gun.

However, over the next year or so one or two things done or said in the course of the Princess's travels would temporarily tarnish her image. It started on that trip to Australia when she said she would not want to live there. Outspoken like her father, she was doubtless giving no more than a straight answer to a straight question, but

Australian newspapers promptly labelled her 'rude'. In Canada, later, when her face showed distaste at having to clamber onto a too-high jetty in a too-short skirt, she was termed 'sulky'. So the new image was established and, once established, was inclined to stick, at least for a time. So she would find herself described as 'snobbish' in the United States and 'arrogant' in Kenya. But later still, through her adventurous and sometimes risky travels on behalf of the Save The Children Fund, a very different image would emerge.

It was seven years since the Queen was last in Fiji, due to achieve independence later that year after ninety-six years of British rule, and so great was the rush to see her that her senior security officer, Commander Albert Perkins, was bowled over – quite literally – in the forward rush of enthusiastic Fijians.

It was even longer since she was last in Tonga. There was no reunion with the massive and immensely likeable Queen Salote, for she had died meantime, and the Queen was greeted instead by her son, King Taufa'ahau Tupou IV. Taking after his mother in stature, turning the scale at close on 300 pounds and a mighty trencherman, the King entertained his British visitors with a feast of gargantuan proportions. Among the ingredients were 1,368 suck- ing pigs and the same number of chickens. The Queen found herself served with not only her own personal pig but a turkey, two lobsters, a giant watermelon, yams, bananas and a coconut. She contented herself with no more than a sample tasting, though she did observe local custom by eating with her fingers.

The subsequent tours of Australia and New Zealand were to be different from any that had gone before. Taking a leaf out of Prince Philip's book, and probably at his urging, the Queen decided that the time had come when royal visits, if they were to have any real impact, needed to be more down-to-earth. In future, using a phrase employed to describe her change of policy at the time, she would meet 'fewer blue-rinsed matrons and more horny-handed men of the soil'. It is highly unlikely that the Queen herself even thought in such terms, but it sums up exactly what she had in mind. As her Press Secretary of the time, William Heseltine, put it: 'The criticism of previous trips has been that the Queen is always disappearing into town halls with officials. We are doing our best to change that this time.'

97

The main innovation was the now popular royal walkabouts. It was not, of course, the first time the Queen had walked among people, pausing to exchange a few words here and there with some stranger in the crowd, instead of simply cruising past in her car. There had been the occasional expedition on foot before, in New Zealand and in Malta. But they had been rare and entirely spur-of-the-moment. From now on they would be a planned feature of royal tours, though those responsible for the Queen's safety were not always happy about them. On one occasion in Australia, for instance, she was almost completely hemmed in by security men when she went walkabout. As she said herself afterwards, there was little point in the whole business if the only people she got near enough to talk to were those detailed to protect her.

The first of the planned royal walkabouts was in New Zealand, in Wellington. Following a drive to the town hall, the party of the Queen, Prince Philip and Princess Anne split up, much as had long been their practice at Buckingham Palace garden parties, and they went their separate ways to 'meet the people'. Prince Philip, who had done this sort of thing before on his solo tours, was in his element, taking the whole business in his long-legged stride, stopping even to exchange bantering words with a brace of New Zealand hippies. 'You just bumming around?' he asked, grinning. The reply was a monosyllabic 'Yeah.'

The Queen and Princess Anne found the business of striking up casual conversations with complete strangers rather less easy. The Queen, who does not possess her husband's talent for casual chit-chat, was visibly tense and, indeed, would continue to be so for a long time to come. She was nevertheless determined to continue with something she felt was very worthwhile. Anne too was initially inhibited by inherited shyness, though encouraged at one point by a series of wolf-whistles from a group of topless workmen.

The experiment was repeated the following day, by which time Prince Charles had joined the royal party. This time the venue was a sports field. Instead of simply driving round in the customary fashion and thereafter occupying seats of honour, the Royals wandered around on foot to watch the various events. If the Queen looked less tense than on the previous day, though by no means completely at ease, Charles seemed distinctly nervous.

All in all, the consensus of opinion was that the new 'meet the people' approach was working well, despite banners bearing such remarks as 'Monarchy Is A Joke' and a small group of jeering students encountered when the Queen visited Wellington's Taita College. Loyalists in the crowd were quick to boo the students, and a party of 'blue-rinsed matrons' even set about them, belabouring them with parasols and ripping their banners to pieces.

The New Zealand part of the tour included many of the customary ingredients. There was a day at the races, including the New Zealand St Leger, which the Queen thoroughly enjoyed, as she does anything connected with horses. In Auckland there was a visit to the Easter Show, where one wily exhibitor laid his own stretch of red carpet to link up with the planned royal route round the exhibits and so lured the Queen into inspecting his two-room holiday bungalow. Charles and Anne spent a weekend on a sheep station. Like his father before him, Charles was invited to try his hand at sheep-shearing. And like father, he declined. 'I tried it in Australia,' he said, 'taking strips of skin and all.' There was a night at the theatre despite a threat from a group calling itself 'the Revolutionary Activists' that a bomb had been planted in the building. There had previously been bombs at Army and Air Force depots, and the Supreme Court building in Auckland would later be damaged by gelignite. So the theatre became the object of a careful search. Nothing was found and the Royal Family went there as planned.

The crossing from the North to the South Island of New Zealand in the royal yacht was a rough one. So bad were conditions that three sailors were swept overboard from the escorting frigate *Waikato*. Two were rescued, but the third, sadly, was drowned. Aboard *Britannia* several members of the crew were injured, among them the First Officer, Lieutenant-Commander D. J. Bird. The Queen was looking decidedly pale by the time the sea-crossing was over. 'I did not enjoy the experience,' she admitted, though maintaining that she had not been seasick.

Bad weather marred a walkabout at the Christchurch showground, but the Queen squelched around under an umbrella to talk with children. Anne also took advantage of an umbrella, but Philip and Charles scorned such protection. At Gisborne, where Captain Cook first landed just over two centuries before, the Queen again met Maoris, addressing them briefly in their own tongue. 'Greetings,' she said, according to translation. 'Greetings to you of the old world and greetings to you of the new world.' The assembled Maoris roared their approval, but later, at Waitangi, that traditional Maori meeting-ground, came the first of the protests with which she would become increasingly familiar on subsequent visits to New Zealand. A man sought to hand her a petition 'on behalf of the Maori people' but was dragged away by the police.

Arriving in Australia, the Queen started as she meant to go on, leaving the official reception area to talk with people in the crowd. It was again a day of heavy rain and blustering wind. 'You must be soaked and chilled,' she said to one group. 'I hope you don't catch cold.' Prince Philip was wearing admiral's uniform, and a small boy, fascinated by his array of medals, asked, 'How many medals have you got there?' Philip shook his head. 'I don't know,' he replied. 'I've never stopped to count them.'

Walkabouts continued to come thick and fast. There was one, admittedly brief, along one of Sydney's busiest shopping streets, another at Sydney's Royal Easter Agricultural Show. It was here that Australian security men, more nervous about the business of walkabouts than their New Zealand counterparts had been, hemmed the Queen in so closely that she was moved to protest.

If Britain's entry into the Common Market had resulted in an upsurge of republicanism in Australia, there was little sign of it among the vast crowds which flocked to see the Queen. Indeed, a public opinion poll revealed that only twenty-five per cent of Australians were in favour of a republic, as against sixty-five per cent (with the remaining ten per cent undecided) for a continuance of the monarchy. Even among the younger section of the population the voting was fifty-three per cent in favour of monarchy.

So large was the crowd for a walkabout in Melbourne, so great the crush and so frantic the jostling, that two people died, a girl of seventeen and a man in his mid-thirties. It was an aspect of the whole business which had not been anticipated, pointing to the need for better crowd-control.

Prince Charles left the family to fly to Japan, where he would be attending Expo 70 in Osaka. From there he planned to go on to Ottawa before rejoining his parents and sister for a visit to the Canadian Arctic.

The Queen celebrated her forty-fourth birthday that year with a barbecue party on Snapper Island, an uninhabited outcrop forming part of the Great Barrier Reef. Also in the party was John Gorton, the then Australian Prime Minister, who would later reveal how close the Queen came to celebrating her birthday with a ducking. Speaking at a luncheon in Melbourne some two years later, he said, 'Half the crew went ashore before us to spray everything so that there were no mosquitoes or sandflies. The chef started grilling spits and handing food around – a really *de luxe* picnic.

'It started quietly but soon developed into a lot of fun. Somebody decided everybody should be thrown into the water. Princess Anne was thrown in. Then Prince Philip.

'I was sitting next to Her Majesty. I was about to throw her in, but I looked at her, and it was something about the way she looked back.'

So the Queen's famous look, presumably the one it is jokingly said 'can kill at ten paces', saved her from a birthday ducking.

The following day found her at Cooktown, on the Queensland coast, where Captain Cook first went ashore to claim possession of Australia for Britain. The occasion was marked with a re-enactment of that historic event, with a longboat pulling ashore at the mouth of the river named after Cook's ship *Endeavour* and a make-believe Captain Cook being carried ashore by a party of his seamen. Fortunately, with the Queen watching, the latter-day Captain Cook was not dropped in the water, as had happened when the pageant was being rehearsed.

The new-style royal walkabouts continued right up to the moment the Queen left Australia. On the day of her departure, instead of heading straight for her aircraft, she veered off to walk among and talk with people in the crowd. Prince Philip and Princess Anne did the same. Commented the Sydney *Sunday Telegraph*: 'The success of the Royal Tour surprised the optimists and staggered the pessimists. Australians will regard the Royals in a different light after this tour. No more will they appear remote figures removed from the realities which face ordinary men and women. They have been seen as warm and human, full of fun and laughter, and intensely interested in and proud of Australia.'

Australia was followed almost immediately by Canada, a ten-day tour to mark the centenary of the North-West Territories and Manitoba Province. After the upsets of some previous Canadian visits, pregnancy on one and riots on another, it would have been understandable if the Queen had viewed this latest tour with some small degree of trepidation. As it turned out, it proved to be a trip of which she would long retain pleasant memories. She was again accompanied by Princess Anne, as well as Prince Philip. It was the sort of tour in which Philip delights most, taking the royal party to such places as Resolute Bay, Yellowknife, Fort Smith and Fort Providence – 'Right out into the wilds', as a royal spokesman put it.

At Frobisher Bay, a township with a largely Eskimo population of some 1,500 inhabitants, they met up with Prince Charles. Also there to welcome them was Pierre Trudeau, the Canadian Prime Minister. The temperature was 30° below, and polar bears could be seen roaming about on the frozen ice of the bay. While the Queen joined in the hymn-singing at the site of a new cathedral and went walkabout among the Eskimos, Charles took the opportunity to go fishing. This involved going out onto the ice and drilling a hole down, through which to drop a line. He caught twelve fish and had one for breakfast the following morning.

Then it was further north still to a tiny Eskimo settlement with the almost unpronounceable name of Tuktoyaktuk. Here the Royal Family stayed up for eighteen hours in the hope of seeing the midnight sun, but bad weather meant that all they got to see of it was a slight gleam through heavy cloud. Disappointed, they flew to Inuvik in a small twin-engined plane to spend the night in a boarding-school. Behind them they left an unfortunate group of about eighty reporters and photographers. The accompanying aircraft having failed to start in the intense cold, the pressmen found themselves sleeping as best they could on the floor of a gymnasium.

Shots of the Queen among the Eskimos, and previously in Australia, were included that year in a television travelogue which accompanied the Queen's traditional Christmas Day message to the Commonwealth. 'The Queen Show,' Prince Philip called it, jokingly.

9 SUMMONED HOME

Twice during her reign events in Britain have obliged the Queen to interrupt an overseas tour and return home unexpectedly.

Australia was the country to miss out on each occasion. She was on her way there in 1952 when the death of her father and her own accession to the throne caused the tour to be aborted. Then in 1974 she was already in Australia but had time only to open the Australian Parliament before the constitutional crisis in Britain following the downfall of Edward Heath's Government again caused her to abandon her programme and fly home. Hardly had that crisis been resolved than a state visit to Indonesia was interrupted by news from London of the attempt to kidnap Princess Anne.

By then the Princess was a married woman.* But marriage was still in the future during those earlier years of the 1970s when she accompanied her parents on further Commonwealth tours and state visits as she had already accompanied them in Austria, to Fiji and Tonga, to New Zealand, Australia and Canada. She was again with them in Canada in 1971, accompanied them on a state visit to Turkey the same year and was with them for a six-week tour of South-East Asia and the Indian Ocean in 1972.

The 1971 visit to Canada was linked to the centennial celebrations of British Columbia. The Queen was not in the best of health at the time. She had been suffering from one of those heavy colds to which she had been subject from childhood, but she doggedly refused to curtail her planned programme. In fact, it was Anne who was missing from a number of functions later during the ten-day visit, when she went down with a stomach upset.

Despite her own state of health, the Queen crammed a lot into

* She had married Captain Mark Phillips in November 1973.

those ten days. One day saw her fulfilling public engagements non-stop over a period of eighteen hours, while several other days' schedules extended to twelve hours or more. Especially hectic was a thousand-mile tour of the backwoods, with eight stops crammed into eight hours of travel by air and road. One of the stops was for a rodeo and barbecue at Williams Lake, where accompanying pressmen had to scramble hastily over a high fence when four bulls stampeded in their direction, a spectacle which caused both the Queen and Prince Philip to chuckle.

That was in May. In October the same year came the state visit to Turkey. The Queen flew to Ankara, where Prince Philip and Princess Anne were waiting to greet her. They had arrived only twenty minutes earlier from Izmir (formerly Smyrna), where they had spent the night aboard the royal yacht following a visit to Iran for the 2,500th anniversary celebrations of the Peacock Throne, soon to be no more. Together, the three of them visited the tomb of Kemal Atatürk, the founder of modern Turkey, as well as watching a fashion show and a cavalry display. There was also a day at the races where the Queen's knowledge of horses enabled her to pick the winner of a new race named in her honour. The crowds were almost overwhelming. At Izmir the Queen's car was bombarded with flowers during her six-mile drive from the airport. 'It's like the charge of the Light Brigade,' she joked as the thickness of the crowd impeded her entrance to an hotel where she was due to have lunch. 'No, more like a rugger scrum,' she decided when the same thing happened again later on a visit to a car factory.

There was also a visit to the battle sites of Gallipoli, where the Queen saw the shallow remains of the World War I trenches and laid wreaths at the memorials to the dead of five countries, Britain, Australia, New Zealand, France and Turkey.

At the Topkapi Palace in Istanbul the Queen was shown round the 400 rooms of the harem with their luxurious carpets and tapestries and richly jewelled sixteenth-century ornaments. To entertain her, musicians dressed in period costume played love songs from the days of the Ottoman Empire. There were also visits to St Sophia Cathedral and the Blue Mosque, where the Queen conformed to custom by wearing over-slippers while Prince Philip simply slipped off his shoes and walked around in his socks. The state visit over, the family split up again to head in different directions. Prince Philip was off to visit British troops in Germany, Princess Anne was heading for Hong Kong in her capacity as President of the Save the Children Fund, and the Queen was returning home.

The following year, 1972, was another busy one, with a ten-week tour of South-East Asia as well as state visits to France and Yugoslavia.

The South-East Asia tour started with a visit to Thailand. The Queen, along with Prince Philip and Princess Anne, flew into the U Tapao air base and from there a car took the royal party to the port of Satahip, where *Britannia* was waiting to take them on the 400-mile cruise to Bangkok.

A small hiatus marked their arrival in the Thai capital. Their host, King Bhumipol (not only royal but divine, known among other things as Brother of the Sun, Half-Brother of the Moon and the Possessor of the Four-and-Twenty Gold Umbrellas), had decided to fill in time by receiving various Thai dignitaries. So engrossed was everyone in all this that no one noticed the Queen's launch coming upriver until the Queen was actually on the point of stepping ashore. Queen Sirikit promptly hastened to greet her, with the country's diminutive King almost breaking into a trot in his effort to catch up. 'These things do happen,' said Queen Elizabeth as apologies and explanation were tendered to her. From then on she was welcomed in characteristic style, walking to the royal pavilion over a carpet of yellow flowers and sheltered from the glare of the King's brother, the sun, by one of the four-and-twenty gold umbrellas.

The Queen was plainly fascinated by this *King and I* country of tinkling temple bells and small, dainty people (Prince Philip positively towered over King Bhumipol). But, as so often on royal tours, appearances were somewhat deceptive. Out of sight of the Queen, Thai troops were patrolling the surrounding jungle against the possibility of attack from Communist guerrillas as the royal party flew north to Chiang Mai. Nor, of course, did the Queen see anything of the drug-trafficking of which Chiang Mai is the centre. But she did get to visit a leper colony. She has been deeply concerned for lepers ever since her 1947 visit to South Africa, when she was still a princess, and since then both she and Prince Philip

have 'adopted' individual children suffering from leprosy for various periods. Indeed, at the time of their visit to Thailand she and
Prince Philip each had an 'adopted' leper child, a Ugandan girl of
thirteen and an Indian boy of ten.

In Thailand there were visits to a handicrafts exhibition, a display
of traditional dancing and a logging display by elephants. The
elephants had the Queen busily clicking away with her camera,
with Princess Anne doing the same. On her own, Anne was shown
round a school of classical dancing, while Prince Philip went to
meet British Buddhists at a monastery in Bangkok. Behind all this
lay the hope that British exports might benefit in a country where at
that time they were running a poor fourth to the products of Japan,
the United States and West Germany.

At King Bhumipol's winter palace in Chiang Mai there was a
banquet at which the Royals ate with their fingers and were served
by girls down on their knees. There was also a picnic lunch beside a
waterfall in the jungle, where local tribesmen danced in their
honour. The tribesmen's costumes were adorned with silver coins
dating back to the days of Queen Victoria, and Victoria's great-
great-granddaughter thought it would be a nice gesture to add some
bearing her own image. Unfortunately, there was a slight snag.
Except when she goes to church on Sundays, the Queen herself
never carries money. So she turned for help to members of her
entourage. However, they could muster only a few British coins.
Not enough, the Queen thought, and she appealed for help to the
pressmen accompanying the royal party. A search through pockets
finally mustered sufficient 5 and 10 pence coins, silver in appearance
if not in content, for the Queen to make a satisfactory distribution.

At the local airport, as the Queen boarded her Comet to fly back
to Bangkok, some 450 girls performed the country's traditional
fingernail dance in her honour and, looking back as the Comet
became airborne, she was delighted to see, what had not been
apparent at ground level, that their red, white and blue sarongs
formed the pattern of Britain's national flag.

From Thailand, where she had found herself eating with her
fingers, it was on to Singapore, where she was supplied with
chopsticks for a banquet which included shark's fin dumplings,
deep-fried chicken, Peking duck, Chinese cabbage and yam cake.
The Queen is not often beaten, but the chopsticks defeated her and

she ended up eating with a spoon. Part of her three days in Singapore was spent visiting a new high-rise block of flats built to re-house people from the city's slums. Her Rolls Royce, manœuvring in an attempt to avoid hitting anyone in the throng around, ending up colliding with a bollard. The accident dented the nearside door so badly that it would not open and the Queen was obliged to slide across the seat and get out on the other side before paying a call on a family on the eighteenth floor.

There was again a day at the races. The Queen saw Lester Piggott win the new Queen Elizabeth II Cup on a horse named Jumbo Jet, and herself presented the trophy to the winning owner. But the highspot of those three days in Singapore was a visit to Chinatown. Milling crowds surrounded the Queen as she walked along Pagoda Street, pausing here and there to take a closer look at stalls selling cakes, sweetmeats and costume jewellery. There was also a pause at a flower stall, whose proprietor took advantage of the occasion to present her with a pot of tulips. They turned out to be plastic. More to the Queen's liking was an official gift: a new camera, gold-plated. Prince Philip and Princess Anne each got one too.

Ahead of the Queen still lay Malaysia, Brunei, the Maldive Islands and the Seychelles. In Malaysia (where she partnered the Prime Minister, Tun Abdul Razak, in the *joget*, a traditional dance which can be likened perhaps to the cha-cha) there was a small moment of panic during a walkabout in Kuala Lumpur, the capital. So big was the crowd pressing in on the Royals from every direction that Princess Anne was momentarily cut off from her parents. 'Where's Anne?' the Queen asked, slightly alarmed. It required the combined efforts of members of the Queen's entourage and the local police to force a passage through the crowd and enable the Princess to rejoin her parents. There was also a visit to a local mosque. Well accustomed by now to Moslem tradition, the Royals quickly shed their shoes and were already inside the mosque while their accompanying police were still unlacing their regulation boots. As a result, they were almost mobbed by Moslem worshippers before their police escort caught up with them.

There was a flying visit to Kelantan State on the east coast of the peninsula to see what is known locally as 'the Beach of Passionate Love'. Fortunately perhaps, Moslem law has now prohibited the sort of loving which gave the beach its name, and the Queen witnessed nothing more erotic than displays of dancing and wrestling and fishermen mending their nets. There was also a display by an orang-utan trained to climb trees and collect coconuts. But the orang, named Jambol, totally unimpressed by his royal audience, initially declined to perform for their benefit, so the Queen waited . . . and waited . . . and waited while Jambol's owner alternately wheedled, coaxed, coerced and threatened his reluctant coconut-picker. Finally, after about an hour, Jambol relented and went to work for the Queen's benefit.

A demonstration with a blowpipe, during a visit to the Bajau tribe, fell even flatter. Prince Philip, in particular, was keen to inspect this ancient weapon, much to his wife's alarm. 'Darling, do be careful. Remember it's poisonous,' the Queen called out as he handled one of the darts. Poisonous or not, a subsequent demonstration of marksmanship failed to send the dart whizzing from the blowpipe, though the embarrassed marksman huffed and puffed with might and main. 'It's probably full of fluff,' joked Philip.

Also in the royal party on that tour was Prince Philip's uncle, Earl Mountbatten of Burma, who had been Allied Supreme Commander in South-East Asia during World War II. For him, in particular, arrival at Kota Kinabalu in Sabah (formerly North Borneo) was a poignant experience. It was there that his wife, Edwina, visiting the area in her dual capacity as Superintendent-in-Chief of the St John Ambulance Brigade and President of the Save the Children Fund had died in her sleep some twelve years previous. Back in London, Mountbatten had received news of her death by telephone in the early hours of the morning. Visiting what had once been Government House, where Lady Mountbatten died, the royal party found that it had since been turned into offices. The rest of the party stayed discreetly outside while Mountbatten went in on his own, emerging again shortly after to ask the others to join him. 'It brings it back very vividly,' he told them. 'In some ways twelve years seems a long time, but in others it is like only yesterday.'

From Sabah the Queen doubled back to the tiny west-coast state of Brunei and its larger neighbour, Sarawak. In Brunei she found herself being hauled around in a massive golden chariot mounted on the chassis of a six-ton truck with forty-eight hefty members of the Royal Brunei Regiment providing the necessary manpower. Sarawak, like Thailand, was an 'area of unrest', with fighting going on not far from where the Queen was staying. In 1842 the Sultan of Brunei had ceded Sarawak to its famed 'white rajah', Sir James Brooke, in return for his help in quelling a rebellion. Now, in 1972, the country was again in a state of rebellion, and the Queen, watching a colourful procession of dragon boats during her one-day stay in the capital, Kuching, was given the protection of a 3,500-strong security screen because of the nearby jungle fighting between government forces and guerrillas seeking to achieve secession from the Malaysian Federation.

A second brief stop at Singapore before visiting Malacca and Penang in Malaya enabled Princess Anne to leave the party and fly home. With the Badminton Horse Trials coming up, she was eager to resume training – and perhaps even more eager to resume her budding romance with Mark Phillips.

It was in Malacca, incidentally, that the Queen stood beneath a coconut tree to watch a display of dancing. A breeze sprang up and a large bunch of coconuts suspended immediately above her began to sway ominously. A member of her entourage spotted what was happening and had a quick word with Prince Philip, who, in turn, looked up at the swaying bunch of coconuts and whispered to the Queen, who promptly took two paces forward out of harm's way. In the event, the coconuts stayed where they were until after the Queen had left.

The journey home was by way of the Maldive Islands, Gan (the mile-square island just south of the Equator in the Indian Ocean which Britain leases as a Royal Air Force staging-post), the Seychelles and Mauritius, where the Queen opened the island's Parliament. At Mali, capital of the Maldive Islands, she served as sort of postwoman – or, at least, others did on her behalf, delivering a set of textbooks sent out from schools in Dorset to John Housley, a Dorset man who was principal of one of the local schools. The Queen also visited the local hospital, the only one in the islands, where she was shown brand-new anaesthetic equipment in the operating theatre. Royal questioning elicited the fact that it had never been used because the hospital staff hadn't the faintest idea *how* to use it. Returning to *Britannia*, the Queen promptly sent for the yacht's medical officer, Surgeon Lieutenant-Commander Ronald Snow, and arranged for him to be ferried ashore to give the hospital staff a teach-in.

Signs of unrest again awaited the Queen at Mahé in the Sey-chelles, where there had been three bomb explosions during the previous four weeks, the last only two nights before her arrival. Nevertheless she went ashore for a lunch which included *coco-de-mer*, the legendary forbidden fruit of the Garden of Eden and believed by the islanders to possess aphrodisiac properties. The Seychelles, at that time, were still a British colony, a fact about which not all the islanders were entirely happy. Red flags of the left-wing Opposition vied with the red, white and blue of Britain during the period of the Queen's visit, and at least one banner of welcome made the reason abundantly plain. It read: 'Welcome Queen – Come Back For Our Independence.' However, it was to be another four years before independence would be granted.

By the time she arrived back in London, the Queen had travelled another 25,000 miles. Her flight home included a touch-down in Kenya. It was the first time she had been there since she became Queen while staying at the Sagana royal lodge in 1952. 'It is hard to believe that twenty years have slipped past so quickly,' she said.

The Queen had originally planned to stay only two hours in Kenya, but Jomo Kenyatta, the country's octogenarian President, insisted that it required at least four hours for her to be given a proper welcome. The royal aide responsible for the Queen's travel arrangements thought two hours quite sufficient. The Queen would quite understand if she was given 'a quiet welcome', he said.

'The Queen may understand,' Kenyatta retorted, 'but the Kenyan people will not, and neither will our African neighbours.'

He got his four hours.

Later that same year, 1972, came state visits to republican France and Communist Yugoslavia.

The old *entente cordiale* between Britain and France had become rather less than cordial as a result of General de Gaulle's vetoes of Britain's application to join the European Economic Community in 1963 and 1967. Then President Pompidou took over and there was a change for the better. He arranged a referendum on the question of an enlarged European community to include Britain. Thirty-six per cent of the French people voted *oui*, twenty-four per cent *non*, and forty per cent did not bother to vote at all. The voting figures were sufficient to clear the way for Britain's entry and, as a thank-you gesture, the Queen paid a state visit to France a month after the referendum. It was her second state visit to that country – she had been there before in 1957 – and the first time she had paid a second state visit to any country.

The French went into a positive frenzy of excitement at being singled out for such special treatment. French television showed the film *Royal Family*. *Le Figaro* published daily previews of the visit for a full two weeks ahead. Shopkeepers in the Faubourg St-Honoré told the story of the Queen's life in a collection of 360 pictures displayed in windows the length of the street. The road surface opposite the residence of the British Ambassador was torn up so that a special pedestrian crossing could be laid for the Queen, with the royal coat-of-arms depicted in tiles of Limoges porcelain. The Rue Royale planned to greet her arrival by releasing 500 pigeons, but this idea was vetoed by the Paris police. 'They've dragged up an absurd old rule,' grumbled one of the Rue Royale pigeon-fanciers. 'Just because pigeons were used by the enemy when in sight of Paris in 1870, they seem to think that we shall be using them for an attack on Her Majesty.'

Well-to-do French matrons almost came to blows in their efforts to get invitations to a state dinner and reception held at the Palace of Versailles. Many were disappointed. There were only 150 invitations to the dinner, though a further 2,000 people managed to get invited to the reception.

President Pompidou, in his speech at the state dinner, verged on the lyrical. 'For the first time in more than ten centuries,' he said, 'from the Sea of Norway to the Mediterranean, from the shores of the ocean to the banks of the Elbe, the peoples of Western Europe are committed to the path of economic integration and political co-operation.'

The Queen's speech, if less lyrical, was no less enthusiastic. 'We may drive on different sides of the road, but we are going the same way,' she said. 'Words like "friendship" and "co-operation" are sometimes part of the debased currency of diplomacy, but there is something deeper between our two countries which needs no label. . . . We should seek to lead by our standard of human civilization, by our example, and to influence by our success in confronting the great problems of our times: poverty, pollution and the neglect of the quality of life in the reckless pursuit of material

111

gain. In all this the European Community will have a heavy responsibility, and to these great tasks my country can bring her long traditions and her wide experience and her links overseas, especially with the Commonwealth.'

Her speech displeased at least one person, however. Labour Member of Parliament William Hamilton complained in the House of Commons that she had spoken like 'a clockwork doll' and accused Edward Heath, the then Prime Minister, of 'excessive obsession' with the Common Market. 'Don't you think it would have been more dignified and more honest,' he demanded of the Prime Minister, 'if you had chosen to make the official speeches in France?' Not so, Heath retorted. 'Her Majesty on state occasions makes speeches herself, on the advice of her ministers.'

The French, on the other hand, were wildly enthusiastic about the speech and every other aspect of the visit. In particular, both the Queen and Prince Philip delighted their French hosts by speaking in French, not only at the official welcoming ceremony but in casual conversation in walkabouts. 'The Queen has a slight accent, but we understood her quite easily,' commented a Frenchwoman to whom she spoke during a visit to Arles.

For a reciprocal dinner at the British Embassy the Queen flew over a dinner service made originally for Queen Victoria, gold cutlery that was even older – it had been made for George III, six members of the Household Cavalry to stand with their swords at the salute as guests arrived, and four Scots pipers and a Royal Marines band to provide the music. With her, as a gift for President Pompidou, she took a painting by Graham Sutherland. For Madame Pompidou there was a gold and topaz brooch, and some children's books for her grandchildren. In return she received a hand-embroidered tablecloth and bedspread, while for Prince Philip there was an outsize grasshopper in Sèvres porcelain.

The royal couple stayed at the Grand Trianon, a *château* in the grounds of Versailles, where the Queen elected to use the consort's bedroom rather than the vast and rather overpowering imperial bedchamber. Her interest in horses was well catered for during the visit. There was a display of classical horsemanship by riders from the Saumur Cavalry School and a day at Longchamps racecourse. The Queen would probably also have liked to see the wild horses of the Camargue, but it was Prince Philip on his own

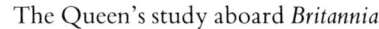

Her Majesty's Yacht *Britannia*

The Queen's study aboard *Britannia*

Prince Philip and Jomo Kenyatta at the Independence Day celebrations in
Kenya, 1963

The Queen inspecting troops in Germany, 1965

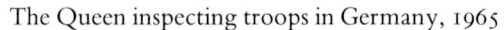

Inspecting a Guard of Honour in Trinidad, 1966

With King Taufa'ahau Tupou IV of Tonga, 1970

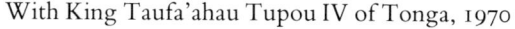

Chatting to President Tito of Yugoslavia during her State visit in 1972

(*Opposite*) Arriving in Thailand, 1972

Receiving exquisite gifts in Thailand with Princess Anne, 1972

The royal couple with Princess Anne and Prince Charles during the Canadian tour, 1970

Feeding a koala bear in Australia, 1970

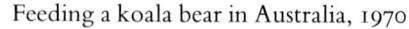

A walkabout in New Zealand during the 1977 visit

Dazzling her hosts in Mexico, 1975

A tea ceremony at the Katsura Imperial Villa, Kyoto during the visit to Japan, 1975

Carried on a golden chariot in Borneo, 1972

who was taken to see them while the Queen had to be content with viewing the Roman remains at Arles, Avignon and St-Rémy.

Prince Charles joined his parents for the last three days of the visit. He was now in the Royal Navy, a sub-lieutenant on HMS *Norfolk*, and his ship was conveniently visiting Toulon. Generous-hearted as he is, Charles had long wanted to patch up the generation-old rift between the Duke and Duchess of Windsor and the rest of the Royal Family. Two years before, visiting France to represent the Queen at the memorial service to General de Gaulle, he had taken the opportunity to call upon the Windsors at their home in the Bois de Boulogne, the first of his immediate family ever to do so. It was perhaps in consequence of that call by Prince Charles, or perhaps because the Queen knew that her uncle was dying, that she decided to pay a similar call during her 1972 visit to France. Prince Charles and Prince Philip went with her.

Delighted at the prospect of the visit, the Duke had planned to receive his niece in the library and afterwards pose with her for photographs on the terrace outside. But his health did not permit. Instead, it was the Duchess who met the visitors at the door and took them into the library, where they had afternoon tea before going upstairs to see the Duke in his first-floor sitting-room. He was up and dressed but too frail even to get to his feet as the Queen entered. Altogether, her visit lasted some forty minutes. It was the last time she was to see the uncle who had been briefly King Edward VIII. He died ten days later from cancer of the throat.

That the Queen should have received such an enthusiastic welcome from the French people was perhaps no more than was to be expected. More surprising was the fact that five months later she should receive an almost equally enthusiastic welcome on her first visit to a Communist country, Tito's Yugoslavia.

Accompanied by Prince Philip and Princess Anne, she drove the fifteen miles from the airport into Belgrade through a gangway of cheering crowds. People were massed six deep in the main street of the capital, while her visit to Belgrade University saw her accorded a warmer and certainly more polite reception than she had received from students at Scotland's Stirling University a week before.

However, bad weather resulted in a degree of confusion over her visits to Dubrovnik and Titograd. At Dubrovnik the official reception committee was already assembled complete with band, guard

113

of honour and cars for the planned motorcade when word was received that because of the weather the Queen's aircraft would now land at Titograd. So off they all went. But when a change in the weather saw the original schedule restored, not everyone in the royal party was informed of this. As a result, some members of the Queen's entourage, along with British Embassy officials and accompanying pressmen, landed at Titograd, where the official reception committee was now waiting, while the Queen arrived at Dubrovnik to find herself unexpected and was obliged to remain sitting in her aircraft for some twenty minutes while a small and unofficial reception committee was hastily assembled.

Visits to the major countries of the old British Commonwealth – Canada, Australia, New Zealand – were becoming more frequent. In 1973 the Queen was again in Canada, her third visit in four years. In fact, she flew to Canada twice that year. 1973 found her also in Australia, her second visit in four years. She was there again – and in New Zealand – in 1974, though this time events back home would curtail her visit.

Principal reason for her first visit to Canada in 1973 was to attend the centennial celebrations of Prince Edward Island, though she also stayed on to tour parts of Ontario, Saskatchewan and Alberta. Prince Edward Island, on Canada's eastern seaboard, is the cradle of the country's nationhood, the setting in 1864 for the Confederation conference. However, it was not until nine years later that the island itself actually joined the Confederation. Hence the Queen's 1973 centennial visit. She has since attended centennial celebrations in Ottawa, the North-West Territories, Manitoba and British Columbia, though it will fall to a future monarch to attend those in Newfoundland, which did not become part of the Canadian Confederation until as recently as 1949.

Prior to the Queen's arrival in Canada, the Toronto *Star* had published a leading article advocating that the country should have its own Canadian head of state. Normal royal policy is for the Queen not to become involved in newspaper politics. But this time she took the unusual step of replying in a public speech. The Crown, she said, should be seen as 'a symbol of national sovereignty belonging to all . . . not only a link between Commonwealth countries but between Canadian citizens of every national origin and ancestry'. The Canadian Prime Minister, Pierre Trudeau, who joined the Queen in Charlotteville on 1 July for the festivities celebrating Canada's National Day, also spoke out strongly in support of the monarchy. Speaking in a radio broadcast, he said that Canadians should realize when they were well off. Monarchy had served Canada well in the past and was probably the only form of government acceptable to the vast majority of Canadians.

As though to underline what he said, Trudeau also invited the Queen to return to Canada later that same month for the Commonwealth Heads of Government meeting, being held that year in Ottawa. It was the first time the Queen had been invited to such a meeting outside Britain and, enthusiastic as she is about the concept of the Commonwealth, she was delighted to accept. With other Commonwealth countries quick to tender similar invitations in later years, it was the start of a new royal tradition.

Royal travel had come a long way since the Duke of Windsor, as Prince of Wales, made his show-the-flag visits to countries like Japan and Chile in the 1920s. Air travel and, since the 1960s, jet travel now made it possible for the Queen to cover in hours distances which had taken her uncle weeks in a battleship. So by 1973 she thought nothing of flying back to Canada for the few days of the Commonwealth Conference and, not long after, flying to Australia.

This visit was to open the spectacular new Opera House at Sydney which the Queen had first seen ten years before in its early building stage. Completed at last, after nearly fifteen years and at a cost of £62 million, it was, said the Queen, a project which had 'captured the imagination of the world'. More than one million people, it was estimated, crowded the Sydney foreshore on the day of the opening ceremony, during which the Queen mixed and talked with construction workers and their wives as well as with civic dignitaries. That evening she attended a gala concert to mark the opening and stayed on to see a performance of Mozart's *The Magic Flute* before returning to London.

Brief though the Queen's stay was, it also included a ceremony of considerable constitutional importance: the signing in Canberra of the Royal Styles and Titles Act passed by Gough Whitlam's Labour

115

Government. Henceforth, on visits to Australia, she would no longer be Queen of the United Kingdom and of Her Other Realms and Territories (which included Australia, of course), as she was on the day of her Coronation, but simply Queen of Australia – a nice point but, to Australians, an important one. To mark the occasion, the Queen, for the first time, personally administered the oath of office to an Australian Government Minister, Dr Rex Patterson, the new Minister for the Northern Territory.

The Queen was to visit Australia again the following year, again only briefly (though through force of circumstance this time). First there would be a visit to New Zealand for the Commonwealth Games and, following in Prince Philip's adventurous footsteps, stop-overs at various islands and outposts, the Cook Islands (where she opened the new Rarotonga airport), Norfolk Island, the New Hebrides, the Solomon Islands and Papua New Guinea. Because the New Hebrides are an Anglo-French condominium, protocol required that the Queen could make a speech there only in the presence of the French President. The French President not being about at the time, protocol was deftly circumvented by having the Queen's speech, couched in the local pidgin, read out by a member of her entourage.

On Pentecost Island, one of the New Hebrides group, tragedy occurred. Those who host the Queen go to great lengths to come up with something fresh and novel by way of entertainment, and on Pentecost Island they decided on a tree-diving display. A tower some seventy feet high was constructed, from whose top the young men of the island took it in turns to hurl themselves earthwards. Stout jungle vines tied to their ankles brought them to a juddering halt only a few feet from the ground. But the vines which should have checked the dive of one young islander unfortunately snapped under the strain, so that he plunged into the ground only feet from where the Queen was watching, leaving him unconscious and seriously injured.

Waiting to greet the Queen when she arrived in New Zealand were Prince Philip and Prince Charles. Charles had now been promoted to the rank of lieutenant and was communications officer on HMS *Jupiter*. Princess Anne and Mark Phillips also flew out to join the family gathering. For them, not long married, it was by way of being a second honeymoon. Also there was Prince Philip's uncle,

Earl Mountbatten. 'Quite a family gathering,' the Queen said, happily.

For Mark Phillips, that visit to New Zealand was something of a baptism into public life. All things considered, he acquitted himself well, revealing the same sort of wit his father-in-law, Prince Philip, has displayed on so many occasions. Invited at a horse show to decorate the winning pony with a garland of carrots, he proceeded to feed them to the animal instead. Elsewhere, presented with a basket of fruit, he spotted one shaped rather like a microphone. He promptly took it out of the basket and held it towards the nearest commentator. 'Care to say a few words?' he invited.

New Zealand's Maoris again took the opportunity of the Queen's visit to campaign for their rights. Campaigning placards greeted her when she arrived in Waitangi, and a group of extremist Maoris started a number of small fires and attempted unsuccessfully to blow up a flagpole. But they were small in number compared with the several hundred Maori dancers and singers who took part in a pageant for the Queen's benefit.

In Australia too there were demonstrations. Aborigines booed and chanted outside as the Queen opened Parliament in Canberra.

Opening the Australian Parliament was about all the Queen had time for before events back in Britain required her immediate return to deal with what was perhaps the biggest domestic crisis of her reign, to date. In Australia it was high summer; back in Britain it was midwinter, with striking miners 'holding the country to ransom'. Factories were on a three-day week, homes and offices were subject to electricity cuts, and the nation's fuel stocks were calculated to run out altogether by mid-March. Edward Heath, the Prime Minister, decided to call a General Election, confident that the result would vindicate the Government's policy which had led to confrontation with the miners. In this he was mistaken. The result of the election showed the nation to be about evenly divided between those who wanted to fight it out and those prepared to concede the miners' demands. The ruling Conservative Party obtained the most votes but, under Britain's first-past-the-post electoral system, not the most seats. The composition of the new Parliament would be: Labour 301 seats, Conservatives 296, Liberals 14, Nationalists and others 26.

The possibility of a General Election had been foreseen and

contingency plans made. The Queen cut short her visit, apologized to her Australian hosts and flew home on 28 February, leaving Prince Philip to carry on alone. She would rejoin him on 6 March for the remainder of the tour, she said. But things did not work out like that.

Arriving back in London on 1 March, the Queen received Edward Heath in audience the same evening – but not to receive his resignation as Prime Minister, as she may have expected. Instead, he informed her that it was his intention to seek an alliance with the Liberals, whose fourteen seats could provide him with a majority over Labour in the House of Commons, though not an overall majority. Until he resigned (or was dismissed), he was still Prime Minister, and the Queen felt he was entitled to try. She is not in the business of dismissing prime ministers, though her Governor-General in Australia, shortly afterwards, would exercise that particular royal prerogative on her behalf and without her knowledge. In the event, the Liberals were not amenable to Heath's terms for a coalition. They wanted future government policy to include a switch to proportional representation, and this Heath was not willing to concede.

The Queen's hopes of resuming her Australian tour on 6 March were dashed as negotiations between the Prime Minister and Jeremy Thorpe, the Liberal leader, dragged on over the weekend. It was not until the Monday evening – 4 March – that Heath again sought an audience of the Queen, this time to report his inability to form a coalition government and tender his resignation. Within minutes the Queen had summoned Harold Wilson,* the Labour leader, and appointed him Prime Minister for the second time.

The change of government obliged the Queen to remain in London in order to announce the new Government's policies in her Speech from the Throne at the opening of the new Parliament. With a state visit to Indonesia planned to follow the Australian tour, there was now nothing for it but to let Prince Philip continue to substitute for her in Australia. She opened Parliament in London the following Tuesday (12 March) and flew out to Bali to link up with her husband for the Indonesian visit the next day.

Britain's relationship with Indonesia had been an uneasy one

* Later Lord Wilson of Rievaulx

since the country discarded its Dutch allegiance and proclaimed itself a republic at the end of World War II. As recently as 1963 the British Embassy in Jakarta had been attacked and burned. So the Queen's 1974 visit was intended on both sides, British and Indonesian, as a gesture of reconciliation. But there were problems. With Indonesia still in a state of unrest, a visit by the Japanese Prime Minister only two months previous had seen him virtually imprisoned in his guest house because of the demonstrations, sometimes erupting into riots, which had gone on. Determined that the Queen should not suffer a similar fate on her visit, the Indonesian authorities put some 5,000 police and troops on the streets of Jakarta. Even such a large show of security did not prevent schoolchildren swarming round her car in such large numbers that on one occasion, at least, they forced it to a halt. But this was enthusiasm, not protest.

The Queen's visit was almost over when Prince Philip was awakened by one of his aides in the early hours of 21 March with news that Princess Anne was on the telephone from London. She had an almost incredible tale to tell. She and Mark had been driving back from a charity film show when an armed man attempted to kidnap her. Four people, including her bodyguard and chauffeur, had been wounded and she herself almost dragged from the car before a passing stranger intervened and knocked the gunman to the ground. Prince Philip, in turn, awoke the Queen – at five in the morning – to tell her what had happened. Satisfied that Anne was unharmed, and with only one day of her visit still to go, the Queen decided to fulfil her few remaining public engagements in Indonesia as planned. The only small hitch in proceedings was that she was half an hour later than scheduled in visiting an arts and handicrafts exhibition.

10 GREEN TEA CEREMONY

If it had taken Britain twenty years after the end of World War II to forgive Germany sufficiently for the Queen to visit her sisters-in-law there, it was to be even longer before she visited the Far Eastern enemy, Japan. Nearly thirty years after Prince Philip, then a young naval officer, boarded the American flagship *Missouri* in Tokyo Bay to witness the formal Japanese surrender, he accompanied the Queen on a five-day state visit to Japan. It was 1975 and he was coming up to his fifty-fourth birthday.

Before that, in 1974, shortly after returning from Indonesia, the Queen had made one of her rare *private* visits abroad. Usually she travels abroad only in her official role, though there have been occasions when a state visit has been extended into a private holiday, as in Sweden in 1956 (when she stayed on to see the equestrian events of the Olympic Games), Denmark in 1957 and Italy in 1961. In 1962 there had been a visit to the Netherlands for the silver wedding celebrations of Queen Juliana and Prince Bernhard, though this was listed in the Queen's engagement diary as 'semi-private'. So her flying visit to France in the summer of 1974 was actually her first time abroad in a completely private capacity since becoming Queen. Few people will require even three guesses to gauge the nature of the trip. Horses? Correct. In fact a horse-race, the Prix de Diane, in which her filly Highclere was running. Bred in the royal stud, great-granddaughter of a yearling bought by the Queen's grandfather forty years before, Highclere romped home first to the Queen's great delight, notching up the franc equivalent of around £90,000 in prize money.

February 1975 found the Queen on her way to Mexico by way of Bermuda, Barbados and the Bahamas. She had called at the Bahamas during her Caribbean tour of 1966 but had not been to either Bermuda or Barbados since her round-the-world tour of 1953–4. Bermuda's Prime Minister, Sir Edward Richards, reproved her respectfully. 'We would like Your Majesty to know that we have been feeling somewhat neglected these past twenty-one years,' he said. There had, of course, been visits during that time by Princess Margaret and Prince Charles. 'Wonderful and popular though they are,' said Sir Edward, 'and welcome as they will always be, they are not the Queen. We would therefore be exceedingly happy if you are able in the future to squeeze some time out of your busy schedule to visit us more often.'

Bermuda at the time was in the grip of unseasonably cold weather and in the throes of a general strike. Despite these two factors, large crowds of both local people and visiting tourists turned out to see the Queen, though the strike had its effect on a visit to the old Royal Naval Dockyard to mark the official opening of the Bermuda Maritime Museum. It had been planned that the Queen and Prince Philip would arrive there in a tug tender, but this had to be changed because of the strike and they went by car instead. Arriving at the dockyard, they found their way barred by pickets. To the Queen's amusement, the pickets sang a calypso version of 'We shall not be moved' before themselves moving aside to allow the royal car to proceed.

Royal aides who were with the Queen on that tour still recall her arrival in Mexico City as perhaps the liveliest and most spectacular welcome she has been accorded anywhere. It is estimated that more than a million excited Mexicans lined the route and jammed the streets, waving flags and banners, as she drove into the city. Bands played along the route, Mexico City was festooned with bunting, hundreds of balloons were let loose to bob into the sky, and confetti showered down on the Queen's flower-bedecked car. In Constitution Square 5,000 schoolchildren formed slogans and pictures with coloured placards, and twice that number of teenagers performed athletic routines while the Queen and Prince Philip watched from a balcony. One side of the square was taken up with giant portraits of the Queen, Prince Philip and Mexico's President Echeverria.

Elsewhere, members of the Queen's entourage were coping with the sort of problems which crop up on most royal tours. The royal yacht *Britannia* (which would also serve as a conference centre for British and local businessmen during the course of the royal visit) had run into near gale-force winds and been forced to seek shelter in calmer waters. A helicopter was called in to air-lift the Queen's luggage ashore but broke down in the process, so that the rest of the luggage had to be landed by boat in choppy seas. Mexico's leading ladies faced a problem of a different kind. For months past they had been busy importing expensive gowns from London, New York, Paris and Rome in preparation for the state banquet. Then, at almost the last moment, President Echeverria decreed that banquet guests should wear national costume.

The Queen herself was suffering at the time from another of the heavy colds to which she is prone. Nevertheless, she insisted that there should be no alteration in the official programme, which included a visit to the picturesque old Indian town of Oaxaca and another to the archaeological site at Uxmal, where, fortunately, she and Philip had the shelter of an alcove when a torrential storm broke during an outdoor pageant of Mayan history. The rest of the audience, not unnaturally, made a frantic dash for such cover as was available while the performers carried on bravely.

The visit to Mexico involved the Queen in 16,000 miles of travel. Two months later came the state visit to Japan, an even longer round trip of slightly over 26,000 miles.

The Queen had originally intended to fly to Japan by way of Jamaica, Guam and Hong Kong, but Honolulu was substituted for Guam as a rest place when it was realized that Guam was crammed almost to overflowing with Vietnamese refugees on their way to new homes in the United States.

The Jamaica visit, which lasted four days, was linked to that year's conference of Commonwealth leaders. As was to become her practice, the Queen received the Commonwealth leaders, in turn, in private audience, seeking to smooth out differences, as well as entertaining them to dinner *en masse* aboard the royal yacht. While in Jamaica, she also visited the University of the West Indies to open a new law school named after the former Jamaica premier Norman Manley. A threatened demonstration by university students who would have preferred the new school to be opened by Manley's widow did not take place, though some students boycotted the opening ceremony. Not so Mrs Manley. She both attended the ceremony and posed for a picture with the Queen and Prince Philip in the doorway of the new building.

The Queen's arrival in Hong Kong coincided with the Festival of Tin Hau, goddess of the sea. In consequence, there were Chinese lanterns everywhere, as well as the usual flags and bunting, and the harbour was filled with decorated junks. The Queen stayed three days in Hong Kong, during which time she visited both the English-speaking university and a family re-housed in a new tower-block home, went shopping in one of the colony's street markets and saw something of the picturesque fishing community of Aberdeen. Like any ordinary tourist, she also took advantage of Hong Kong's reputation for turning out fashions in double-quick time to have two dresses and a coat run up for her almost overnight.

Her call on the re-housed family was made during a visit to a new estate where some 46,000 people would eventually live like battery hens in tower blocks twenty storeys high. Those already in residence watched from balconies festooned with washing, television aerials and bird-cages as the Queen arrived and made her way up to the fourth floor to call upon a harbour ferry fare-collector, his wife and eight children. On her street-market shopping expedition, she was particularly intrigued by a display of hundred-year-old eggs. 'What are they exactly?' she asked and was told that they were duck eggs pickled in a mixture of lime and bran for a hundred days (not years) during which time they turned black and were then judged 'ripe' for eating.

Fortunately perhaps, there were no eggs, hundred-year or hundred-days old, on the menu for an official lunch at which the Queen was entertained. But everything else was Chinese style: shark's fin soup, crab in a swallow's nest, honey-roasted chicken and grouper fish, rice in lotus leaves, wheat noodles in oyster sauce, lotus seeds in almond syrup and oyster sauce. She ate with chopsticks, on this occasion wielding them with a dexterity which suggested a degree of practice since her experience in Singapore.

Throughout the Queen's visit security was kept as low-key as possible. Despite that, the visit was marred by one very small demonstration. This came when Prince Philip, on his own, arrived at the colony's Chinese university, where a group of left-wing students shouted anti-royal slogans from a distant vantage-point on a small hillock. There was also a last-minute change in the route he should have taken – 'because of the weather' was the official explanation. Rain did indeed threaten, but a more probable reason for the change was the discovery along the planned route of two brown paper packages labelled 'Keep clear'. However, upon further investigation the packages proved to contain nothing more lethal than old jam jars filled with water.

Security in Japan was in striking contrast to the low-key version mounted in Hong Kong. With terrorism on the increase around the world, the Japanese were determined that the Queen should not be exposed to the slightest possible danger. Ahead of her visit, Crown Prince Akihito's personal bodyguard, Inspector Takao Iguchi, had been sent to Britain to accompany her on one of her provincial tours, to Norwich, and study how his British counterparts went about their task of safeguarding her. One can hardly imagine that 50,000 security men – or even one-hundredth of that number – guarded the Queen when she visited Norwich, but that was the total assigned to protect her in Japan.

Her arrival in Tokyo was in marked contrast to the cool reception Londoners had accorded Japan's diminutive and bespectacled Emperor Hirohito on his visit to Britain four years before. As a special mark of respect to the Queen, the guard of honour was given commands in English, there were flags everywhere as she drove through the city, the crowds turned out in their thousands, and ticker tape floated down on her open car in a fashion that rivalled New York. Nearly every important shopping centre and depart-mental store had its 'Made in Britain' promotion, and there were British exhibitions and cultural events at some seventy-five different locations. These included an exhibition of twenty-three paintings and sketches loaned by the Queen herself, as well as performances by the Royal Ballet Company and the Royal Shakespeare Company. The Queen also took advantage of her speech at that state banquet to put in a plug for British industry. 'Britain has a strong and broadly based industry,' she said. 'It has kept vigorously in the forefront of scientific research and develop-ment. So we have much to offer.'

Unlike Prince Charles when he visited Japan five years earlier, the Queen was not served the raw fish dish known as *sashimi*. (Charles thought it tasted rather like 'rubber hose'.) Instead, the banquet menu consisted of turtle soup, cold salmon, stuffed quail and roast lamb, perhaps the Queen's favourite meat dish. But later, at a traditional tea ceremony held in the imperial villa at Kyoto, she was served with a bowl of green tea whipped to a froth with a small bamboo brush. She was observed to grimace slightly as she sipped it, but her one-word comment was restricted to a diplomatic 'Surprising'.

She and Prince Philip stayed at the Akasaka Palace, a state guest-house built in imitation of Versailles. To make the Queen feel more at home, the enthusiastic Japanese even had a police patrolman dress in Highland regalia to play 'Scotland the Brave' for her on his bagpipes.

The Queen met members of the Diet, Japan's Parliament, and lunched with a group of leading Japanese businessmen, again plugging British industry in a few well-chosen words. Trade between the two countries had grown by 650 per cent in the past ten years, she said, with British industry 'now giving serious attention to the large and growing Japanese market'. However, a sharp-eyed journalist noted that, in striking contrast to the large numbers of Japanese cars to be seen in London, the Queen's Rolls Royce was the only British car to be glimpsed about the streets of Tokyo.

Almost inevitably perhaps, she was taken to see round a factory turning out cameras, to see a traditional drama, *Kabuki*, at the national theatre and a display of *Ikebana* (flower arranging). That display was held in a pavilion behind the palace at which the Queen was staying. She arrived there wearing slippers. 'Do I take these off?' she asked. Answered in the affirmative, she quickly nudged off the slippers and proceeded to inspect the flowers in stockinged feet.

With Prince Philip, she drove to the Hodogaya War Cemetery on a wooded hillside outside Yokohama where are buried some 1,500 Commonwealth servicemen, many of whom died from malnutrition or lack of medical attention while in Japanese prison camps. Husband and wife stood in silence before the memorial which dominates the cemetery while the Anglican rector of Yokohama, the Reverend John Berg, uttered a brief prayer: 'We remember the sacrifice of these men in the service of their country and pray it may not have been in vain.'

There was also a visit to the Shinto shrine at Ise – which brought a degree of criticism from those Japanese who equate Shintoism with Fascism. The shrine at Shinto, tucked away in the centre of a pinewood, consists of three stockades, one inside the other. A few members of the royal entourage were permitted to accompany the Queen and Prince Philip when they entered the outer stockade, but only the royal couple were allowed to enter the second. And even they could not enter the third stockade containing the sacred mirror which Shintoists believe was brought to earth by the Deity. Only the Emperor, believed to be a descendant of the Deity – though he himself has disclaimed such belief – can enter the third stockade, and he was not with the Queen on this occasion.

It had been planned that the Queen should travel to Kyoto on the famous 'bullet train', but a transport strike put the train temporarily out of service and she went by air instead. There was also a visit to Toba to see a demonstration of pearl-diving – which seems to have caused the Queen a small degree of embarrassment.

Japanese pearl girls normally dive topless, but such a display of feminine attributes, it was felt, might offend Britain's Queen. So on the occasion of the royal visit the girls were outfitted in thin, thigh-length cotton overalls. However, even the ever-so-efficient Japanese had overlooked the small fact that thin cotton clings transparently and seductively to flesh once it is wet. As a result, the girls, respectably covered when they dived in, left little to the imagination when they surfaced again. Prince Philip could not entirely suppress a grin, but the Queen looked a shade disapproving. There was perhaps compensation for that embarrassment in the pearl necklace and a single rare black pearl which the Queen was given by the proprietor of the pearl company before leaving.

Mexico and Japan in 1975 were followed, in 1976, by state visits to Finland and Luxembourg and by further visits to Canada and the United States.

For her visit to Finland the Queen decided against crossing the North Sea in the royal yacht. Instead, *Britannia* went on ahead to await her arrival by air at Maarianhamima, capital of the Ahvenanmaa (Åland) Islands. To allow the Queen's aircraft to land there, the runway had first to be cleared of its resident ducks and swans while the islanders themselves, unaccustomed to royal visitors, seemed hardly to know how to take it all.

'What shall we do?' the Queen was heard to ask her husband as they strolled together through the main street of the island's capital (population 6,700). What they did do was wander round the town's maritime museum and drink champagne at a small, informal and hastily convened reception at the local sailing club. Among those they met at the reception were a British doctor and his Finnish wife. They were 'refugees' from Britain's National Health Service, they told the Queen.

Things were better organized in Helsinki, where a crowd of 20,000 people, said to be the biggest Helsinki had seen since declaring its independence from Tsarist Russia in 1917, turned out to greet the arrival of *Britannia*. In addition to the customary ceremonies linked to any state visit, including on this occasion the laying of a wreath on the tomb of the national hero Marshal Mannerheim, there was a picnic in a pine forest and a boat trip across the country's second largest lake. There was also a visit to the Haukanmas Forest, where the royal visitors were offered protective helmets to wear because of the tree-felling going on nearby. Prince Philip sensibly donned one, but the Queen declined. Philip also found time to talk to Finnish businessmen about trade relations with Britain and to enjoy the relaxation of a sauna. 'A marvellous device,' he termed it, adding, 'I am taking it entirely for pleasure and not for any therapeutic value.'

The year 1976 (when the Queen celebrated her fiftieth birthday) marked the 200th anniversary of American Independence. The great-great-great-great-granddaughter of King George III, who reigned at the time of the War of Independence, could hardly be expected to participate in that country's 4 July bicentennial celebrations: President Ford's invitation for her to do so was graciously declined. But two days later *Britannia* with the Queen aboard sailed into Philadelphia, the city where the American Constitution was framed and where the Liberty Bell was rung to proclaim independence from Britain.

Ahead of the Queen's visit, there had been discussion in royal circles as to whether it would be more appropriate for her to fly over in Concorde, at that time sorely in need of some gesture to boost its reputation in the United States. But the restricted landing rights imposed on the aircraft by the (perhaps slightly envious) US authorities created problems and, in the final analysis, it was decided to use the royal yacht, which the Queen could board in Bermuda and which could serve as a floating conference hall for British and American businessmen when she went on to Washington.

Philadelphia, at the time of the Queen's arrival, was crowded with Americans who had stayed on to see her following the Bicentennial celebrations. Nearby Valley Forge Park, for instance, was still filled with the covered wagons of people from all parts of the country who had trekked there for the celebrations. In consequence, crowds were thick along the banks of the Delaware as *Britannia* sailed in, and thousands more lined the route into the city.

The Queen was welcomed by the state governor, Milton Shapp, and by Philadelphia's mayor, Frank Rizzo. With them she went to see the original Liberty Bell, cast in Whitechapel more than two centuries before but unable to be rung since it cracked in 1835. As a gift to the city the Queen had brought with her another bell, cast in the same foundry, but slightly larger and considerably heavier. Instead of the Biblical text engraved on the original, 'Proclaim liberty throughout the land unto all the inhabitants thereof,' the Queen's new bell bore the simple inscription 'Let freedom ring.' So it was not quite an exact replica, and certainly not intended as a replacement, as official spokesmen on both sides of the Atlantic were quick to point out. Yet seldom can a royal gift have aroused such opposition. Religious fundamentalists led by the Reverend Carl McIntire, a preacher of Ulster Protestant origins, paraded the streets with posters proclaiming 'Bicentennial Bell A Counterfeit' and demanding 'Send The Bell Back.'

Presenting Philadelphia with its new bell, the Queen said she did so 'as a direct descendant of George III . . . the last crowned sovereign to rule this country'. It seemed to her, she went on, that Independence Day should be celebrated as much in Britain as in America. 'We lost the American colonies because we lacked the statesmanship to know the right time and manner of yielding what it is impossible to keep. But the lesson was learnt. In the next century and a half we kept more closely to the principles of Magna Carta which have been the common heritage of both our countries.'

She was to develop the theme further in a subsequent speech in Washington. 'Both of our peoples believe in the world of the individual and the family, in freedom of religion and expression, and the right to change a government by the ballot box rather than the gun, perhaps the best definition of democracy. That is why time and time again, in the testing days of war and the constructive years of peace, we have stood together on the things that matter.' She concluded her Washington speech: 'One thing is certain, and that is the strength and permanence of the Anglo-American Friendship. It has grown and prospered down the years. It has brought with it benefits beyond measure to our peoples. May it long continue to flourish for the sake of both our countries and for the greater good of mankind.'

The Queen's desire to indulge in walkabouts and talk to ordinary people caused not a few headaches for Americans responsible for her security. Having got through the Bicentennial holiday weekend without serious trouble, they did not want to see their copybooks blotted during the Queen's visit. As one police chief put it when the question of royal walkabouts was being discussed, 'We have a lot of kooks in this country.' Both 'kooks' and the average Joe Citizen were to cause trouble before the tour was over.

Among the 'kooks' was the bank robber who fled into Andrews Air Force Base, hotly pursued by police, just as the Queen and Prince Philip flew in from Philadelphia. Security men assigned to protect the Queen drew their handguns as the pursuing police cars, lights flashing, raced past only a few hundred yards from where she was standing. The fleeing bank robber was finally cornered and arrested. 'I don't know how much the Queen saw,' said a police spokesman later, 'but the secret service agents certainly saw it all and almost had heart attacks.'

Rather like an American tourist visiting Europe ('This is Thursday, so it must be Rome'), the Queen found herself being whirled at dizzy pace from one public engagement to another. She was taken to the National Gallery in Washington to see an exhibition depicting the Life and Times of Thomas Jefferson, and to the Smithsonian Institute, where she saw, among other things, an exhibition of Leonardo da Vinci drawings from her own collection at Windsor Castle which she had loaned for the occasion. There was a ceremony to present her with the keys of the city, a service to dedicate the nave of Washington Cathedral and a wreath-laying ceremony at the tomb of the Unknown Soldier in Arlington National Cemetery. There was a luncheon at the Capitol, where she commented that America's founding fathers had acted in a 'typically British fashion' when they broke from Britain in 1776, and a gala banquet in a pavilion erected in the rose garden of the White House, where she danced with President Ford to the tune of 'Getting To Kow You'. All this in the space of two days – and she still found time to host a reciprocal banquet held at the British Embassy and, as Queen of New Zealand, to lay the foundation stone of a new chancellery building at the New Zealand Embassy.

The reception and banquet at the British Embassy were in true royal style. There was music by the pupils of the Yehudi Menuhin School from Cobham, Surrey, and a Bach solo by the great violinist himself. By contrast, the Grimethorpe Colliery Band played in the embassy garden, and later the band of the Royal Marines performed the ceremony of Beating the Retreat.

While the Queen was chatting to selected guests in the garden there was an unexpected intervention. A man barged through the crowd of people around her, grabbed her hand, shook it and asked, 'How are you?' It was the boxer Muhammad Ali.

For a moment the Queen was clearly taken aback. 'I'm all right,' she said. Then, recovering her composure and recognizing the former World Heavyweight Champion, she said she was glad to see him and showed her knowledge of sporting matters by asking after his leg – Ali had been undergoing treatment in a Californian clinic for a blood clot which developed following a contest with a Japanese wrestler in the World Martial Arts Championship.

'I'm fine now,' he told the Queen. That said, his old loquacity seemed to desert him for once, and he withdrew as abruptly as he had arrived.

While the Queen was viewing her own Leonardo da Vinci drawings at the Smithsonian, Prince Philip flew by helicopter to Wolftrap Farm in Virginia to watch a Scottish military tattoo which was another gift from Britain to mark the independence Bicentennial of its former colonists. It would have seemed sensible, while the royal couple were in Washington, for them to have visited Monticello, the Virginian home of Thomas Jefferson, author of the Declaration of Independence, which was also on their itinerary, but time did not permit, and this visit was sandwiched in later, following their stay in New York.

If Washington had been frenetic, New York was to prove riotous in the extreme. The Queen sailed into New York aboard *Britannia*, which she had boarded at Bayonne following a flight from

Washington. Some of those in a crowd estimated at three-quarters of a million came to blows – quite literally – in their determination to see her. Police and security men had to form themselves into a flying wedge to get her safely inside Trinity Church on Wall Street. Outside the church, on the corner of Wall Street and Broadway, fights broke out. A man with a camera, shouting 'Let me get to the Queen', was grabbed by the police, pinned against the doors of a Wall Street bank and, in American police parlance, 'frisked'.

The Queen's programme of public engagements, less jam-packed than for Washington, was busy enough. She was made an Honorary Citizen of the city, was guest of honour at a luncheon given by the Pilgrims and the English-Speaking Union, and gave a reciprocal reception and dinner aboard *Britannia*. She was taken to Harlem to see Jumel Mansion, the oldest house in Manhattan and George Washington's headquarters during the War of Independence. Despite the doubts of US security chiefs, she went on a brief walkabout before visiting Bloomingdale's, the famous New York department store.

With Prince Philip, the Queen flew south to Charlottesville for the visit to Monticello, then they doubled back to Rhode Island for brief stops at Providence and Newport. The Queen entertained President Ford at a farewell dinner aboard *Britannia* before sailing to Boston, that hotbed of Irish Americanism, where the state governor, Mike Dukakis, called out the National Guard as a precaution against the possibility that demonstrations in support of the IRA might get out of hand. Whether because this precaution was unnecessary or more than adequate, demonstrations were limited to the parading of a few banners and Irish tricolours.

However, the Queen found herself listening to what was more a protest speech (though she was not the target) than a sermon when she attended a service at the Old North Church, from whose steeple, two centuries before, Paul Revere had hung a lantern to warn 'The Redcoats are coming.' This time it was Dr Robert Golledge who used the pulpit to denounce rather than warn. Much of the 'sermon' must surely have puzzled the Queen. She will have understood Dr Golledge's denunciation of those who raised funds for the IRA, but much else of what he said required an intimate knowledge of local politics, a denunciation of those organizing the sometimes violent white protests against the bussing of children to schools in black areas.

If the Queen did not understand all this, the city's civic leaders, who were with her in church, surely did, as Dr Golledge thundered: 'We in Boston have more than our share of false men and women who are called leaders but are actually cowards, running away from the challenge of reconciliation and accommodation. They are loud, cruel people who think themselves brave but who are weaklings. They are petty people who accept their petty acclaim so easily won by petty slogans, but who, as they are now, cannot earn any standing beyond their own small group.' He mentioned the Queen, but only to praise the speech she had made in Philadelphia concerning the lessons Britain had learned from the events of 1776. 'Perhaps Your Majesty's comments,' he said, 'can teach us a similar wisdom and decency here in Boston, a lesson to guide us in our reconciliation and in our growth as a community.'

From the United States the Queen went on to Canada, her eighth tour of that country in the nearly quarter-century since she succeeded to the throne – her ninth visit if you include the brief stops made in Edmonton and Vancouver while *en route* to Australia and New Zealand in 1963, and her tenth in a lifetime if you also add in her 1951 tour when she was still Princess Elizabeth.

Primary object of the 1976 visit was to open the XXI modern Olympic Games in Montreal, an exercise which did not meet with the complete approval of the city's majority French-Canadian population. The Queen's twelve-day stay was also designed to include visits to Nova Scotia and New Brunswick, where Anthony Francis, chief of the Micmac Indians, taking a leaf out of the New Zealand Maoris' book, seized the opportunity to protest to her concerning the erosion of rights granted to Canadian Indians by her great-great-great-great-grandfather, George III. On the Queen's behalf, New Brunswick's Premier, Richard Hatfield, accepted from the Indians a copy of the 1763 royal proclamation in which their rights were spelled out.

As on a previous tour Down Under, that visit to the Olympics turned into a family affair. Prince Andrew, then only sixteen, had flown out to join his parents. Princess Anne was already there, a member of Britain's three-day eventing team. With her was husband Mark, the team's reserve rider. Prince Charles, now

132

commanding the small and ancient minehunter *Bronington*, was due for a spot of leave and would fly out to join the rest of the family a few days later. So would twelve-year-old Prince Edward, though it was not planned that way originally. 'Why should I be left out? It isn't fair,' he grumbled to brother Charles. So Charles made a telephone call to the Queen in Canada and she agreed they should fly out together.

Focal point of family interest was Princess Anne. Five years earlier she had won the 1971 European eventing championship and they now hoped to see her perform equally well in the Olympics. Alas, it was not to be. The clapping of loyal supporters served to upset her horse during the dressage section and she ended it with sufficient penalty points to push her back into seventh place. Not bad perhaps, but not as good as she herself would have liked. Then in the cross-country section of the event she took a nasty fall at the nineteenth obstacle. Slightly concussed though she was, she re-mounted and completed the course but accumulated more penalty points. A time-fault in the final show-jumping section completed the series of disasters, and she finished in twenty-fourth place.

It was Andrew, not Anne – nor, for that matter, Prince Charles – who emerged as the star of the show. Tall and ruggedly handsome at sixteen, he quickly attracted the attention of teenaged girls, pushing and jostling in their efforts to see him, the more bold among them even pressing love poems and notes giving their telephone numbers into the hands of accompanying royal aides. And all of them envying blonde Sandi Jones, whose father, Colonel Campbell Jones, had the task of organizing the Olympic yachting events. She was Andrew's companion for the period of the royal stay and was to see more of him later, when he went to school in Canada.

Andrew's spell of schooling in Canada stemmed from that visit to the Montreal Olympics. It was while the family was there that the idea was mooted by Pierre Trudeau, the then Canadian Prime Minister, who perhaps saw it as a useful political boost. Prince Charles had had some of his schooling in Australia and Edward, some years later, would have a similar spell in New Zealand. In between, and following Trudeau's suggestion, Andrew went to Lakefield College, some ninety miles from Toronto. While there, he invited Sandi to a school dance, went skiing with her and took her to a jazz concert in Toronto. There was a degree of teenage romancing involved and they continued to write to each other for a time after Andrew's return to Britain. But, contrary to the proverb, absence did not serve to make the Prince's heart grow fonder, and the romance eventually fizzled out.

Despite some initial degree of opposition from French-Canadians to the Queen opening the Montreal Olympics, there were no major separatist demonstrations during her stay there. The crowds gathering to see her, small at first, grew in numbers as the days passed, and the end of her visit saw several hundred people waiting into the small hours outside the hotel which was the venue for the farewell banquet. French- and English-speaking Canadians were at long last beginning to bury their differences, the Queen must have thought. 'My great-grandfather, Edward VII, was one of the far-sighted creators of the *entente cordiale* between France and Britain which has stood the test of time and war,' she reminded guests at the banquet in her farewell speech. 'As Queen of Canada it gives me great pleasure to witness, nearly a century later, your own *entente cordiale*, because it lies at the very foundation of Canada's personality – an enduring belief in the encouragement of human diversity and an acceptance of the rights of others to be fully and proudly themselves.' Events on subsequent visits to Canada would show that she was being perhaps a shade over-optimistic.

Royal travels that year ended with a four-day state visit to Luxembourg which would be extended by a further two-day private visit which would lead, in turn, to rumours that the Queen's eldest son would marry the Grand Duchy's Princess Marie-Astrid. So strong and persistent did these rumours become that Buckingham Palace twice took the unusual step of denying them. As Ulster Unionist MP Enoch Powell pointed out at the time, however, constitutional law prohibits the heir to the throne from marrying a Catholic, however unreasonable this may seem in this day and age. In any event, Charles himself had not even met Marie-Astrid and, as we now know, would marry for love.

The Queen took with her, on that state visit to Luxembourg, which also included visits to the administrative centre of the European Economic Community and the European Court of Justice, a special gift for the orphaned children being cared for at the Rham Children's Home – a Victorian-style rocking horse. She had been cautioned before leaving Britain not to expect the sort of frenzied welcome to which she has become accustomed. The people of Luxembourg, she was told, were inclined to be undemonstrative, more likely to stand in respectful silence than to cheer and clap. In the event, even the 'undemonstrative' Luxembourgers surrendered to the Queen's *mystique*, waving flags and balloons, clapping and cheering, much to the surprise of Grand Duchy officials. 'We have never known anything like it before,' said one of them.

And the Queen herself was visibly moved by a speech of welcome from Madame Colette Flesh, the Burgomaster, who spoke of those World War II days when 'many of our people found refuge on Britain's friendly soil, when hope came from the skies, from the broadcasts of the BBC and the planes of the Royal Air Force'. Said Madame Flesh: 'You did not fail us then, and we have never forgotten.'

11 SILVER JUBILEE

The year 1977 marked the celebration of the Queen's Silver Jubilee. She had reigned for a quarter of a century over Australia, Canada and New Zealand as well as the United Kingdom, along with those former colonies which had continued to recognize her as Queen on achieving independence.

The question was, how best to involve those overseas monarchies and other countries of the Commonwealth in the celebrations? To mark his Silver Jubilee, her grandfather, gruff old King George V, to whom 'abroad' was 'awful', had invited the leaders of what was then the British Empire to London. The Queen, by contrast, decided that she would celebrate in the countries of the Commonwealth – or, at least, in as many of them as could be sandwiched into two lengthy overseas tours totalling 56,000 miles.

Curiously enough, the first two places to be honoured in this way were countries which do not hail her as Queen – Western Samoa (which is a republic) and Tonga (which has its own monarch), though both acknowledge her as Head of the Commonwealth.

The visit to Western Samoa was perhaps also designed to assuage the hurt feelings of the head of state, His Highness Malietoa Tanumafili II, who had turned up unexpectedly in London the previous autumn and been both surprised and somewhat offended to find that the Queen was on holiday at Balmoral. The hurt feelings of His Highness were further soothed when he was invited to join the Queen aboard her royal yacht and made a Knight Grand Cross of the Order of St Michael and St George. Not to be outdone, he now bestowed upon the Queen the Grand Order of Vailima, a new honour specially devised for the occasion and named after the princely residence which had once been the home of Robert Louis Stevenson. This exchange of honours was later celebrated ashore with a drink of mouth-numbing *kava* and a feast of which the principal components were roast pig, lobster, pigeons and coral worms.

There was to be another feast on Tonga at which the Queen was served with her own sucking pig, a turkey, two lobsters, sweet potatoes, a watermelon, a pineapple and a coconut. Needless to say, perhaps, she contented herself with a few token mouthfuls. However, her host, King Taufa'ahau Tupou IV, tucked in happily, despite an earlier warning from his doctor that, at something like 300 pounds, he would be well advised to eat less.

On Fiji, ahead of the Queen's arrival, there was torrential rain. Fearing that it might mar the ceremonies planned for the royal visit, a curiously worded appeal was sent to the chief of the Waimaro tribe, believed to have power over the weather: 'Please let it rain heavily when the Queen comes.' In some strange fashion, it was supposed that the weather would then work in reverse. The chief promptly proceeded to work his weather magic, which involved going without food, strong drink and the comfort of a woman for a period of three days. But either the appeal was incorrectly worded or the chief did not abstain for the full three days or the gods of the weather were not listening. As the rain continued, the Governor-General, Sir George Cakobau, sent for the chief to ask, 'What went wrong?' It was still raining in torrents on the day of the Queen's arrival, though, oddly enough, there was a brief dry spell during the welcome ceremony.

A delegation of chiefs boarded *Britannia* to present her with the traditional whale's tooth. Yet again she drank the traditional *kava.* There were other gifts for her too, among them a table and six chairs. 'Beautiful examples of Fijian craftsmanship,' said the Queen. 'You may be quite sure that we shall use them.' She stayed in Fiji two days. On the second day, on Vanua Levu, the second largest island, she watched a display of native dancing which included an erotic little number performed by a group of girls in swinging skirts and bras fashioned from coconut shells. Back in Suva, the capital, late that night, massed choirs sang the hauntingly sweet 'Farewell-isa Lei' as the Queen left the island to sail for New Zealand.

It was raining too when the Queen arrived in New Zealand, and she won extra applause when she declined to use an umbrella while driving around the review ground in an open Land Rover, though wearing only a sleeveless *crêpe-de-chine* dress, and then sat on a dais in her wet dress to watch a display by units of the Army, Navy and Air Force. The rain continued for a walkabout in Auckland, obliging the Queen to pick her way through puddles of water, while Prince Philip revealed a surprisingly long memory when he spotted a man in the crowd and asked him, 'Are you still in the Navy?' John Forrest had been a naval cadet at HMS *Royal Arthur* in Corsham when Philip was an instructor there during those immediate post-war years before he married the then Princess Elizabeth.

Odd things seem to happen to the Queen in New Zealand, as witness that earlier visit when her jewels went astray. This time, on her very first day in the country, she entered the private rooms set aside for her at a restaurant where she was the guest at a civic lunch to find another woman going through her handbag. However, the incident proved to be innocent enough, if embarrassing. The handbag-searcher turned out to be a young policewoman who had been told: 'Check the Queen's suite and don't miss a thing.' She had been in the process of doing a thorough job when the Queen intervened. The Queen reclaimed her handbag, and the police-woman withdrew, apologetic and red-faced.

During her two weeks in New Zealand the Queen visited twenty cities and executed nineteen walkabouts. The walkabouts involved many small, and often amusing, incidents. At a place called Mystery Creek the Queen was waylaid by an elderly Maori woman who promptly proceeded to tell her, with magnificent gestures and loud bursts of laughter, an old Maori legend. The Queen smiled happily and seemed to be very much enjoying the encounter, but when the Maori woman arrived at the stage of resting her head on the Queen's shoulder, an accompanying detective felt it was time for discreet intervention. In Napier a woman in the crowd showed the Queen and Prince Philip a souvenir newspaper picture of the two of them standing on the Buckingham Palace balcony following the Queen's Coronation. 'Obviously you haven't lit a fire lately,' joked Prince Philip.

It was in Napier, incidentally, just prior to the Queen's arrival, that civic leaders learned, to their horror, that there was not room for *Britannia* in the harbour. It was unthinkable that the royal yacht should be told to remain out at sea, but that seemed a distinct possibility until local dockers volunteered to work overtime in pouring rain so that a Russian freighter could clear the harbour and make way for *Britannia*. 'Normally we don't work in the rain. It's a strict union rule,' one docker explained. 'But Liz is a great lady and we thought, "To hell with unionism. Let's put the Queen first."'

At Gisborne there was the traditional welcome from New Zealand's Maoris, with the Queen resplendent in her Maori cloak of kiwi feathers. She was amused to learn that the leading 'warrior' in the ceremony, hissing at her and flicking his tongue in and out, was named Callaghan, which also happened to be the name of her Prime Minister back in Britain. Later she was visibly moved to tears as massed Maori choirs sang the psalm 'The Lord Is My Shepherd'.

In Wellington there was a heart-stopping moment for those responsible for the Queen's security on the day she opened Parliament. She had just climbed the red-carpeted steps to enter the Parliament buildings when a man in the crowd produced a gun (later found to be a .22 air rifle) from under his raincoat. Security men on the roof of the building spotted him through binoculars but were powerless at that distance to intervene directly. However, the surrounding crowd included an off-duty detective, William Hooper, who was as eager as anyone else to see the Queen. He too saw what was happening and made a grab at the air rifle. The ensuing scuffle brought uniformed policemen to the scene and the man was arrested. He was later found to be mentally ill and was recommended for psychiatric treatment.

Despite the security scare, the Queen continued with her planned programme of walkabouts. Everywhere she went she was given flowers and small gifts by people in the crowd. By now she was well accustomed to that. But she was somewhat taken aback, during a walkabout in Christchurch, when a small girl dashed up to her and thrust a lollipop into her hand.

While in Christchurch, the Queen visited Lincoln College and arrived at its laboratory to find a lecture in progress. The subject was the reproductive qualities of mares, with the lecturer, Dr Margaret Evans, reportedly using 'fairly vivid' photographs to explain the use of a new synthetic hormone. In no way embarrassed, the Queen intervened with a question. Was there, she wanted to know, trouble with early abortion on the part of mares treated with the new hormone? 'Yes,' Dr Evans told her. 'It is one of the worst problems.'

The air-rifle incident apart, the New Zealand tour was among the pleasantest parts of the Queen's Silver Jubilee celebrations. Her subsequent tour of Australia was, at times, to be somewhat less pleasant.

Many Australians had resented and had not yet forgotten the manner in which the Governor-General, Sir John Kerr, had so summarily dismissed the country's Labour Prime Minister, Gough Whitlam, some sixteen months previous. The Queen herself had had nothing to do with Whitlam's dismissal and, indeed, had known nothing about it until it was a *fait accompli*, but the Governor-General had acted in her name and, Silver Jubilee or not, she was to get the backlash. A public opinion poll conducted among 1,600 people in the various state capitals just prior to the Queen's arrival elicited the astonishing response that fifty-eight per cent of Australians, on the basis of the poll, felt that the country no longer needed a queen. Subsequent events might tend to show that the poll, for whatever reason, did not echo the true feelings of the majority of Australians, but with so many undercurrents there was clearly no question of the Queen's paying heed to any hint from Malcolm Fraser, who was now Prime Minister, that Prince Charles should be despatched to Australia to serve as the next Governor-General. What might once have been possible, and would probably have delighted Charles himself earlier on, had been effectively ruled out by the Crown's involvement, in the person of Sir John Kerr, in the political scene.

That the Australian tour would have its problems was apparent from the moment of the Queen's arrival. The teacher in charge of one contingent of schoolchildren taken to see her land at Fairbairn air base, near Canberra, tried to persuade them to boo her. However, the youngsters insisted on clapping and cheering instead. A few awkward moments arose with the formal presentations following her arrival, to be made by Sir John Kerr in his role of Governor-General, for among those he was due to present was the Prime Minister he had sacked, Gough Whitlam. When it came to his turn to be presented, Whitlam pointedly ignored Sir John while bowing to and smiling at the Queen. Mrs Whitlam went one degree further. 'I will treat the Governor-General as though he didn't exist,' she had promised earlier, and this she did. Without waiting for him to present her, she took a brisk pace forward and began talking to the Queen. 'We had a nice natter about the weather and how nice it was to see each other again,' she said after.

The following day, when the Queen arrived to open Parliament, there were boos from a small group of demonstrators, said to be a rent-a-mob bussed in from Sydney and Melbourne, though whether the booing was directed at the Queen or at Malcolm Fraser was unclear. Later, a larger group of some 300 demonstrators sought to interrupt the Queen's review of the Australian armed forces outside Parliament House. They waved banners proclaiming 'Kerr Is A Traitor' and urging 'Sack Kerr', squatted and sang 'Waltzing Matilda' when the National Anthem was played, and hoisted the Eureka flag of the republican movement, a star-pointed cross on a blue field, said to have been first used by gold-diggers in Victoria during their battles with the colonial authorities over a century before.

Gough Whitlam's action in greeting the Queen showed that he himself in no way linked her to what had happened. He was also among those present at a reception in Parliament House during which he essayed a joke which some people misunderstood. Referring to the fact that the Queen would also become Queen of the Solomon Islands when they became independent the following year, he asked, 'What next? Queen of Sheba?' If there were some people who thought the remark 'a gross insult', as members of the Norwich Mediaeval Society apparently did when they read about it, the Queen herself did not. She laughed several times during Whitlam's speech and responded to it in light-hearted fashion. Commented a member of her entourage: 'The Queen thoroughly enjoyed the speech. It was extremely witty, linking the name Solomon with the Queen of Sheba. It is absolute rubbish to suggest that the Queen was annoyed.' Nor could she conceivably have been. Speeches to be made in the Queen's presence are usually submitted in advance to her Private Secretary, and there is no reason to think that this did not apply to Gough Whitlam's speech. Had there been anything in it which might have offended the Queen, it would have been deleted.

There was to be more trouble in Sydney. The Queen was on her way in an open Rolls Royce to unveil a plaque commemorating

141

a new waterfront driveway when a demonstrator, not content with holding aloft a heavy placard demanding 'Independence for Australia', hurled it at her. She raised an arm in an attempt to ward it off, but it struck her on the shoulder before falling into the car. Prince Philip seized it angrily and hurled it out again. Said a senior police officer who was with the royal couple, 'It caught the Queen a heavy blow on the shoulder and, what is more, it hurt her.' The demonstrator, an unemployed marine chemist, was later fined $A100 for offensive behaviour. He could not be charged with the more serious offence of assault, it was explained, because, 'If he decided to plead not guilty, there could, have been difficulty over Her Majesty coming to court to give evidence.'

Eureka flags and placards demanding that the Queen sack the Governor-General were in evidence too when she arrived at Government House for lunch with Sir Roden Cutler, Governor of New South Wales. The demonstrators were still there, jeering and booing, when lunch finished ninety minutes later. By this time loyalists in the crowd had had more than enough. They decided to set about the demonstrators, whom they clearly outnumbered, and ended up throwing three of their number into a nearby pond.

It is easy for a vociferous minority to convey a wrong impression, and the demonstrators during that Silver Jubilee tour of Australia were undeniably vociferous. But for every demonstrator who booed the Queen, thousands of loyalists cheered her. The placard incident in particular served to stir loyalist feelings and brought thousands more who might otherwise have been content to watch the Queen's progress on television out onto the streets to cheer and clap her.

There was to be another protest – for a totally different reason – in Newcastle, where the Queen re-boarded the royal yacht. Local Sea Cadets had been given the honour of mooring *Britannia*, but this upset the unions. In protest they banned the handling of other shipping and jeered *Britannia*'s crew members when they went ashore. The Queen and Prince Philip went aboard without incident, but Prime Minister Malcolm Fraser and his wife had their car bombarded with tomatoes and empty beer cans.

The Queen's visit to Brisbane was viewed with some degree of trepidation by those responsible for royal security. The city had a reputation as a hotbed of radicalism, and it was known that one

142

group was circulating a hit-list of names, addresses and telephone numbers. Security was accordingly tight, and it was perhaps due to that that the visit passed off without incident. Queensland, at that time, had been devastated by floods, and after formally welcoming the Queen the State Governor, John Bjelke Petersen, flew north to see the flooded region for himself and ascertain what aid was needed. Prince Philip wanted to go with him but was persuaded otherwise because there was no twin-engined helicopter available and the single-engined machine the Premier would be using was deemed too hazardous for a royal passenger.

Tight security continued for the Queen's visit to the island state of Tasmania. In particular, her insistence on continuing to go walkabout and her continued use of an open Rolls Royce gave cause for concern. There was some booing from a small group of republican demonstrators during her walkabout in Hobart, but again it was loyalists to the rescue. Their cheers drowned the boos, and the demonstrators found their republican banner and protest placards wrenched from their hands.

Back on the mainland, in Melbourne, a city the Queen always enjoys visiting, she was given a rousing reception by some 30,000 cricket fans when she went to the Melbourne Oval to watch part of the centenary test match between England and Australia, 'the latest encounter in the hundred years' war', as she termed it, jokingly. It was in the Long Room of the Melbourne Cricket Club that she held a royal investiture and bestowed upon Sir Robert Menzies, the former Australian premier, the Knighthood of the Order of Australia.

In Adelaide there were visits to a couple of stud farms, and at one of them the Queen saw the stallion Without Fear, sire of the unborn colt which would be Australia's Silver Jubilee gift to her. Only one small incident marred the Adelaide visit. While the Queen was being welcomed by the State Premier, a solitary demonstrator ran onto the platform, waving a Eureka flag and shouting some sort of protest against 'colonialism'. He was quickly seized by the police and arrested.

The Australian tour was briefly interrupted to enable the Queen to spend four days in Papua New Guinea, an Australian-administered protectorate when she was last there and now an independent state with the Queen – 'Misis Kwin', as she is styled in the local pidgin – as its monarch. Papua New Guinea, said the Prime Minister, Michael Somare, in his speech of welcome, had 'surprised the world' when it had not become a republic on achieving independence. 'But the people wanted the Queen as head of state because she represented the Commonwealth.'

If the Queen had been briefly embarrassed by the girl pearl-divers she saw on her earlier visit to Japan, she showed little or no sign of embarrassment at the bare breasts which frequently confronted her in Papua New Guinea. In Alotau, where royal transport consisted of a somewhat battered Mercedes, topless dancers manned the doors of the car. In the village of Gabaeabuna, which is also a pearl centre, there were a lot of bare breasts in the crowd which watched her as she walked past the hulks of Japanese landing craft on her way to a local pearl farm. However, she *was* apparently embarrassed at the pearl farm when she was invited to seed an oyster and thus start the process which leads to a pearl. 'I don't want to do it,' she said, blushing. 'You do it and pretend it's me.'

Back in Australia again, at Perth, there was another incident when the Queen's speech was interrupted by a group of demonstrators. The demonstration erupted into fighting as loyalists pulled down the Eureka flag the demonstrators were waving. The Queen waited patiently until order had been restored and then calmly carried on with her speech. That day was among the longest and busiest of the tour, starting at 10 a.m. and still going on with a reception aboard the royal yacht over twelve hours later. There were two walkabouts that day, and a third, unplanned and carried out on the spur of the royal moment, among schoolchildren in Kings Park the following day.

While it is the purpose of this book to chronicle only the Queen's Commonwealth and foreign travels, it should not be forgotten that each year she travels many thousands of miles in the United Kingdom also. Her Silver Jubilee year was naturally an extra busy one in this respect. Returning from the first leg of her Commonwealth tour, she paid visits to various parts of Scotland and Wales, visited Northern Ireland, made progresses through Lancashire and Merseyside, East Anglia, Humberside and Yorkshire, the North-East, the West Midlands, Derbyshire and Nottinghamshire, Devon, Cornwall and Avon, as well as making two tours of

The Queen in one of her special full-length dresses at the start of her tour
of the Gulf States, Saudi Arabia, 1979

With Prince Andrew during their visit to Zambia in 1979

Accompanied by King Hassan during the 'bloody' visit to Morocco and looking far from happy, 1980

Royal walkabout in Switzerland, 1980

Progressing at a walking pace with tough security in Tunisia, 1980

The Queen and Prince Philip visiting Pope John Paul in the Vatican, 1980

(*Opposite*) At the Scripps Institute of Oceanography, San Diego, USA, 1983

Revisiting the place where she became Queen: game warden Richard Prickett points out the site of the original Treetops which was burned down. In the background is the present building, 1983

At a dinner in San Francisco with
President Reagan, 1983

Inspecting the view at Qutub Shahi
Tombs in India, 1983

Receiving gifts from Princess Haya and Prince Hamzeh, Jordan, 1984

Welcomed by President Li Xiannian in Beijing, China, 1986

In 1986 the Queen left an unusual and special gift with this family in Hong Kong – her autograph

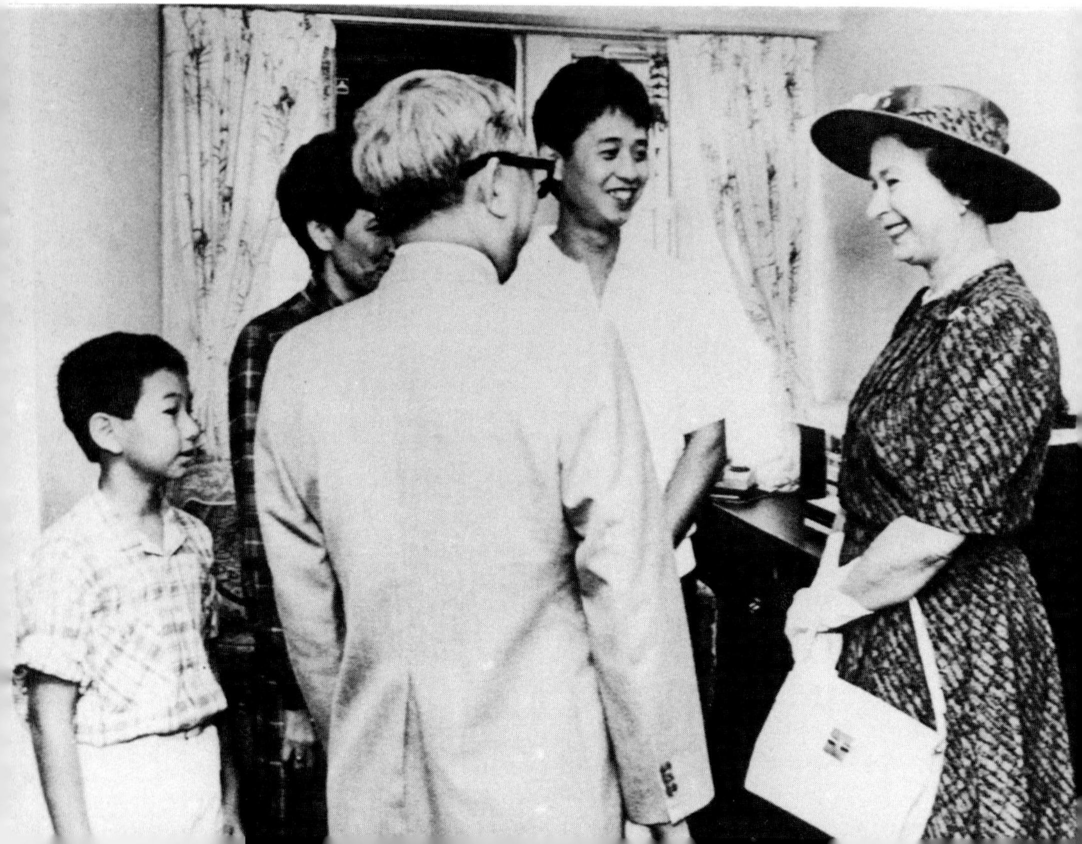

London. There was also a flying visit to West Germany where units of the 4th Armour Division staged the biggest display of tanks in Britain's history, on a heathland gunnery range near Hanover. The air was filled with the roar of engines and the rumble of tracks as 573 armoured vehicles, including 120 Chieftain tanks, passed by, while Gazelle and Scout helicopters hovered overhead. The Queen was seen to brush her eyes, though perhaps more on account of the dust and diesel fumes than from a show of emotion. Some 800 musicians grouped into twenty-four bands swelled the turn-out, at their centre a drum-horse bearing the silver drums captured at the Battle of Dettingen when the Queen's ancestor George II became the last British monarch to lead troops into battle.

That autumn, with celebrations in Britain over, the Queen set out again to share her Silver Jubilee with the countries of the Commonwealth: with the people of Canada, the Bahamas, the Virgin Islands, Antigua and Barbados.

Arriving in Ottawa she and Prince Philip were amused rather than alarmed by the dire predictions made by a so-called 'wheel of fortune' during their visit to the Museum of Man. 'The ship catches fire and you are burned to death' was the Queen's somewhat alarming fortune, while Prince Philip's future was just as grim: 'You are attacked on the dock of Quebec and die.' The wheel of fortune would have been more accurate had it predicted that the royal visit would again stir the now customary controversy over separatism. Even before the Queen arrived in Canada, René Levesque, Premier of Quebec, was on record as saying that the monarchy was 'irrelevant' to Quebec.

Levesque's views did not prevent his accepting an invitation to lunch with the Queen at the country home of Pierre Trudeau, one of ten provincial leaders to do so. It would have been discourteous to have refused, he said by way of explanation, adding that he was not hostile to the Queen personally, only to the institution she represented. Care was taken not to seat him near the Queen at the luncheon, and it was presumably by design on someone's part that he found himself sitting next to Prince Philip, whose views on the whole business of the monarchy and Canada had been expressed publicly in the course of a previous visit: 'The monarchy exists in Canada for historical reasons . . . also because it was thought to be a benefit to the nation . . . we do not come here for our health . . . if at any time people feel that it has no future part to play, then for goodness sake let's end the thing on amicable terms without having a row about it.' Which of the two men, prince or politician, raised the subject in lunch-time conversation is not known, but it was inevitable that one of them would – inevitable too that they should disagree, as Levesque said later. 'But subtly,' he added.

A televised speech by the Queen was equally subtle, though it carried the imprint of Pierre Trudeau rather than Prince Philip. There was no direct mention in the speech of Quebec's desire to secede, but clearly that was what it was about. 'One of Canada's greatest assets,' the Queen said, 'is that you have not one but two basic traditions, French and British, each of which represents a mainstream of Western thought and enlightenment.' Confederation was not a French idea or a British idea, she went on, but 'an idea born of this land', and she ended with a strong plea for continued Canadian unity: 'In a world divided by differences of colour, race, language, religion and ideology, the Canadian experience stands out as a message of hope. My prayer is that it will continue to offer this message to mankind.'

It was a speech which cut little ice with René Levesque. In a comment clearly aimed at Trudeau, he said: 'To use a symbol for political purposes in a stressful situation like ours is to risk de-valuing the symbol.' Despite such risk, the Queen was again 'used' to repeat the call for national unity when opening the Canadian Parliament.

After Canada, the Bahamas must surely have come as a welcome relief. The atmosphere there was much more in keeping with the Silver Jubilee which the tour was intended to celebrate. Nassau, the capital, had been given the equivalent of a springclean ahead of the Queen's arrival, and any small objection to the money spent on this was answered with the view that the various improvements would 'last long after the Queen has been and gone'. Her arrival was greeted with one of those colourful West Indian carnivals, a mixture of exotic costumes, zippy music and calypso dancing, known as *junkanoos*. There was a similar carnival, a spontaneous outbreak of excitement and joy, to speed her on her way when she left again two days later.

Jamaica, which might normally have expected a visit from the Queen during the course of a Caribbean tour, did not get to share in her Silver Jubilee celebrations. Disappointing though this was to the people of the island, the Queen could hardly be expected to call there at a time when Michael Manley, the Prime Minister, was suggesting that the country should become a republic. In the absence of the Queen, Manley invited Cuba's Fidel Castro. To the average Jamaican, it was not at all the same thing.

On its way to the Virgin Islands, where the Queen opened the two-centuries-old legislature and laid the foundation stone for a new hospital wing, the royal yacht dropped anchor off Little Iguana so that the royal party could go ashore for a beach barbecue. Some of the party, though not the Queen, were taking the opportunity to swim in the sea when a basking shark was spotted. The alarm was raised and the swimmers headed hurriedly back to the beach. Later in the day, with the shark gone, the Queen herself ventured into the sea for a quiet dip.

On the small island of Antigua, at that time still a British colony though it has become independent since, the Queen again found herself embroiled in political controversy. Opponents of the Prime Minister, Vere Bird, took advantage of her arrival to distribute a pamphlet headed *Welcome To A State In Bondage* which was directed more against the depressing state of the island's economy, with unemployment at something over forty per cent, than against colonialism. The Prime Minister's speech of welcome was drowned by the loud and persistent wailing of demonstrators, though this stopped when the Queen rose to reply.

Advantage was taken of the royal itinerary to pay a private visit to the island of Mustique, at that time a focus of Press attention because of Princess Margaret's holidays there with Roddy Llewellyn. It was the Queen's first visit to the island and the first opportunity she had had of seeing her sister's holiday home, *Les Jolies Eaux*. Princess Margaret, separated from Lord Snowdon and soon to be divorced, was waiting to greet her sister and brother-in-law when they went ashore. So were most of the rest of the island's population, perhaps a hundred people. Diplomatically, Roddy Llewellyn was not among them, though due to fly in to join Princess Margaret later.

The Queen was at sea again, heading for Barbados, when Concorde flew over. With Prince Philip, she waved to the crew of the supersonic airliner as it made two passes over the royal yacht at a height of only a few hundred feet before making its first-ever landing in Barbados in readiness to speed her back to London the following day. Arrangements for the royal visit to the island had to be hastily reorganized when a tropical storm knocked out power lines, flooded roads and all but flooded the recreation ground which was to have been the centre of celebrations. The Queen was more than able to cope. To the delight of the crowd, instead of driving round the recreation ground, as had been originally intended, she walked among them.

Then it was home to Britain. The 3,686-mile flight from Barbados to London in Concorde took only three hours and forty-two minutes. It was the first time the Queen had flown supersonically.

12 ARABIAN NIGHTS AND AFRICAN SAFARIS

Among the many Silver Jubilee gifts presented to the Queen was a new Rolls Royce, a special Phantom VI limousine built at a cost of £60,000. With a rear seat four inches higher than in a normal limousine and a transparent dome to the rear roof quarters, it was ideally suited to allowing the Queen to see and be seen. Due to an industrial dispute, it was not delivered to the royal mews at Buckingham Palace until Silver Jubilee year was some months in the past, but it was in good time for the Queen's 1978 state visit to West Germany, her second in thirteen years.

With terrorism rampant in many parts of Europe, the German authorities were determined that no harm should come to the Queen while she was in their care. Indeed, so thorough were their planned security measures that it looked as if she would be boxed in almost completely by armed guards wherever she went. When news of this reached Buckingham Palace, the Queen reacted characteristically. She wished to see and be seen by the German people, she said, to move amongst them on walkabouts and talk with them. The result was to modify German security arrangements, at least to the extent of making them less obvious than they would otherwise have been.

Unobtrusive though it was in the final analysis, security was still on a massive scale. Members of a German commando unit who had successfully stormed a hijacked Lufthansa airliner at Mogadishu were amongst those who guarded the Queen. A helicopter hovered protectively overhead as she travelled by train from Bonn to Mainz, where some 40,000 enthusiastic Germans braved a rainstorm to welcome her. 'E-liz-a-beth,' they chanted as some of them even clambered over barriers for the privilege of a royal handshake. 'We

149

have seen nothing like it since her last visit all those years ago,' commented a senior police officer.

In West Berlin, where the Queen was joined by Chancellor Helmut Schmidt, armed marksmen were perched on rooftops. She had flown into the Royal Air Force base at Gatow where she was greeted by a threefold guard of honour, British, French and American. Some 20,000 Berliners, including, it was said, some who had ventured across from East Berlin, heard her speak from a dais erected in front of the Blue Church. As on her previous visit to the city, her speech had a distinctly political content. 'Your city has compelled our sympathy and admiration,' she said. 'You have kept burning the flame of freedom. In Berlin we test the peaceful intentions of others. We have lived through difficult and danger-ous times together. My Government and my people stand beside you. My soldiers and airmen stationed in Berlin embody the British commitment to defend your freedom for as long as need be, until the divisions in Europe and your city can be healed.'

As though to underline her words and reinforce British commit-ment, the Queen took the salute at a Trooping the Colour ceremony held in the Maifeld Stadium, which once echoed to the rantings of Adolf Hitler. It was the first time the ceremony had been held anywhere outside Britain itself.

As well as her new Rolls Royce, the Queen also had with her the royal yacht, boarding it to sail through the Kiel Canal to Bremerhaven and Bremen. Among the things she saw on this last leg of her visit were models of Kaiser Wilhelm's Navy. 'Wouldn't you like to play with these?' she teased Prince Philip.

Two months later the Queen again flew to Canada, where she was to open the Commonwealth Games in Edmonton as well as touring Newfoundland and Saskatchewan. It had become almost habitual for her Canadian visits to be dogged by controversy, and this one was to prove no exception. It began the moment she arrived there in the company of Prince Philip and her two younger sons, Andrew, now eighteen, and Edward, fourteen. With Pierre Trudeau, the Prime Minister, out of the country on holiday (though he would be back in time to meet the Queen in Edmonton later), she was met at the airport by the Governor-General, Jules Leger. If the Queen herself did not feel slighted by the

Prime Minister's absence, as was stated in an attempt to cool the ensuing argument, others clearly felt so on her behalf. It was 'extraordinarily rude' of Trudeau, said an official of Canada's Monarchist League. 'He damned well should have come back.' The long-running issue of separatism was also quick to rear its head. The official English translation of a passage in French forming part of a speech the Queen made at St John's was queried by French-speaking journalists. With an election coming up, they accused the Trudeau Government of speaking with two voices on the question of separatism, strongly opposing it in the English version but less opposed to it in the original French.

Republicanism as well as separatism was also the subject of argument and newspaper comment, though the Queen's popularity among the vast majority of Canadians, judging by the reception she received in Edmonton and elsewhere, seemed un-diminished. An estimated crowd of 100,000 turned out to see her when she went walkabout in Edmonton, while the numbers greeting her on her whistle-stop tour of sparsely populated Saskatchewan, if smaller, were no less enthusiastic.

Coincident with the tour of Saskatchewan came the leaking of a report on the constitution by the Canadian Bar Association which suggested, among other things, that the Queen should be re-cognized as Canada's head of state only when she was actually in Canada. Publicly, Pierre Trudeau took the view that this was no more than enshrining in constitutional law a situation that already existed, with the Queen represented in her absence by a Canadian Governor-General exercising her royal prerogatives, functions and authority. Privately, it was said, he saw it also as a move to counter separatism. Which of these arguments he put to the Queen is not known, but it was alleged that she raised no objection. Others, however, objected vociferously. Pro-monarchists saw it as a step along the road to republicanism. Former Prime Minister John Diefenbaker said he would campaign against any such proposal 'all over Canada', and a meeting of ten provincial premiers unanimous-ly rejected it as 'a constitutional change' which the federal govern-ment had not the legal power to make. Even Quebec's Premier, René Levesque, was opposed to it, though his motive may have been somewhat different.

151

Before and after that tour of Canada with its controversial over-tones the Queen found herself facing a problem of a very different kind. She was going, early the following year, on a tour of the states of the Arabian Gulf – Kuwait, Bahrain, Saudi Arabia, Qatar and Oman – and the problem was what to wear in countries where even a woman's bare arm is construed as immodest or worse.

Faced with the necessity for conforming as nearly as possible to Arab custom, the Queen, with the aid of her fashion designers, assembled a tour wardrobe unlike any that had gone before, day dresses as well as evening dresses high enough to conceal the throat, long enough to hide the ankles, and long-sleeved to cover the arms.

The same went for the ladies-in-waiting who would accompany her.

It was, the Queen feared, going to be one of the most sensitive tours of her reign, with some degree of awkwardness, given the Arab attitude towards women, on the part of the sheikhs and others who would be hosting her. In the event, the tour passed off remarkably well, even if some of her Arab hosts, confronted with a situation in which they had to treat a woman as an equal, and more than an equal, resolved the dilemma by pretending that she was not a woman at all, speaking of her as 'he' rather than 'she'.

The Queen flew in Concorde to Kuwait, where she was greeted, somewhat stiffly perhaps, by the Emir, who entertained her to a banquet of spiced lamb in a hall hung with silk draperies to give the impression of a tent, and presented her with a three-strand pearl choker and a silver model of an Arab dhow. The Queen, in return, gave him a silver salver bearing an engraving of the royal yacht, and entertained him to a reciprocal dinner abroad *Britannia*, with filet of beef as the main course and orange juice to drink instead of the customary wines. She stayed in Kuwait two days – 'Such a short time,' as she said, certainly too short for the Emir to overcome the engrained habits of Arab tradition, though he seemed to relax more in the Queen's presence towards the end.

She remained aboard *Britannia* for the onward journey to Bahrain, where she was again greeted by an Emir. In Japan she had taken part in the traditional green tea ceremony; in Bahrain it was Arab coffee followed by rose water. She was taken to see the gardens at Budiya, which local legend maintains were the original Garden of Eden, and the prehistoric burial mounds at Dilmun which date back to 3000 BC. While Prince Philip went to see a centre for falcon-breeding, the Queen had lunch with the ruler's wife and her ladies. There was also a day at the races which whipped up rather more dust than is seen on British racecourses.

Then it was aboard Concorde again for the flight to Saudi Arabia, where King Khalid, as a gesture of goodwill, had pardoned twenty-five Britons previously jailed for transgressing the country's strict no-drinking laws.

To conform with Islamic custom, the Queen arrived in Riyadh dressed (in blue) from top to toe, though it was noticed that she wore a shorter, albeit still modest, dress for later visits to a local hospital and museum. She was required to wear long dresses only in the presence of the King, it was said by way of explanation. So it was a long dress again for a desert feast for which the King had flown in orchids from Holland, lobsters, turkeys, beef and pine-apples from other parts of the world, as well as ordering the spit-roasting of fifty lambs. The Queen wore a long dress too for her visit to the University of Petroleum and Minerals, where the British and American wives of various professors and graduates, having sat down beside their husbands, found themselves ordered to move and sit in a segregated bunch elsewhere. In none of the Arab states were women permitted to play a part in the public functions linked to the Queen's visit. Even the customary royal bouquets were always presented by men. But she did get to see something of the leading ladies, lunching with Sheikha Hassa in Bahrain, taking tea with Queen Sita in Saudi Arabia, with the senior of the four wives of the Emir of Qatar and with Sheikha Fatima, one of the wives of Sheikh Zaid, President of the United Arab Emirates.

Two months prior to the Queen's arrival in Qatar, the Emir had decided that it would be nice to show her round a zoo. Qatar had no zoo at the time, but such a thing was not difficult to organize in a country which, in terms of income per head of the population, was the third richest in the world. A zoo suitable to show the Queen was constructed and stocked in six weeks flat. Abu Dhabi, for its part, laid on another desert feast, with Sheikh Zaid himself joining in the folk dancing which greeted the Queen's arrival. Indeed, he even tried to encourage her to join in, but laughingly she declined. At the tea party with Sheikha Fatima the Queen found herself the recipient of a wonderful necklace, one of several she was to be given in the course of her tour. In return she gave Fatima a silver-framed photograph of herself, and a pendant for which she felt it necessary to apologize – as being 'rather small'.

Before the tour ended the Queen had been heaped with gifts, if not more numerous, certainly more valuable than those of any previous tour. So lavish were the gifts from Sheikh Rashid in Dubai – a diamond and sapphire necklace with matching ring and ear-rings, together with a miniature oasis fashioned in gold, with rubies as the dates on its miniature palm trees – that even the Queen could not suppress a gasp of delight. Elsewhere, in addition to the pearl choker in Bahrain and the necklace from Sheikha Fatima, she was given two more necklaces, two magnificent carpets, a double string of pearls, a ruby brooch, a watch, a gold coffee-pot, gold goblets, a gold fruit bowl and what can only be described as a pinafore, except that it was fashioned in gold chainmail and studded with sapphires and amethysts. For Prince Philip there was a platinum watch with matching cufflinks and not a few ornamental swords, including one in a diamond-and-ruby encrusted scabbard. The entire collection of royal gifts was estimated to have a value of around £1 million.

In Dubai the Queen heard a reading from the Koran, switched on a new desalination plant and was taken for a trip round the port in a barge while dancers and musicians provided entertainment on two accompanying dhows. Prince Philip was busy taking photographs of it all while the Queen for once was content to relax in an armchair on deck.

In Oman, as the tour neared its end, scented aerosol sprays were used to freshen the air ahead of the Queen's visit to a local *souk*. There was also, during the course of a visit to an ancient fort, one of those outbursts from Philip to which he is prone when concerned for the Queen's safety or well-being, when the couple had become separated by an onrush of local tribesmen eager to see the royal visitors. 'Where's the Queen? Where's the Queen?' Philip shouted, elbowing his way through the mob. Unable to locate her im-mediately, he banged on the roof of a police car which had its siren going and shouted, 'Switch that bloody thing off.' Having found the Queen, he decided to join her in her car – his own, he complained, was 'like a bloody oven' – for a drive to yet another desert picnic for which the main course turned out to be roast goat.

Later that year came another long, hot and demanding trip, this time to the African states of Tanzania, Malawi, Botswana and Zambia. But first there was a briefer, cooler and more relaxed state visit to Denmark, the second of the Queen's reign. On her last visit, in 1957, she had been welcomed by King Frederick IX. Now, in 1979, it was his daughter, Queen Margrethe, and her husband, Prince Henrik, who greeted her. Queen Margrethe, a talented artist, presented the Queen with a copy of Tolkien's *Lord of the Rings* which she herself had illustrated. In return, the Queen gave her a gilt carriage clock.

With one aboard *Britannia* and the other on *Dannebrog*, the Danish royal yacht, the two Queens sailed for Aarhus, where banner-carrying protestors staged a pro-IRA demonstration. However, police ensured that they were kept well away from the royal visitors. It was during that visit to Jutland that members of the Queen's entourage, though not the Queen herself, were entertained at what was styled 'a Viking feast'. One of them told the Queen about it afterwards, listing the various traditional dishes served, among them smoked salmon. The Queen laughed. 'I'm sure the Vikings never had smoked salmon,' she said. She was touring a local museum at the time, and a member of the museum staff, chancing to overhear, was quick to put her right: 'Yes, they did, Ma'am.'

As the time approached for the Queen's visit to Africa, whose focal point would be that year's Commonwealth Conference in Lusaka, there was a difference of opinion between Buckingham Palace and Downing Street as to whether she should go there. With sporadic fighting taking place on the border separating Zambia from Zimbabwe-Rhodesia, Prime Minister Margaret Thatcher took the view initially that it was unsafe for her to go. Disliking fuss about her safety as much as ever, the Queen saw it as a Commonwealth matter on which she did not necessarily have to accept the advice of her British Prime Minister. Like her father before her, who saw no reason why he also should not sail with the D-Day invasion fleet if Churchill was going, the Queen saw no reason to be absent from Lusaka if Mrs Thatcher was going. In the case of her father and Churchill, wisdom prevailed and neither King nor Prime Minister accompanied the invasion fleet. In the case of the Queen and Mrs Thatcher, both monarch and prime minister went to Lusaka for the Commonwealth Conference. A Rhodesian undertaking that there would be a cease-fire while the Queen was in Zambia helped to sway the issue.

She was already in Tanzania when news reached her that Zimbabwe-Rhodesian forces had again crossed the border to strike at guerrilla bases only 200 miles from Lusaka, but she did not see this as a breach of the undertaking, which would apply once she was actually in Zambia, and still saw no reason to cancel the rest of her tour. Sir Seretse Khama, President of Botswana, would later praise her 'great personal courage and commitment in visiting southern Africa at this most difficult period in the history of the area'.

As though to underline her sense of commitment, the Queen had not only her husband but also her second son, Prince Andrew, with her, just as she had taken him to Northern Ireland with her in defiance of the IRA during her Silver Jubilee year.

Nineteen that year, Andrew had already had some experience of royal travel, though such experience was limited to Canada, which he had toured extensively, both on his own and in the company of one or both parents, over the previous two years. But this was his first exposure to the emerging states of Africa, and a startled look came over his face when six youngsters of the revolutionary Young Pioneers goose-stepped towards him prior to popping a garland of flowers about his shoulders. He threw a quick glance at his father, who grinned encouragingly, and the startled look gave way to a smile.

If black Africans were eager to see the Queen, whites of the feminine gender were as eager to see her tall, handsome second son. In Dar-es-Salaam, during the course of a royal walkabout, a group of British-born wives held up a banner inscribed 'Hi Andy, Come And Have Coffee.' There was no opportunity for that, but later, when Andrew was eating out at a restaurant in Blantyre, a young wife dining in the same restaurant bet her husband that she would ask the Prince to dance with her. She got her dance and won her bet. Perhaps Andrew was too surprised to refuse. But he was quick to flee the restaurant afterwards before anyone else could get in on the act.

Dancing seemed to be the fashion in Malawi. When the Queen first arrived in Blantyre, Hastings Banda, the country's autocratic President, welcomed her by dancing along the red carpet towards her, fly whisk in one hand, ivory cane in the other. As the band played on, he tried to persuade the Queen to join him in his little dance. She sidestepped the issue as adroitly as she had with Sheikh Zaid's folk-dancing in Abu Dhabi, but did beat time to the music with her hand – an action so out of keeping with her customary regality that both Philip and Andrew looked frankly astonished. Or perhaps it was the newly invented costume of the country's women which astonished them, with its portraits of President Banda displayed over ample bosoms.

On a visit to Lilongwe the Queen was greeted by a group of Zulu warriors in leopard skins and lions' teeth, chanting as they flourished their war-like hide shields. One warrior presented to her turned out to be a former government minister, which suggests that today's 'Zulu warriors', like the Maori warriors of New Zealand and, indeed, Britain's own morris dancers, are really bank workers and civil servants keen to keep old traditions alive.

The royal party flew from Malawi to Botswana by a route designed to avoid flying over Zimbabwe-Rhodesia. It added an hour to the flight time, but they did get to see the Victoria Falls from the air. Andrew, in Botswana, also saw the bare breasts of some native dancing girls, but only briefly. Aware that photographers were waiting with cameras at the ready, he sensibly decided to avoid the dancing girls in favour of what was presumably a meaningful conversation with two local officials. There was another slightly embarrassing moment for the young Prince when the royal party reached Zambia. Taking a leaf out of his father's book, he strolled casually into what he thought was a village hut with the idea of chatting to the occupants. He was hurriedly eased out again. 'No, no, this is for goats,' he was told.

With the Queen's arrival in Lusaka, the Zambian capital, African politics began to intrude on the tour, with placards displayed attacking Bishop Abel Muzorewa, Prime Minister of neighbouring Zimbabwe-Rhodesia, and his predecessor, Ian Smith, and urging 'No Sell-Out On Zimbabwe'. The Queen was welcomed by Kenneth Kaunda, the Zambian President. Joshua Nkomo, the guerrilla leader, had been invited to join in the welcome (or so he said), but was not there. He had no wish to treat the Queen as 'a political football', he said. Sam Mwema, the Mayor of Lusaka, had no such inhibition. He subjected the Queen to a tirade against 'the less able whites' across the Zambesi and 'the racist governments' which protected them. Invited to reply, the Queen discreetly declined. Later she received an apology from the President's secretary-general: 'This should not have happened, Your Majesty. We try to keep you out of politics.'

Security was on a scale so massive as to verge on the ridiculous. There was one occasion when Andrew was cut off from his parents not by the crowd but by a whole mass of scuffling security guards; another when Prince Philip was treated by security men as a member of the accompanying Press corps. He did not lose his temper, as he had in Oman, but he did make some tartly witty comments. 'Now they're arresting each other,' he commented acidly at one point.

There were twenty-four hours of peace and quiet at a lodge on the Luangwe game reserve before the serious business of the Commonwealth Conference. However, the Queen was up even earlier than usual. Five o'clock in the morning saw her climbing into a Land Rover, binoculars in hand, to go on a game-spotting safari. Andrew too went on safari, with President Kaunda's nineteen-year-old son as his guide. Then, while the Queen was engaged in her 'healing touch' talks at the Commonwealth Conference, Andrew and Prince Philip went to a 'Save the Rhino' meeting. As always, the concept of the Commonwealth touched something deep in the Queen's emotions and there was a moment later, when the conference was over and the Zambian crowd was chanting 'Bye-bye Queenie', when she was visibly close to tears.

Travel-wise, every year had long since become a busy one for the Queen and 1980 was to be as full as all the rest, with state visits to Switzerland, Italy and the Vatican, to Tunisia, Algeria and Morocco, a five-day flying visit to Australia, a trip to Belgium and another to Germany.

The visit to Switzerland was slightly marred by the presence of demonstrators at a horticultural show in Basle – but it was the demonstrators who suffered most: police had to charge into the crowd to rescue them as a group of irate Swiss matrons belaboured them with handbags. That small incident apart, the visit was a considerable success, though the Queen was somewhat disappointed that Swiss security was so strict as to prevent her indulging in her now customary 'meet the people' walkabouts. However, she did get to cruise Lake Lucerne in a paddle steamer, as had Queen Victoria when she visited Switzerland over a century before, going ashore at one point to see a field blue with forget-me-nots, climbing a hillside at a brisk pace which left some of her entourage puffing and blowing in her wake.

She presented the Swiss President, Georges-André Chevallez with a copy of the Magna Carta – not that she was suggesting, she told him, that the Swiss had anything to learn in that direction. 'Indeed,' she said, 'yours is a harmony the whole world might seek to emulate.' Among the several gifts she received in return was the promise of a holiday in Switzerland for thirty British children. 'A touching gift and a thought the Queen likes,' it was said on her behalf. However, the Swiss were disappointed that the Queen herself did not select the thirty children. That was left to the Department of Education.

The flying visit to Australia, a month later, was principally so that the Queen could be presented with the Silver Jubilee gift promised three years earlier, though, as usual, other engagements were tacked on. The stallion Without Fear having done his duty, the Queen became the happy owner of a two-year-old filly which, to the delight of her Australian subjects, she decided to name Australia Fair (after the country's new national anthem) before having it shipped to Britain for training at the Newmarket stables of William Hastings-Bass.

The presentation ceremony went off well. Not so the royal opening of a new High Court building in Canberra. Protesters packed the forecourt, an estimated 2,000 of them, waving anti-monarchy banners and placards while a balloon overhead trailed a giant streamer proclaiming 'Monarchy Out – Australia Republic Now.' So persistent was the jeering as the Queen planted a commemorative tree that, for once, she looked a shade apprehensive. That night the commemorative tree was stolen and a smaller, ailing specimen – presumably intended as some sort of protest symbol – planted in its place.

Sydney compensated the Queen with a warm welcome, a crowd of some 50,000 chanting 'Good on you, Queenie' and 'God save the Queen' when she opened a new city square there. Then it was on to Melbourne, where the crowd was twice as large and even more enthusiastic. 'Nothing could be more heart-warming than to be back among the Melbourne crowd,' said the Queen.

It was nearly twenty years since the Queen's last state visit to Italy when she went there in 1980. Her new Rolls Royce and the royal yacht set out ahead of her, with *Britannia* again to play its now customary dual role as a floating palace and a conference centre for businessmen and bankers. If the yacht made the trip without incident, the car did not. The royal car does not display registration plates, and this created some small difficulty with European customs officials. Once in Rome, however, it attracted large crowds, as it was driven empty through the streets to make sure its bulk – it is nineteen feet ten inches long and six feet seven inches wide – could safely negotiate certain twists and turns.

As so often, rumour also travelled ahead of the Queen. An early visit to Australia saw the rumour spread that she liked only biscuit-coloured tablecloths (which is not so). Tablecloths of that shade not being readily available, white ones were quickly dyed to what was thought to be an appropriate colour. In Italy the rumour spread that ladies presented to the Queen must not wear either red or black. As a result, the British Embassy was inundated with panic calls from fashion-conscious females.

At a state banquet in the Quirinale Palace the Queen extended Britain's thanks to Italy for its support in the European Economic Community. Her visit included trips to Genoa, Naples, Palermo in Sicily and, at her own request, the ruins of Pompeii. In Sicily, where she was entertained by the Princess San Vincenzi, she had the unusual experience of lunching by candlelight because her hostess would not permit daylight into the dining-room.

There was also, in the middle of all this, a state visit to the Vatican, oddly the Queen's first such visit though she had been there twice before. The reason for this seeming anomaly lies in the protocol surrounding royal visits. Her earliest visit to the Vatican, in 1951, could hardly be a state visit because she was still a Princess. In fact, it is listed in the royal archives as 'private'. Her 1961 audience with Pope John XXIII (who showed her some of the love letters written by Henry VIII to Anne Boleyn), during her previous visit to Italy, was apparently not a 'state visit' either, though the visit to Italy was. The Vatican visit on that occasion was listed simply as 'official'.

But her 1980 audience with the Pope, though little different from that of 1961 except that the Pope was now John Paul II, merited the title 'state visit'. For it the Queen wore a long dress of black taffeta designed by Ian Thomas, with a black veil, a diamond tiara and the sash and star of the Order of the Garter, in view of which it was perhaps appropriate that the Pope should present her with a facsimile manuscript of Dante's *Divine Comedy* with its illustration of the Order of the Garter as worn by Edward IV in the fifteenth century. In return, the Queen gave him a book about Windsor Castle together with signed and silver-framed photographs of herself and Prince Philip.

From Italy it was straight on to Tunisia and Algeria, and to what one royal aide would later term 'a bloody trip' to Morocco.

The Queen's visit to the Gulf States the previous year had given her experience of meeting Arab rulers, and the fact that she was female would cause no problems in either Tunisia or Algeria. Indeed, the Tunisian President, Habib ben Ali Bourguiba, welcomed her with tears in his eyes as he recalled the days of 'imprisonment, exile and dark prospects' which had seen him seek sanctuary in London nearly thirty years before. Together they drove into Tunis in a Rolls Royce so ancient that it carried the number plate 13, with Bourguiba urging the Queen to stand on the seat so that people could see her better. With some help, she did, laughing and waving as she went along.

During her two days in Tunisia the Queen visited the North African war cemetery at Bourj al Amri where she particularly asked to be shown the graves of two holders of the Victoria Cross, Lord Lyell of the Scots Guards and Captain Sandys-Clarke of the North Lancashires. There was also a visit to the seventh-century mosque at Kairouan where accompanying reporters wrote that the Queen 'looked surprised' at being asked to remove her shoes before entering. Surely not, given the other mosques and holy places at which she had done the same thing several times during her years of travel?

Algeria, the next stopping-place on the tour, had experienced a disastrous earthquake in which thousands died just prior to the Queen's visit. Indeed, she had sent a message of sympathy to President Chadli before leaving London. While the Queen performed the routine functions of a state visit, Prince Philip flew to the stricken area at the controls of an Andover, making a tricky landing on a small, bumpy runway near El Asnam, to meet and talk with survivors of the earthquake.

And so on *The Road To Morocco* for a state visit during which the Queen would experience more upsets than Hope, Crosby and Dorothy Lamour did in the film of that title.

Two things seem to have governed King Hassan's odd treatment of his royal visitor. One was his inability to come to the terms with the fact that this particular mere woman was at least his equal. The other was an obsession with security stemming from previous attempts on his life. Princess Margaret, who had visited Morocco four years earlier, had warned her sister what to expect. Driving with King Hassan, she told her, was 'rather like being kidnapped'.

The Queen discovered the truth of that for herself when there was an abrupt change of cars during a state drive through Marrakesh. 'Security', she was informed. But it can hardly have been security which saw the King go off for a round of golf instead of attending the welcome luncheon laid on in the Queen's honour. His first meeting with her saw some high-handed treatment meted out to her ladies-in-waiting, the Duchess of Grafton and Mrs John Dugdale: they were unceremoniously dismissed from the royal presence.

Security may or may not have been the reason why a state banquet was unexpectedly put back half an hour without either explanation or apology to the Queen. She arrived at the banquet to be left kicking her heels in her car and was eventually welcomed not by King Hassan himself but by two of his children. With a multi-million pound engineering contract for Britain in the balance, and dependent upon King Hassan's goodwill, the Queen could hardly afford to show the anger she is said to have felt, though this must surely have required every ounce of her experienced self-control as things went from bad to worse.

The King was again absent from an arranged lunch with the Queen on a visit to Casablanca. A planned visit to Fez was abruptly deleted from her itinerary. A trip to the Atlas Mountains echoed the 'kidnap' experience about which Princess Margaret had warned her sister. The King's obsession with security led to several changes of car, as a result of which the party was some two hours late in reaching its destination where the Queen was ushered into an elaborate tent complete with red carpet and silver tea urns. But if she was expecting lunch, she was to be disappointed. Leaving the Queen and Prince Philip to their own devices, King Hassan disappeared into an air-conditioned trailer, presumably to rest. An hour went by before he appeared again, with the Queen getting hotter by the minute, fiddling with her handbag in the absence of anything more constructive to do.

While the Queen could hardly display the anger she must have felt, others could react on her behalf. A discreet tip-off to accompanying British journalists ensured indignant headlines in Fleet Street newspapers the following day. It was promptly and officially denied that the Queen was in any way put out. Well, it would be, wouldn't it? But that could not prevent King Hassan being informed of what was being said about him in the London newspapers and taking umbrage. In consequence, he was nearly an hour late turning up for a farewell banquet aboard the royal yacht. His anger apparently mounting as the meal proceeded, he suddenly announced his intention of leaving. Somehow the Queen prevailed upon him to finish his meal and stay on to witness the ceremony of Beating Retreat by the yacht's contingent of Royal Marines. But by then she herself had seemingly had enough, and her leave-taking of the King is said to have been not only formal but brief and cool. Reaching the quayside, the King, apparently in better humour, turned to wave a last goodbye. Too late. The Queen had already gone below.

As though seeking to make amends, King Hassan decided next day, at almost the last minute, that he would see the Queen off personally from Casablanca. The result, true to form, was to cause delay in her departure for London.

However, the visit was not entirely without compensation. While in Morocco the Queen met the ageing Field Marshal Sir Claude Auchinleck, Allied Commander-in-Chief in both the Middle East and India during World War II, and there was a gift for her of four Arab horses from the unpredictable King Hassan. Together with her preceding state visits to Italy and the Vatican, her tour had lasted seventeen days, during which time she attended eighteen receptions and five banquets, inspected eight guards-of-honour, laid five wreaths and was shown round thirty-six schools, factories, museums, churches, palaces and historic sites.

A month after returning from her strange visit to Morocco, the Queen was off to Belgium.

It is difficult to realize that Belgium has existed as an independent state only since 1830. Before that it was dominated in turn by Austria, Spain, France and the Dutch. The Queen's visit was to mark the 150th anniversary of independence.

As she was going to Brussels anyhow, the British Government of the day thought it would be a good idea if she looked in also at the headquarters of both the EEC and NATO, and anti-marketeers in Britain thought to detect the handwriting of Margaret Thatcher in the Queen's response to a speech made by Roy Jenkins, at that time President of the EEC Commission. The Labour Party, at its annual conference, had voted for withdrawal from the Common Market, and the Queen's speech was seen as countering that vote and re-emphasizing Britain's continued membership. 'The foundation of the Community will surely prove to be a turning point in the history of our continent,' the Queen said in her speech. 'Economically, the Community has made its mark on world production, trade and finance, and as a friend and helper of those countries which are still in the early stages of material development. Politically, the pooling of the traditions and experience in world affairs of nine separate nations has given an authority to their common policies and views which individually they could not have expected to wield.'

In a second speech the following day the Queen similarly underlined Britain's commitment to NATO. 'Because of the strength and determination of the Atlantic Alliance,' she said, 'we have been able to bring up our children free from the fear of war and free to enjoy the rich heritage of our common civilization in peace and in growing prosperity. The threat which brought this Alliance into being was here in Europe and it has by no means diminished. But recent events* have reminded us all that the vital interests we share as allies are under threat in other parts of the world as well.'

However, even allies do not always see things the same way, and German farmers around Lemigo were less than happy when the Queen flew there a week later to visit the 1st Battalion Royal Welch Fusiliers, of which she is Colonel-in-Chief. To entertain her, a

* Presumably a reference to the Soviet invasion of Afghanistan.

mock battle was arranged. For convenience, a snow-covered hill-side close to the barracks was used instead of the normal exercise area some distance away. In consequence, there was a picket line of some twenty local farmers as the Queen watched her troops in action. 'They're ruining my winter crops of wheat and barley,' lamented one. 'I know I'll get compensation, but it's the principle of the thing.'

13 SENTIMENTAL JOURNEY

Largely, though not entirely, through the match-making tendencies of her great-great-grandmother, Queen Victoria, the Queen is related, if sometimes distantly, to most of the royal houses of Europe, reigning or otherwise. For instance, both King Juan Carlos of Spain, a country the Queen has not yet visited, and his Greek-born wife, Queen Sophie, are similarly descended from Queen Victoria. So, through her mother, is Queen Margrethe of Denmark. So is King Carl XVI Gustaf of Sweden. And King Olav V of Norway whom the Queen visited again in the spring of 1981.

King Olav's mother, Queen Maud, was the youngest daughter of King Edward VII, the Queen's great-grandfather, so it was appropriate that the Queen should call him 'Uncle' on arrival in Norway and that he should greet her with a kiss instead of the customary formal handshake. It was her second state visit to Norway since ascending the throne, though there had been at least one private family visit in between. On her first state visit, back in 1955, the Queen had been proud to show her new royal yacht to Olav's father, King Haakon VII. Now, in 1981, *Britannia* had been in service for more than a quarter of a century, though looking as pristine as ever.

In Norway, as elsewhere, the period between state visits had been a quarter-century of considerable change. There, as in Britain, the Prime Minister presented to the Queen was a woman, Mrs Gro Brundtland. So was the British Ambassador, Miss Gillian Brown, who would be elevated to the status of Dame before the Queen left again. Noticeable too in Norway, as elsewhere on the Queen's travels, was the increasing tendency to protest. Raucous chanting greeted her arrival in Oslo, and some ketchup was thrown, fortu-

166

nately missing its intended target. It was in keeping with the changing times too that the Queen should be taken to Stavanger to see what was, certainly at that time, the world's largest offshore oil platform in operation and that she should leave Norway to sail for the Shetlands where she was to inaugurate the Sullum Voe oil terminal.

The September of that year found the Queen flying out (in a Boeing 707 of the Royal Australian Air Force) to yet another Commonwealth conference, this time in Australia. Almost her first request when she touched down at Melbourne was to be shown round the conference centre. As Head of the Commonwealth, her visit proved to be a considerable success. She had lunches with some of the Commonwealth leaders, received others in audience aboard *Britannia* (which had arrived in Australia ahead of her) and entertained all to dinner.

As Queen, however, her sorties ashore met with what was generally felt to be a 'subdued' reception. The crowds were nothing like they had been during the early visits of her reign. Partly this was doubtless due to the fact that people could now stay comfortably at home and see her on television. But there were other factors. The sacking of Gough Whitlam by the Governor-General was still a sore point with many Australians. Others objected to the multi-million-pound cost of hosting the Commonwealth Conference. The Queen had had no say in either matter, but suffered the after-effects of both. Political leaders, like the Australian public, differed in their views of the resulting situation. 'The monarchy has never been stronger,' insisted Prime Minister Malcolm Fraser. 'The monarchy is in decline,' retorted Labour leader Robert Hawke (soon to be prime minister). 'I don't believe it will last in Australia beyond the end of the century.' However, it was united Ireland sympathizers, not Australian republicans, who flaunted their banners outside the National Gallery when the Queen went there for a state reception.

Despite this surrounding hassle, the Queen enjoyed a day at the races, opening a new racing museum while there, and an evening at the ballet. Backstage after the ballet, she sought out one of the company who had been obliged to limp off with a sprained ankle during the performance. 'It was very sad,' the Queen sympathized with her. 'I saw you disappear in the first act.'

Tasmania too afforded a pleasant interlude, including going

167

ashore from the royal yacht at Wineglass Bay for a barbecue picnic after which the Queen set out to 'stretch her legs'. By the time she returned she had walked seven miles.

During a flight from Hobart to Launceston she passed the time glancing through a magazine, pausing at an article which posed the question of possible abdication. 'Are they trying to put me in my grave?' she asked, jokingly, of those around her.

Back in mainland Australia, a visit to Perth passed off without incident except for the small girl who, having given the Queen a bunch of red roses, asked if she could kiss her. Whatever the Princess of Wales might do later, the Queen is not the type to kiss or hug small children. 'No, dear – I'm sorry,' she told the girl. In Adelaide the Queen again found herself the focal point of protest. 'Brits out,' shouted demonstrators flourishing imitation coffin lids (meaning out of Northern Ireland rather than out of Australia) when the Queen attended a reception at the Festival Centre.

There were to be more demonstrations in New Zealand, at both Dunedin and Wellington. In Dunedin a royal walkabout ran into banners of almost every description waved by united Ireland sympathizers, Maori rights protesters, republicans, the unemployed, even a group of lesbians and a faction opposed to the policies of Prime Minister Robert Muldoon. With an election in the offing, there were those who saw the royal visit as politicking on behalf of the Prime Minister. 'I have to remain neutral on these occasions, but to adapt a well-known saying, "The best of New Zealand luck to you all,"' said the Queen, amidst laughter, at a state luncheon. In Wellington, where the Queen did another walkabout, the protest banners took a more personal turn, not only 'Brits Out', but also 'Royal Fat Cats Go Home.'

Despite such incidents – and a heavy cold from which she was suffering at the time – the Queen insisted on her planned programme of engagements. Much of the tour was pleasant enough, in particular a visit to the Middlepark Stud where she saw the chestnut filly born to one of the mares which she had shipped to New Zealand to be mated with the stallion Balmerino. She inspected the filly with an expert eye, commenting, 'She is well grown, walks very well and has the family colour.' She decided upon the name Annie, a choice which would hardly have commended itself to her grandfather, King George V. It was because he disliked the name

Ann that Princess Margaret's name was changed from Ann Margaret to Margaret Rose.

Before returning home, there was also a state visit to Sri Lanka, the first time the Queen had been there for more than a quarter-century. It was Ceylon when she last visited the country during her round-the-world tour of 1953–4 and she was its Queen. Now it was a republic and she was Queen no longer, though still recognized there as Head of the Commonwealth. A welcoming crowd of more than a million people, given a public holiday to mark the duality of the Queen's visit and the fiftieth anniversary of universal suffrage, turned out to see her drive through Colombo, many of them fainting from a combination of the intense heat and the pressure of those around them.

The Queen was taken to Anuradhapura, the country's ancient capital, to see the Buddhist shrine of the sacred Bo-tree. Given a pair of navy-blue socks to wear instead of shoes before entering the shrine, she slipped them on to find they carried an advertisement for Air New Zealand. There was also a visit to Kandy to see the traditional parade of painted and caparisoned elephants, and to the nearby Victoria Dam project where she met a number of British workers employed there. But there was one Briton she did not get to meet. Bernard Sarjeant, the father of the boy jailed the previous year for firing blank shots at the Queen as she rode on horseback towards Horse Guards Parade for the annual ceremony of Trooping the Colour, had been given a day off to avoid possible royal embarrassment.

In April the following year, two weeks before the Queen was due to pay another flying visit to Canada, Argentine troops invaded the Falkland Islands. Four days later the vanguard of the British Task Force which was to recapture the islands sailed from Portsmouth. It was led by two aircraft-carriers, HMS *Hermes* and HMS *Invincible*, and aboard the latter was the Queen's second son, Prince Andrew, now twenty-two and a helicopter pilot in the Royal Navy. The result was a situation with which the Queen was concerned as both monarch and mother. To enable her to keep in touch with developments during her three days in Canada, a hotline linking her directly with the Prime Minister's office at 10 Downing Street was installed in her apartment in the Governor-General's residence in Ottawa.

This visit to Canada was no ordinary see-and-be-seen royal tour.

169

One hundred and fifteen years after Queen Victoria approved the British North American Act which gave Canada its first constitution, her great-great-granddaughter was flying there to sever the country's last colonial links with Britain. From now on Canada would be able to enact its own laws without seeking approval from the London Parliament, and a crowd of some 50,000 people braved the rain to witness the proclamation of the new constitution at an open-air ceremony on Ottawa's Parliament Hill.

French-Canadians did not approve of the new constitution. The province of Quebec boycotted the proclamation ceremony and in Montreal there was a protest march through the city. The new constitution, said Quebec's Premier, René Levesque, would serve only to weaken the province and increase the powers of the central government. The Queen, in her speech at the proclamation ceremony, made reference to the 'differences and rivalries' existing in Canada. They were part of the country's history, she said, and would probably always exist in such a vast and vigorous land.

The brief but bloody conflict for the Falkland Islands was already fading into memory when the Queen again visited Australia the following October, her third visit in three years. Memories of Gough Whitlam's dismissal, which had lingered long in the Australian consciousness, were finally beginning to fade also. Sir Ninian Stephen, who had replaced Sir John Kerr as Governor-General, was with Malcolm Fraser, the Prime Minister, to greet the Queen when her aircraft landed at Darwin after the twenty-one hour flight from London. As always, the welcome ceremony was preceded by that small Australian legality which not even a royal visitor can escape. Officials of the Agriculture Department boarded the Queen's aircraft and sprayed it with insecticide.

Among the Queen's public engagements during that visit to Australia was the presentation of the Royal Humane Society's gold medal, awarded only seven times in more than forty years, to a thirteen-year-old schoolgirl, Peta-Lyn Mann, for her bravery in saving a man who was being savaged by a crocodile. In fact, the man was twice attacked by the crocodile, being bitten on the thigh and the buttock, and twice the diminutive thirteen-year-old engaged in a courageous tug-of-war as the reptile sought to drag its potential victim into deeper water. Later, visiting a local museum, the Queen was shown a preserved specimen of the type of crocodile involved. The specimen was somewhat longer than the real-life twelve-footer which had attacked Hilton Graham, but even a twelve-footer, the Queen realized, was extremely formidable. 'I saw that little girl earlier today,' she recalled. 'Quite remarkable. Quite remarkable.'

In Brisbane she attended the Commonwealth Games, though Aborigine dancers were disappointed when her timetable was altered so that she missed their performance. To make up for this, they were invited to a gala theatre show which the Queen attended. However, not all Aborigines were so easily satisfied. A land-rights protest mounted to coincide with the Queen's visit resulted in over 200 people being arrested – with some consequent embarrassment for the new Governor-General. His thirty-year-old daughter, a supporter of the land-rights movement, was arrested twice in four days.

Advantage had been taken of the fact that the Queen was going to Australia to arrange a tour of Commonwealth islands in the Pacific – Papua New Guinea and Fiji of course, but also the recently independent islands of the Solomons, Nauru, Kiribati and Tuvalu.

At the time of the Queen's visit to Papua New Guinea there was talk of the country's becoming a republic, with a president replacing the Queen as head of state. But such was the enthusiasm of the people – well over 100,000, some of whom had trekked for more than a day through the mountains, turned out to see her – that the chairman of the commission considering the question of the country's constitution was obliged to issue a hasty statement saying that no decision in the matter had yet been taken, while the Prime Minister, Michael Somare, expressed the hope that the Queen (or a member of her family) would return in 1984 to open the new parliament building. As it turned out, that duty fell to Prince Charles.

The only small hitch came during a visit to Mount Hagen in the Western Highlands when a tropical downpour of monster hailstones sent everyone diving for cover in the middle of the Queen's speech. The Queen herself was only partly protected by a shelter of thatched grass which had been erected to shade her from the sun rather than from a fusillade of hailstones. There was no such shelter for her car, and after the ceremony it obstinately declined to start and a replacement had to be found.

171

In Honiara, capital of the Solomon Islands, the Queen was greeted with an equal display of enthusiasm and serenaded with conch shells. A hospital walk-round during the course of the visit saw Prince Philip waxing eloquent on one of his pet themes, the subject of birth control. Learning that the islands' birth-rate had a five per cent inflation rate, he did a quick spot of mental arithmetic and pointed out that the population would have doubled to 400,000 by the year 2000. 'You must be out of your minds,' he said. 'You'll be blaming everyone else for the problem you have on your hands.' Unarguable, one would have thought, but he did not go unchallenged for once. 'With respect,' a hospital doctor pointed out, 'you yourself are the father of four children.'

A heavy swell was running when *Britannia* arrived off Nauru, causing the royal barge to rise and fall some six feet as it lay alongside. Undaunted, the Queen descended the companionway, waited calmly for the barge to rise with the next wave and then made a deft and experienced transfer from yacht to barge. She made light of the incident, even joking about it in a subsequent speech. Delighted laughter greeted her remark: 'I have wanted to visit Nauru for a long time and am grateful that wind and sea have been kind enough to make this possible.' Wind and sea were equally kind for her visit to the Kiribati (formerly Gilbert) group of islands, thanks – or so it was said – to a local magician weaving a spell to dispel a threatened storm.

On Tuvalu (formerly in the Ellice Islands) a ceremonial dug-out canoe was used to get the Queen ashore, and she looked momentarily alarmed as the canoe, with her still in it, was lifted clear of the water. However, alarm changed to a peal of laughter as she found herself being carried shoulder-high across the beach to the meeting-place. Later, however, as she was being borne in her canoe through the streets of the capital, Funafuti, bad weather struck again. The rain came down in such torrents that even the combined protection of her own umbrella and another held by a small girl perched behind her could not prevent her getting wet. Despite the weather, such was the warmth of her welcome that members of her entourage murmured that she had never enjoyed a visit so much. Gifts too were heart-warmingly simple, a roll of matting and some grass skirts and, for Prince Philip, walking-sticks and tobacco boxes. The Queen herself echoed the whispers of her entourage in her farewell speech, saying that, while Tuvalu might be scarce in natural resources, it was rich in human qualities. 'We have witnessed for ourselves,' she said, 'the wealth of friendliness and happiness that far outweighs the material wealth which is so often over-valued and abused in the world today.'

Nor was there any doubting the 'friendliness and happiness' which greeted her arrival in Fiji, where she opened the Great Council of Chiefs which advises the government of the island. It was the hope and desire of the chiefs, said the Prime Minister, Ratu Sir Kamisese Mara, that Fiji should remain loyal to the Crown 'for all time'. It was perhaps the most moving speech the Queen had listened to during her five-week tour.

It was certainly a speech in striking contrast to remarks made by Michael Manley, former Prime Minister of Jamaica, ahead of the Queen's visit to that island the following year. 'We have the greatest respect for Queen Elizabeth as Queen of England and Head of the Commonwealth and as a very distinguished woman in her own right,' he told an American television team, 'but when she comes here, we do not regard her as Queen of Jamaica.' All the same, Manley was standing beside the current Prime Minister, Edward Seaga, to welcome the Queen when her Royal Air Force VC10 landed in Jamaica. And judging by the welcome she received from the people of Jamaica, his views were somewhat at odds with popular sentiment. To them, she was still 'Good Queen Bess' of Jamaica to be greeted with the exuberant singing of 'Long Time Gal', sung at her own request.

In Montego Bay, when the Queen went there, people blocked the streets and lined the rooftops, and the local mayor, in a speech which rivalled that in Fiji for emotional content, spoke of the island's long and historic association with Britain. The Queen herself, opening the Jamaican Parliament on the twenty-first anniversary of the island's independence, made what many people took to be a pointed rejoinder to Manley's remarks. 'I am delighted to be with you as Queen of Jamaica,' she said by way of introduction.

From Jamaica, before going on to visit Mexico and the United States, there was a call at the largest of the three Cayman Islands, Grand Cayman, perhaps the most curious survival of the old colonial empire.

Taking full advantage of the tax-haven status granted to it by George III for succouring a shipwrecked Londoner, Grand Cayman has prospered to become an offshore trading and banking centre. At the time of the Queen's visit there were 422 banks on the island, 16,000 registered companies and more telex machines per head of the population, it was said, than anywhere else in the world. Today there are doubtless even more banks, more registered companies and more telex machines. Despite having no taxation, the local treasury could report at the time of the visit – incidentally, the first by a reigning monarch in the more than 300 years it has been a British colony – an annual budget surplus and no unemployment. Twice in the previous four years, the Cayman Islanders, who clearly know when they are on to a good thing, had voted against seeking independence, and in 1983 they welcomed the Queen with open arms.

Every village had its flags and bunting, its coloured lights and placards of greeting, as the Queen saw from a second-hand Rolls Royce which had once belonged to the President of Czechoslovakia and was now owned by a wealthy American with a home in the Caymans, who had loaned it to her for the occasion. The mock colonial house in which she stayed during her two days on the island was similarly American-owned. In her speech to the Legislative Assembly the Queen made a point of expressing thanks for the donation of £500,000 – an amazing £28 for every man, woman and child in the Caymans – sent to the South Atlantic Fund in the aftermath of the Falklands campaign, and she rewarded Bert Watler, the Assembly's serjeant-at-arms who organized this 'Mother Needs Your Help' fund, with the Cayman Islands Certificate and Badge of Honour.

With Mexico in the throes of financial crisis, it seemed a rather curious time for a royal visit. Or perhaps not. Almost the first of the Queen's official engagements was to take a look at a new steel mill in which Britain had a £200 million stake, including a government grant of £35 million. She found it still only at the foundation stage and, with Mexico abandoning many other projects because of its mounting foreign debt, at least one newspaper queried whether the Queen's visit was intended more to save the mill than to inspect it. She was told by her Mexican hosts that the mill would indeed be built.

174

The Queen herself had something to say concerning the country's financial problems when she spoke at a state dinner held in the courtyard of a seventeenth-century Spanish fort in Acapulco. Referring to the part Britain had played in the $10 billion rescue operation designed to avoid Mexico's defaulting on its foreign debts, she said, 'We have demonstrated by our actions our wish to help in the most useful way we can. The British Government, banks and other institutions and enterprises have already played their part.'

Whatever the motive underlying the royal visit, the Mexicans were delighted to see the Queen for the second time in eight years. So excited did the crowd become on one quayside where she went ashore that it broke through the restraining cordon of sailors and almost mobbed her. Photographers came to blows with each other in their efforts to secure the best vantage-points from which to take pictures, pressing so closely around the Queen at times that on one occasion her Press Secretary, Michael Shea, had physically to restrain a particularly enthusiastic cameraman.

The Queen had long wanted to visit America's west coast, she told President Reagan during his 1982 visit to Britain. He responded by inviting her to stay at his ranch in California, and it was there that she made her way following her five-day visit to Mexico in 1983.

Like Mexico, the American visit was classed as 'official', but American reporters clearly did not feel bound by the customary rules of royal protocol. It is usually understood, for instance, that anything said by the Royals at a Press reception is 'off the record' and not for quotation. This certainly did not apply to the Press reception given aboard *Britannia* when the Queen arrived in San Diego. Indeed, one television reporter actually dashed away from the reception to go live on the air from the quay at which *Britannia* was berthed, informing viewers that he had asked the Queen if she was looking forward to going horse-riding with the President. 'That's the purpose of the visit,' he reported her as having replied. A reporter similarly quoted an exchange with the Queen concerning the movie *The Prince and the Pauper*. Yes, she'd seen it, the Queen was quoted as saying. According to the newspaper, the reporter had then asked, 'Doesn't Your Majesty sometimes think of changing places with a pauper?' – to which the Queen's perhaps not unnatural answer was 'No.'

Prince Philip received his share of the breaches of protocol. Asked the colour of his underpants, he reportedly 'grinned, tugged out his pants at the belt-line and pretended to look.' And timed to coincide with the Queen's visit, a mass-circulation tabloid came out with a story entitled *Queen Elizabeth's Strange Secret Life* which seemed to owe rather more to journalistic imagination than to hard fact.

The royal visitors were taken to see the Scripps Institute of Oceanography, Silicon Valley and the San Diego replica of the Globe Theatre, where the Queen unveiled a bust of Shakespeare before flying to Palm Springs for lunch with Walter Annenberg, former United States Ambassador to Britain.

At the Queen's own request, Hollywood was also included in the itinerary, and there was a gala dinner on a sound stage previously used for filming the television series *M.A.S.H.*, but converted for this evening into an indoor garden complete with trees and a fountain. The Queen wore a dress specially designed for the occasion, a creation in white chiffon with sequined California poppies on the bodice. Tony Richardson occupied a place of honour next to the Queen, and Julie Andrews sat beside Prince Philip. The large British contingent also included Greer Garson, James Mason and the diminutive Dudley Moore, along with such veteran American stars as Fred Astaire, Ginger Rogers, Bette Davis, James Stewart and Gene Kelly. There was entertainment by Frank Sinatra, Perry Como, Dionne Warwick and George Burns among others. If it was not all of equally high quality, the Queen appeared to be thoroughly enjoying herself throughout.

Freak weather marred the long-anticipated visit to the presidential ranch. The Queen had planned to sail along America's west coast in *Britannia*, but gale-force winds and heavy seas obliged her to fly instead, leaving behind a Los Angeles which would be hit by both a tornado and a slight earth tremor. Lightning played around the aircraft as she flew to Santa Barbara, where she found that creeks criss-crossing the dirt road to President Reagan's ranch had become so swollen with rain that a four-wheel-drive Dodge was the only sure way of getting there. The weather also put paid to the plan for the Queen and the President to ride together in the Santa Ynez Mountains, though there was doubtless some compensation in the presidential gift of a Hewlett-Packard computer, which the Queen said she would use for storing the bloodlines of her thoroughbreds. The President and Mrs Reagan entertained their royal guests to a Mexican-style lunch, after which they sat round the fire chatting. 'Such good company,' Nancy Reagan said of the royal couple, adding that their ready acceptance of changes necessitated by the weather had made their stay 'more like an adventure than a state visit'.

Further changes were necessary as the bad weather continued. Instead of sailing to San Francisco, the Queen was obliged to fly there, with Mrs Reagan along for company. In the absence of the royal yacht, she had to make do with the St Francis Hotel, with other hotel guests being asked to change rooms to make way for the Queen and her entourage. In all, the royal party filled forty-six rooms of the hotel, with the Queen occupying the Presidential Suite on the thirty-first floor, its gilt decor hastily refurbished, table lamps adorned with the royal coat-of-arms, and baskets of flowers dotted here and there. 'And we have stocked up on the Queen's favourite Malvern water,' said the manager, Robert Wilhelm.

A total of 230 secret service men had been assigned to guard the Queen while she was in the United States, and the switch from the absent royal yacht to the St Francis Hotel was a cause for concern to some of them. With several pro-Irish groups active in the city, which has a twenty-five per cent Irish population, the Queen found herself shepherded through the hotel lobby by a mass of body-guards while other hotel guests, eager to see her, were kept at bay by police equipped with truncheons and riot-control stun-guns. A bullet-proof limousine in a cavalcade of fourteen vehicles was used to convey her and Mrs Reagan through the streets of San Francisco for a meal at a Polynesian restaurant which had, of course, been checked beforehand for possible bombs.

In the event, there were only two demonstrations during the period of the Queen's stay, and both were in a relatively minor key. It had been forecast that a crowd of 20,000 would take part in the second demonstration, mounted in Golden Gate Park on the evening of the state banquet, but the actual number was something under 5,000. For the banquet the Queen wore a perhaps over-elaborate Tudor-style dress with arched shoulders, puff sleeves, lace ruffles, flying bows and a full skirt. 'Glorious chaos' was the verdict of one fashion editor, while another mocked it as being

177

'slightly beyond the call of duty'. If some joked about the dress, the Queen herself joked about the weather. 'I knew we had exported many of our traditions to the United States,' she said in her speech. 'I had not realized that weather was one of them.'

A visit to the Yoshemite National Park was marred by the news that three secret service agents assigned to protect her and travelling about half an hour ahead of her had been killed in a car crash, and the Queen interrupted what had been intended as a relaxing and private weekend to attend a memorial service in a small mountain chapel.

The bad weather having abated sufficiently for *Britannia* to catch up with her, the Queen gave a reception and banquet on board at which President and Mrs Reagan were guests of honour. In fact, there were two parties aboard the royal yacht that night. Some thirty privileged guests were asked to stay on after the official banquet for a private party to celebrate the Reagans' wedding anniversary. The Queen provided the champagne, the yacht's culinary department came up with an iced cake, there was a giant card and congratulations from *Britannia*'s crew, and a pianist from the Royal Marines band provided the accompaniment for Nancy Reagan's singing of 'True Love'.

The Queen's visit to the United States ended in Seattle, where she addressed an audience of 8,000 students, faculty and guests at the University of Washington. She spoke of the shared traditions of Britain and the United States, 'tested in two world wars where our life and liberty were at stake'. She spoke also of the changing world epitomized by what she had seen during her visit to Silicon Valley: 'The shape of the world economy and therefore the shape of our individual lives is being changed beyond recognition. With those changes will come immense human problems, but I am confident that the people of our two countries will be able to transcend them together.'

It was just over three weeks since the Queen had flown out from London, and the tour was not yet over. There was still Canada, with visits to Victoria, Vancouver and the small fishing port of Nanaimo. After the tight and sometimes obtrusive security mounted in the United States, the Queen doubtless found it a relief to be where security, though sound, was rather less obtrusive and where she could again indulge in walkabouts. She had a busy three days in Canada, ending with a banquet which allowed her only five hours' sleep before flying back to London.

The Queen had visited six countries in twenty-seven whirlwind days, and it was still only March, with four more state visits to come in the course of the year. Nearest of these in both time and distance was Sweden, just across the North Sea and due for another state visit only twelve weeks after the Queen's return from Canada.

It was over a quarter-century since the Queen's last state visit. Then King Gustav VI had occupied the Swedish throne. His son having predeceased him, killed in an air crash the same year that the future Elizabeth II made her first flight, it was his grandson, King Carl XVI Gustaf, and Queen Silvia, a German whom Carl Gustaf had met when she was a hostess at the 1972 Olympic Games in Munich, who welcomed the Queen to Stockholm in 1983.

Except in its incidental details, the occasion was much the same as any other state visit to a European country. There was an official lunch at the city hall (with roast reindeer on the menu), a night at the opera, a state banquet, a reciprocal banquet aboard *Britannia* (with tennis star Bjorn Borg, recently retired, among the Queen's guests) and an exchange of gifts. The Queen gave the Swedish royal couple a nineteenth-century oil painting of Lake Windermere. She also bestowed upon Sweden's King the Order of the Garter, Britain's most prestigious order of chivalry.

There was a visit to the Hasselblad factory at Gothenberg where the Queen, keen photographer that she is, was given the company's latest model, a camera retailing in the shops at that time at around £1,300. She and Prince Philip were also taken to see the *Vasa*, a seventeenth-century warship raised from the sea after reposing for 333 years on the bed of Stockholm harbour, now splendidly restored and housed in a specially built museum with controlled humidity. In fact, the Queen had seen the ship before, during her previous state visit in 1956, but she was interested to see it again now that Henry VIII's flagship *Mary Rose* had been raised from the sea-bed off Portsmouth.

The next three state visits, later in the year, were further afield – Kenya, Bangladesh, India – and to be taken in a sixteen-day gulp. Apart from a brief stop-over – extended from two to four hours on Jomo Kenyatta's insistence (see p. 110) – on the way back from her 1972 Far Eastern tour, the Queen had not visited Kenya since 1952, when her stay there was interrupted by news of her father's death. It was, after all, a country which held sad memories for her. But nearly thirty-two years later memory had dimmed sufficiently for her to re-visit the place where she was staying when she so unexpectedly became Queen. First, however, there were the usual engagements of any state visit to be carried out, a state banquet to attend, a service of remembrance at the Commonwealth war graves cemetery, a wreath to be laid at the mausoleum of Jomo Kenyatta and the now almost obligatory walkabout. Then came the sentimental journey up-country to the spot where her reign began.

Conscious perhaps of the historical significance of the occasion, the stationmaster at Nairobi saw the royal train out with the announcement: 'The royal train for Thika is now leaving from Platform 1.' Disappointingly, the Queen was to find that Treetops, the tree-house in which she spent the night of her father's death, had gone, destroyed by fire, with only a pile of stones beside a water-hole to mark where it once stood. In its place, though not occupying precisely the same spot, the Queen found a safari hotel built to accommodate tourists lured there by the combined attractions of history and the big game which frequent the area. 'It's changed so much I can't recognize it,' she told Richard Prickett, the 'white hunter' who was her escort. She spent that night at Sagana, in the stone and cedar-built lodge which was one of her wedding gifts and where she was staying that morning in February 1952 when Prince Philip gently broke the news that her father was dead and she was now Queen Elizabeth II.

14 A HAZARDOUS VISIT

The Queen's thirty-sixth wedding anniversary, like many other of her anniversaries and birthdays, was destined to be celebrated in another country, India, where she was again fulfilling her Head of Commonwealth role at yet another Commonwealth conference (or 'Commonwealth Heads of Government' meeting, as it is officially termed). But first there was to be a visit to Bangladesh.

The Queen had been to Bangladesh before, in the days when it was still part of Pakistan, but this was her first visit since it had achieved independence, and one of her first acts was to lay a wreath on the memorial to the estimated three million who died in the bloody fighting of 1971. Coincident with her visit, General Ershad, the country's military ruler, announced a return to free political activity with elections to follow, but these things, of course, do not necessarily mean the same thing in countries like Bangladesh as they would do in, say, Britain.

There was the customary state banquet and, in striking contrast, a visit to a Save the Children malnutrition unit of desperately under-nourished children, which gave the Queen at least a glimpse of the problems inherent to this impoverished country. There was also a visit to a government-sponsored village co-operative where the village folk took time out from their weaving, craftwork and fish farming to present the Queen with a silver casket containing two bracelets. Each villager had donated the equivalent of 30 pence towards the cost of the gift, a trifling sum by British standards perhaps but a day's wage in Bangladesh.

The Queen's visit to the Save the Children unit reinforced her desire to bestow some form of honour on Mother Teresa, the almost legendary Catholic nun who has spent a lifetime caring for the destitute children of Calcutta, work which had already merited the Nobel Peace Prize. To this, on the Queen's arrival in India, was added the Order of Merit, an honour instituted by Queen Victoria as a reward for distinction in art, literature, science or public service. 'This is not for me,' murmured the elderly nun when the insignia was presented to her. 'This honour is for the poor.'

The presentation took place in the grounds of the Presidential Palace. Once it had been the Viceregal Palace, and much of the splendour of the days of the old British Raj had been specially recreated for the period of the Queen's stay. The suite which she and Prince Philip occupied had been re-decorated in the old style and refurbished with old furniture, including a magnificent four-poster bed normally stored away in the bowels of the building. Lancers in scarlet tunics and blue-and-gold turbans were on guard duty in the corridors, and bearers in scarlet and white liveries attended the Queen just as they had her grandfather, George V, when he was there in 1911 to be crowned Emperor of India.

Some of the entertainment afforded the Queen was in the old style too: a dancing display by gipsy girls and a seventeenth-century India Court scene staged by the youthful descendants of the Nizams of Hyderabad. But she was also shown something of modern India. There was a visit to an engineering firm and an institute for crop research, and a demonstration of one of the thirty British-made computers given to India for use in schools. Invited to try her own hand on the keyboard of the computer, the Queen smiled when a yellow bear appeared on the screen. Meetings with heads of government attending the Commonwealth Conference also occupied her time, among them a meeting with Indira Gandhi, who was assassinated so shortly afterwards.

Prince Philip, who once aroused controversy by taking part in a tiger hunt in India, this time expressed a desire to see something of Project Tiger, which had been set up with the idea of increasing rather than reducing the country's tiger population. This involved him in a 300-mile flight to Gondia, with Philip himself piloting an Andover of the Queen's Flight, followed by a three-hour drive to the Kanha Safari Park and then a ride on the back of an elephant. Having seen something of what Project Tiger was doing, Prince Philip, as President of the World Wildlife Fund, praised it as 'probably the most successful major conservation programme with which the World Wildlife Fund has been associated'.

Early the following year, the Queen was off again, this time on what would prove to be perhaps the most potentially hazardous trip she had ever undertaken. She was going to Jordan, to visit King Hussein.

Officially the visit was said to be nothing more than a further cementing of the already close ties between Jordan and Britain. Unofficially it was equally intended to underline Britain's support for Hussein's moderate attempts to find a solution to the thorny Palestinian problem, one of the many tricky tightropes he has had to walk during his more than thirty years of monarchy. Several times he has come close to being assassinated, as his grandfather, King Abdullah, was in 1951. If he was in no personal danger from the bomb which exploded in Amman, the Jordanian capital, two days before the Queen was due there, nor from two other bombs which were discovered in time and safely defused, there were obvious fears for the Queen's safety once it was established that the bombs had been planted by the Abu Nidal terrorist group, three members of which were serving long terms of imprisonment in Britain for their attempted assassination of the Israeli Ambassador.

News of the situation in Amman reached the British Prime Minister, Margaret Thatcher, while she was attending a Conservative Party rally in Birmingham. Immediately she convened a meeting of a few select ministers at Chequers, the Prime Minister's country residence. Among those present, in addition to Mrs Thatcher herself, were Sir Geoffrey Howe, the Foreign Minister, Michael Heseltine, the Defence Secretary, and Richard Luce, Minister of State at the Foreign Office. A telephone call was made to King Hussein in Amman so that Mrs Thatcher could be informed on the situation there at first hand, and after due consideration of the available facts it was decided that the royal visit should go ahead.

It was a decision which accorded with the Queen's own views. Like all royal visits, the invitation to go to Jordan had been extended and accepted a considerable time ahead. Had it come later, it is questionable whether it would have been accepted. But acceptance was now a *fait accompli*, and the Queen, as she had demonstrated before when visiting Ghana and Zambia, puts royal duty and pride ahead of personal safety. However, bets were hedged by the most stringent security precautions ever taken for a royal visit.

The British Airways Tristar in which the Queen would fly was fitted with missile-deflection equipment. A roundabout flight plan was devised so that the aircraft would fly to Jordan via Egyptian air space, steering well clear of such Middle East trouble-spots as Israel, Lebanon and Syria. It was also rumoured, though officially denied in Jordan, that a unit of Britain's crack SAS Regiment flew out ahead of the Queen to reinforce local security. Whatever the truth of that, there was a last-minute addition to the Queen's entourage in the person of Commissioner Colin Smith, head of Scotland Yard's royalty and diplomatic protection squad. As a final precaution, the flight was broken with an overnight stay at Akrotiri, the British base on Cyprus, affording an opportunity to turn back if the situation in Jordan worsened.

There was a further telephone conversation between King Hussein and Mrs Thatcher while the Queen waited at Akrotiri, with the King urging that the visit should go ahead. He would personally guarantee the Queen's safety, he said. So the visit went ahead, with King Hussein taking elaborate precautions to implement his guarantee. Marka military airfield, where the Queen's aircraft landed, was patrolled by armoured vehicles and ringed with armed guards, while a spotter helicopter hovered protectively overhead. The welcome ceremony was over in minutes, and the Queen was ushered into a bullet-proof car forming part of what was more an armoured convoy than a royal cavalcade. A machine-gun unit was stationed at every road junction along the eight-mile route to the royal palace in Amman, and the convoy travelled at almost breakneck speed, much to the disappointment of a group of British youngsters who had gathered at one point along the way in the hope of seeing the Queen. When she heard about this later, the Queen urged that her schedule should be altered to include a visit to the children's school, and King Hussein himself drove her there in a bullet-proof car.

Security continued on the same massive scale. At Basman Palace, where a state banquet was held, the King's personal guard of Bedouins were on duty equipped with automatic rifles, machine-guns and even rocket-launchers. In a speech which seemed, in part at least, to owe more to Downing Street and the Foreign Office than to the Queen herself, she made mention of the Palestinian problem. 'My Government,' she said, 'will continue to support all constructive efforts to achieve a peaceful, just and lasting solution to this problem in accordance with the Charter of the United Nations.' Political? Certainly not, it was insisted officially. The Queen had simply 'stated facts'. King Hussein's speech was undeniably political as he urged Britain to help 'to eliminate the injustices arising from errors of the past from which the Palestinian people are still suffering and from which Jordan more than any other country has had to pay the price'.

There was no let-up in security during visits to hospitals and universities and during a trip to Petra, that 'rose-red city half as old as time' which is the most famous of Jordan's historical sites. Always there was a ring of armed guards around and a helicopter overhead. There were even tanks standing by for the Queen's visit to the national stud farm, where she was presented with an ornate saddle made, oddly enough, not in Jordan but in Syria. For a picnic on the shore of the Dead Sea, where the Queen was lectured on the political situation by Hussein's younger brother, Prince Hassan – 'We still regard Jerusalem as ours,' he said among other things – there was a security screen which included machine-guns, armoured personnel-carriers, helicopters, ambulances and two battalions of troops. In the middle of all this the royal party picnicked in a tent furnished with Persian rugs and silken cushions from a menu which included lamb roasted over a charcoal brazier, rice laced with almonds and sultanas, sorbets and sherbets, and coffee dispensed from gold pots.

Jordan was followed by another flying visit to Germany, this time to visit the Royal Regiment of Artillery and the Royal Green Jackets, and then came yet another visit to France, though this time not a state visit but a unique and very special occasion, and one which must have brought back memories to the Queen.

In 1944, as a teenaged Princess, she had accompanied her father to a secret location to watch a rehearsal for the D-Day assault on Hitler's European fortress. Forty years later, on 6 June 1984, as a fifty-eight-year-old grandmother, on the anniversary of that momentous day she stood with the leaders of other wartime Allied nations on the French beach known as Utah (after its war-time code-name) where the first assault troops had fought and died to secure the toehold which was to lead to ultimate victory.

Utah was, of course, only one of several beaches where Allied troops fought their way ashore in June 1944. Places elsewhere in

France were written into history that day, among them Pegasus Bridge, under which *Britannia* passed at six in the morning, where in 1944 Bill Millin of the 51st Highland Division marched ahead of the reinforcing troops with bagpipes skirling and Lord Lovat, reaching the bridge, tendered apologies for being 'a few minutes late'.

From *Britannia* the Queen went ashore at Caen, scene of some of the fiercest fighting in the days following D-Day, and on to Bayeux to visit the Commonwealth cemetery where 3,900 British troops and 700 others lie buried. Silently, she walked among the graves, pausing here and there, as she did at the grave of twenty-three-year-old Sidney Bates of the Royal Norfolk Regiment whose bravery in 1944 cost him his life and earned him a posthumous Victoria Cross. She paused also to talk with some of the war-widows who had crossed the Channel to remember their loved ones on that anniversary day, among them Mrs Elizabeth Jenkins, who told the Queen how her young husband, a private in the Royal Army Medical Corps, had been killed while attending to wounded men trapped in a crashed glider. 'Such dreadful tragedies,' the Queen murmured, sympathetically. 'Just dreadful.'

Helicopters are perhaps the only form of transport of which the Queen is slightly nervous. She had flown in one only once before, for security reasons during her Silver Jubilee visit to Northern Ireland. Partly for security reasons again, though also to enable her to squeeze in all the ceremonies she was due to attend, she now boarded one in France, this time for the journey to Utah Beach, looking very different from the churned-up and bloodstained picture it had presented on D-Day. For the anniversary it had been cleaned and smoothed, decked with the flags of the wartime Allies. With the Queen, for the ceremony on Utah Beach, were the current leaders of those Allied nations – America's President Reagan (who had previously visited the Omaha Beach cemetery with its nearly 10,000 American graves), Canada's Pierre Trudeau, President Mitterand of France, King Baudouin of the Belgians, Queen Beatrix of the Netherlands, King Olav of Norway and Grand Duke Jean of Luxembourg. No one represented that other wartime ally, the Soviet Union, nor the old enemy, Germany, though a few individual Germans were to be found on the fringes of the many different ceremonies which took place that day.

Britain's own special ceremony was held later in the day in the town square at Arromanches, with the crumbling remains of the Mulberry Harbour (that prefabricated floating landing stage without which the invasion of Europe might not have succeeded, might not even have been possible) forming an appropriate backdrop just off the beach. As the Queen said in her speech, those taking part in the D-Day landings were 'mostly young men. None wished to die. But they knew that unless they established a bridgehead on the shores of France there was no prospect of an end to Hitler's war.' Those to whom she spoke, those who had survived, were now no longer young, but it was with mingled pride and remembered sorrow that, medals glinting, they marched, limped or were – some of them – pushed in invalid chairs past the Queen, who had herself been only eighteen on D-Day. But if no longer young in years, they were still young in heart, as was plainly shown when the words of the soldiers' wartime version of *Colonel Bogey* were heard as they marched past.

It had been thought that only a few hundred veterans would be in France for the anniversary and that the march-past would last no more than a few minutes. In the event, some 3,000 travelled from Britain to Arromanches and back forty years in memory, and the march-past went on and on and on.

Said the Queen: 'There are only a few occasions in history when the course of human destiny has depended upon the events of a single day. June the 6th 1944, was one of those critical moments.' And she quoted from the message with which Field Marshal Montgomery had bolstered his men for the assault on fortress Europe: 'In the better days that lie ahead, men will speak with pride of our doings.' Then, though the ceremony had already lasted an hour longer than planned, she walked among and talked with – as, indeed, did Prince Philip – those D-Day veterans who, like her, were in the flower of their youth on that memorable day in 1944.

The Queen had planned to go to Canada again the following month for a two-week tour linked to the bicentenary celebrations of New Brunswick and Ontario, but there was an unexpected hitch. At almost the last minute – so late in the day that the royal yacht had already set sail for Canada – John Turner, who had succeeded Pierre Trudeau as prime minister, flew to London to tell the Queen that he planned a snap election. Because it is her policy to steer clear of party politics, the Queen avoids visiting a Commonwealth country over which she reigns when it is in the throes of an election campaign. In Britain, similarly, she will not attend public engagements which might be construed as favouring one party or the other at election time. So the Canadian visit was postponed until late September.

If the Queen was inconvenienced, as she was, the parts of Canada she was to visit were not only inconvenienced but put to considerable extra expense. Unavoidable postponement coming so late in the day, programmes for and invitations to the various planned functions had already been printed. Now these had to be scrapped and new ones put in hand. The estimated cost of this in Ontario alone was put at around £200,000. There was also a further problem. Outdoor functions which it had been thought would be held in summer sunshine would now be taking place during the shorter days and the colder, more uncertain weather of the Canadian fall. None of this was the Queen's fault but it was she who was to suffer the backlash. Turner was no longer around when the postponed visit finally took place. He had sustained a disastrous election defeat, and it was Brian Mulroney, as Canada's new prime minister, who greeted the Queen when she arrived in Monckton, New Brunswick.

The tour got off to a good start. The Queen was warmly welcomed both in Monckton and in the neighbouring village of Shediac, despite the fact that the village is predominantly French-speaking. She received the new Prime Minister in audience. The meeting was scheduled to last ten minutes, but Brian Mulroney had much to discuss and it ran for half-an-hour. There were other warm welcomes for the Queen in Fredericton and Ottawa, though the crowds were smaller than anticipated because of cold weather. In Prescott, Ontario, descendants of loyalists who had fled across the border from America during the War of Independence paraded for the Queen in replica eighteenth-century uniforms.

At Amherst descendants of Mohawks who had fought for the British in that same war presented the Queen with an oil painting depicting the Mohawk landing there in 1784. The presentation came as an unexpected addition to the royal itinerary which those responsible for organizing the tour tried to head off. Things were already beginning to run late, but the Mohawks said they would not perform their dance of welcome (which was in the itinerary) unless the presentation was permitted, and this threat won them the day.

188

As the tour proceeded with its banquets and galas, presentations and unveilings, church services and walkabouts, it became ever more apparent that the gremlins which had dogged so many royal visits to Canada were again at work. The royal schedule, normally timed to the minute, slipped more and more. The extra cost caused by postponement brought grumbles here and there. In Cornwall, Ontario, the canon of a church lamented that it had cost $750 to change the date on a plaque the Queen unveiled. Cold weather resulted in sparse attendance at many events. At Fredericton people had shivered with cold as they waited to see the Queen, while she herself found it necessary to don a mink coat for a military pageant in Toronto.

All this served as grist for newspapers in Toronto which resulted in some of the most blatant criticism ever. The *Star* published an article querying whether the monarchy had become redundant and followed this up with cartoons which were perhaps more pointed than witty. The *Sun* took a whack at the Queen's clothes, which it thought 'unflattering . . . awful . . . dowdy'. The *Globe & Mail* descended to a level of personal criticism of both the Queen and Prince Philip which many people thought in bad taste and went on to accuse them of looking 'tired' and 'bored'. The verdict of the only London reporter accompanying the royal party was that the Queen did indeed appear to be bored at times, but blamed this on the dullness of the arranged events and the sparse turn-out.

However, the criticisms of the Toronto newspapers were by no means shared by newspapers elsewhere, most of which reported with enthusiasm the royal visit to their particular locality, while Canada's new Prime Minister did his best to make amends for the Toronto attacks at a farewell dinner in Winnipeg. 'You have carried out your difficult and onerous duties with a warmth and charm which have endeared you to Canadians everywhere,' he told the Queen. 'The monarchy is a central feature of our national life and of our parliamentary democracy.'

Nevertheless, it must surely have been with a sigh of relief that the Queen found herself crossing the border into the United States for a private visit to the William Farish stud farm at Versailles (pronounced 'Versales' because this one is in Kentucky, not France).

The Queen's interest in breeding and racing thoroughbreds is well known. Over the years she has won every British classic race with one major exception, the Derby, and it remains her great ambition to win that, as her great-grandfather Edward VII did, with a horse she has bred herself. For something like twenty years, in pursuit of this aim, she had been shipping mares to Kentucky to be covered by American stallions, relying on a study of photographs, bloodlines and racing successes in selecting the stallions. A Derby winner having not yet resulted, she was now going to inspect the available stallions for herself.

In the company of her racing manager, Lord Porchester, and her stud manager, Michael Oswald, the Queen spent a pleasant and relaxing few days studying the horseflesh not only at Stallion Station, the Farish home where she stayed, but also at other studs in the area, with more than one breeder generously offering to waive the usual six-figure stud fee. 'It would be lovely to see an offspring of your stallion racing in the Queen's colours,' said one, while all agreed that where horses were concerned the Queen had 'a professional level of knowledge'. There was a further brief stay at the Wyoming ranch belonging to Lord Porchester's American-born wife before returning to London, and it was while there that the Queen received the horrific news of the IRA attempt to assassinate Mrs Thatcher and members of the Cabinet during the Conservative Conference at Brighton.

Early in 1985 came a state visit to Portugal, the second of the Queen's reign. Her marriage, which rumour had hinted was heading for the rocks when she last went there, was now in its thirty-eighth year, solidified since 1957 by the birth of two more sons and the addition to her family of four grandchildren. Yet she was perhaps reminded of that earlier visit as she again flew into Montijo air base without Prince Philip. As on the previous occasion, he was waiting to greet her, having arrived in Portugal on *Britannia* (this time after visiting Madeira). Together they sailed up the Tagus to Lisbon, where the royal yacht would accommodate Portuguese businessmen attending a seminar on British technology while the Queen was ashore.

On her earlier visit flowers and bouquets had been tossed into her open carriage as she drove through Lisbon. Now, in 1985, such demonstrations of welcome were banned by the Portuguese authorities in the cause of security. But there are other ways to say

'Welcome'. People scattered rose petals in the Queen's path when she went walkabout in Evora, and students at the university there removed their long black capes and tossed them on the ground for her to walk on. At the state banquet the Queen essayed a small royal joke. 'I see we have port in which to drink our toasts tonight,' she said. 'Dr Johnson said that claret is the liquor for boys – port for men. I am not sure that that is entirely true.' It was perhaps to enable her to probe the truth of the matter further that the northern city of Oporto, when she went there, presented her with a cask of port.

A host of former British colonies, some of them mere pinpoints on the map, had been granted independence during the Queen's reign, most of them electing to join the Commonwealth, so that by 1985 it numbered forty-nine member nations. In her more than thirty-three years on the throne the Queen had visited most of them. But not all. And later that year, having previously paid another flying visit to Germany, this time to visit the Royal Tank Regiment, she set out to put that right. First stopping-point was Belize, which had become independent only four years before.

Belize welcomed her both for herself and as a sign of continued British concern for a small and impoverished nation which relies upon the presence of British troops and a flight of Harrier jets as protection against possible invasion by neighbouring Guatemala. 'Your Country, Your Majesty,' announced one banner at the airport where the Queen landed, and at a state banquet the Prime Minister, Manuel Esquivel, tendered thanks for 'the much valued and welcome presence of Your Majesty's forces'. On the menu for the banquet was one of the more exotic delicacies the Queen has been required to sample in the course of her world travels, roast *paca*, the *paca* being described as looking like 'a large rat or guinea-pig' and having a flavour 'between that of pork and turkey'.

During her two days in the country the Queen inspected the British base, where she met and talked with troops who had not long returned from relief operations in earthquake-shattered Mexico City. Boarding a small eight-seater aircraft normally used for spotting fields in which the traditional sugar crop has been replaced by marihuana, she also flew inland to see something of Belmopan, the country's new capital, built with British aid at the foot of the Maya Mountains.

Belize was the first port of call in a tour of twelve Commonwealth countries extending over a period of four weeks. From there she flew to the Bahamas, where that year's Commonwealth Conference was being held. In the company of Sir Shridath Ramphal, the Secretary General, she toured the new beachfront hotel in Nassau which would be the conference centre and was doubtless amused to learn that the mahogany table around which discussions would take place had been made by prisoners in the local gaol. The conference proved a somewhat acrimonious affair, with Britain's Margaret Thatcher staunchly refusing to go along with the demands of others for sanctions against South Africa. The Queen, of course, plays no part in the actual debates, but behind the scenes she had much to do, and it was reported in Toronto that she enlisted the aid of Canada's Prime Minister, Brian Mulroney, in her efforts to prevent a breach developing between Britain and other countries of the Commonwealth.

If the controversy over sanctions was a major hiccup in proceedings, there was a smaller and mildly amusing one the evening the Commonwealth leaders were due to join the Queen aboard *Britannia* for the customary heads of state photograph and royal banquet. Thirty-four of those invited, including Mrs Thatcher, duly arrived on time, having travelled from Nassau by road, but a number of others, including the Prime Ministers of the Bahamas, India and Zambia, decided to make the trip from the conference centre to the royal yacht by launch. On the way they ran into a heavy squall and had to heave-to. Aboard *Britannia*, as time passed, the royal chef became worried that the meal would be ruined, and the Queen became more and more impatient, fingers tapping the bridge rail, as she awaited the remainder of her guests. Finally the launch arrived, eighty minutes late and with some of those aboard looking too queasy to enjoy the lamb cutlets which were on the menu. Apologies were tendered as the Queen set briskly about the task of marshalling everyone into place for the traditional 'family photograph'.

The conference over, the Queen sailed for St Kitts. She had been there before, though that was nearly twenty years earlier, when it was a British colony. Now, with its associate island, it had become the newest member of the Commonwealth, an independent country with the more elevated name of St Christopher-Nevis. Determined to live up to its new status, on the day of the Queen's visit the island mustered a guard of honour which included not only the local defence force but police, Boy Scouts, Girl Guides, members of the Boys' Brigade and even a contingent of Brinks security guards, though the effect was rather spoilt by some of them fainting from the heat. It was a blazing hot day. An improvised review stand had been constructed for the Queen to stand on, but she was obliged to step down hastily when it began to sway as though on the point of collapse.

Antigua, with its sister island, Barbuda, had similarly achieved independence since the Queen was last there, and its Prime Minister, Eugenia Charles, had been among the more outspoken supporters of the 1983 American invasion of Grenada, much to the fury of some other Commonwealth states in Africa. On an island so devoted to cricket, it was inevitable perhaps that the official welcoming committee should include Viv Richards and that the Queen's speech should contain a joking reference to him. 'Every summer,' she said, 'you export on a temporary basis the incomparable Viv Richards who gives so much pleasure to cricket-lovers all over Britain.' And before she left the island another well-known cricketer, Andy Roberts, would find himself made a CBE.

Dominica and St Lucia, two more islands which had supported the American invasion of Grenada, were also accorded their royal day apiece. So was St Vincent, where the island's small army of only fifty men, trained by the Americans in the aftermath of the Grenada invasion, demonstrated their new parade-ground skill for the Queen's benefit.

She also went ashore at Bequia in the Grenadines, the chain of small islands with which St Vincent is linked, to visit the huddled, timber-built little township once known simply as 'The Harbour' but re-named Port Elizabeth in her honour at the time of her father's coronation. While there she was given a model of *Britannia* by Lawson Sergeant, who had made it specially for her. 'It's terrific,' she enthused, delightedly. 'It's so difficult to make a model from photographs, but you've got everything right, even the propeller.'

Her visits to the various islands had been marked so far by an atmosphere of relaxed and easy-going informality, with little more than the minimal security afforded by her own entourage. But on Barbados, which was accorded two days of the Queen's time, things were rather different. There was more formality and stricter security, as one might expect of an island which prides itself on being more sophisticated than its smaller neighbours. As so often, however, pride came before a fall, and so it was on the day the Queen was taken to see a new cement works. The plant had broken down and was producing only clinker, not actual cement. 'Murphy's Law,' the factory manager pleaded, jokingly.

As on the 1977 Caribbean tour, *Britannia* dropped anchor briefly off Mustique, where Princess Margaret has her holiday home, for the Queen to go ashore in her 'private' rather than her regal capacity. Then it was on to Grenada, the Commonwealth island invaded two years before by American marines, with the backing of a 300-strong force drawn from other islands belonging to the Organization of Eastern Caribbean States.

The so-called 'Grenada 19', Marxists whose *coup* led to American intervention, were in gaol awaiting trial at the time of the royal visit. (The previous Prime Minister had been murdered in the course of the *coup*.)

The Queen's main engagement on the one day she spent on the island was to open Parliament, an action also seen as formally re-establishing Commonwealth influence in the wake of US intervention. The Speech from the Throne, as it is termed, with which she opens any Parliament, is never her own, of course. It is written for her by the prime minister concerned, in this case Herbert Blaize. However, it proved a relatively low-key affair, making no reference to either the Marxist *coup* or the American invasion.

The tour ended with visits to Trinidad and Tobago, and it was on Trinidad that the only unseemly note intruded. Protesters opposed to apartheid made their chants heard when the Queen visited a factory making Angostura bitters (the 'pink' in pink gin), and students holding anti-apartheid banners lined her route across the campus when she visited the University of the West Indies. The student protesters also handed out a statement saying, 'Any representative of such oppression, no matter how much royalty they are crowded with, is an enemy of the youth and students here in Trinidad and in Tobago also.' As elsewhere on other royal tours, the Queen was suffering the backlash for something which was not her fault.

15 BEYOND THE
BAMBOO CURTAIN

Most royal tours and state visits are a long time on the drawing board. But eight years? That was the length of time which elapsed between the first invitation for the Queen to visit the People's Republic of China and when she actually went there, though there was good reason for such a long delay. The invitation was first tendered as far back as 1978 and issued afresh in 1981, but with sensitive negotiations in progress over the return of Hong Kong to Chinese sovereignty, both had to be diplomatically declined. In 1985, with negotiations concluded (though not everyone in Hong Kong was happy about a future under Chinese domination), the invitation was issued yet again. This time it was accepted.

The Queen's visit to China came towards the tail-end of a year during which she had already been again to Nepal, to Australia and New Zealand, and again privately to the United States in pursuit of her long-standing ambition to win the Derby.

As usual, the royal yacht had sailed ahead of the Queen, this time to New Zealand to await her arrival there by air. It was this fact which found *Britannia* on its way through the Arabian Sea when fighting erupted in South Yemen. Conveniently placed as it was to evacuate British expatriates from the danger area, it was promptly ordered to heave-to in international waters and, two days later, to start evacuating from a beach east of Aden. A shore base was quickly set up and some 340 evacuees, British and other nationalities had already been successfully ferried out to the yacht when it came under fire. Said *Britannia*'s captain, Rear-Admiral John Garnier, 'Just before the final passengers came on board, ricochets were falling. We saw tanks and rebel militia coming down the beach about a mile and a half away. I had to pull out our shore party because there was a battle going on actually at the embarkation point, with heavy shelling of buildings just behind the beach.'

Those rescued were transferred to the frigate *Jupiter* to be taken to Djibouti while *Britannia* remained off the coast of South Yemen where, over the course of the next few days, it successfully plucked several hundred more people to safety from other beaches in the Aden area. The Queen was kept informed of what was going on and expressed herself delighted and proud of what *Britannia* had accomplished.

Her visit to Nepal, some three weeks later, was the second of her reign, though it was a quarter of a century since she was last there. King Mahendra had been on the throne then. Now he was dead and King Birendra, whose coronation Prince Charles had attended, ruled in his place. The diminutive monarch welcomed her to his picturesque capital, Kathmandu, 4,300 feet up in the Himalayas, with scenes of extravagant pageantry. However, the Queen did not get to see the Kumari, the country's six-year-old virgin goddess, permitted to emerge from her Hindu temple only on the occasion of religious festivals, though the Kumari, it is said, was allowed to peep at the Queen from a high window as the royal car went past. But she did get her wish to meet Gurkha holders of the Victoria Cross.

Nepal's Gurkhas have formed part of Britain's armed forces for more than 170 years, curious when you realize that Nepal is an independent state which is not even part of the Commonwealth. Ten regiments of Gurkhas fought in World War I. During World War II they saw service in North Africa, Italy, Burma and Malaya. More recently, their fierce fighting reputation was sufficient in itself to unnerve Argentine conscripts during the struggle to recapture the Falkland Islands. Their exploits have earned them many awards for gallantry, including the staggering total of twenty-six Victoria Crosses. The Queen's known wish to meet ex-Gurkhas saw a turn-out of 150 of them, with 122 medals between them, including five Victoria Crosses. One man even made a ten-day trek through the foothills of Everest to be there. The Queen and Prince Philip posed for photographs with the five holders of the Victoria Cross and arranged that each man should be sent a copy of the photograph.

Keenly interested in wildlife as he is, Prince Philip also took advantage of the visit to Nepal to fly north to the Royal Chitwan National Park where, from the back of an elephant, he watched a rare one-horned rhinoceros being tranquillized with a dart so that it could be fitted with a radio collar to enable its future movements to be tracked.

The visit to New Zealand was dogged almost from start to finish by Maori land-rights demonstrators. At the very outset of the tour, as the Queen stood in a Land Rover being driven round a gathering of schoolchildren in Auckland, two white-coated young women posing as marshals suddenly dashed forward to pelt her with eggs. One egg hit only the windshield of the Land Rover, but a second struck the Queen herself, disintegrating to leave a yellow smear on her pink coat. 'We're bloody protesting, that's what,' yelled one of the women as police pounced on them and hustled them away. 'The Queen's come here and they aren't honouring the treaty.'

The reference was to the Treaty of Waitangi under which the Maoris ceded New Zealand to Queen Victoria in return for guarantees that they would keep their traditional lands, woods and fisheries. But the treaty was never ratified and the guarantees were not kept. This fact led to the Maori wars of 1845–8 and 1860–70 and, all these years later, to the protests and demonstrations of today.

David Lange, New Zealand's Prime Minister, tendered the Queen a public apology for the incident. Shocked though she was at the time, she could joke about it later: 'New Zealand has long been renowned for its dairy products,' she quipped at a state banquet, 'though I myself prefer my New Zealand eggs for breakfast.' It was perhaps her sense of humour which also saw her wearing a coat the colour of egg yolk for a subsequent walkabout.

Though there was to be no more egg-throwing, there were other protests of various sorts. A noisy demonstration when the Queen and Prince Philip were on their way to a civic reception resulted in six arrests. Catcalls and banner-waving punctuated a Polynesian festival the Queen attended. Dun Dun Mihaka, the Maori who had exposed his bare buttocks – a traditional insult known as *whahapohane* – during the 1983 visit of the Prince and Princess of Wales, threatened to go even further on the occasion of the Queen's visit and 'give her a 21-bum salute'. He was presumably intending to do just that when police surrounded his van ahead of the royal

197

motorcade and arrested him. That was near Wellington. Two hundred miles further north, at Clive, another Maori did succeed in baring his buttocks as the Queen passed by. He too was arrested. The Queen's arrival at the botanical gardens in Christchurch was greeted with shouts of 'Honour the treaty!' Scuffling broke out when loyalists in the crowd set about a man who was in the process of exposing his buttocks. As a result, he did not succeed in his efforts. But a number of women did succeed and four were arrested. In contrast to all this, more than a thousand Maoris gathered at Hawke's Bay to sing and dance for the Queen.

Opening the New Zealand Parliament, the Queen, in her Speech from the Throne, said that the Government would continue to implement pro-Maori policies and that there would be legislation forthcoming to recognize Maori as an official language. The speech had been drafted for her, of course, by the Prime Minister, and another of its provisions pointed up the curiousness of her multi-monarchy position. As Queen of New Zealand she found herself announcing legislation to outlaw nuclear weapons, a move which would put New Zealand at odds with its defence partner, Australia, of which she is also Queen. However, since Britain's refusal to go along with other Commonwealth countries in their desire to impose major sanctions against South Africa, she was well accustomed to such divergence of policies between her various 'queendoms'.

Arriving in Canberra, as Queen of Australia now, almost her first duty was to sign the new Australia Act, formally severing the last constitutional links between Australia and the United Kingdom and thus bringing to an end a relationship which began in 1788 with the arrival of the first 1030 British settlers, 736 of them convicts. No longer would the London Parliament have power to legislate for Australia; no longer would the Privy Council in London remain a final court of appeal.

The surge of republicanism which had followed the dismissal of Gough Whitlam seemed to have abated somewhat. A public opinion poll showed that those in favour of replacing monarchy by a republic now numbered less than thirty per cent, and there were large crowds wherever the Queen went. 'More like the good old days of the 1960s,' commented a veteran Queen-watcher. But those in favour of a republic made themselves heard at times. Posters denouncing monarchy confronted Prince Philip when he unveiled a bust of the explorer Matthew Flinders at Flinders University, and there was a shout of 'Long live the republic of Australia.' Prince Philip, who does not take that sort of thing lightly, muttered, 'A good idea' – and a live microphone relayed his words to the audience. There was an outburst of booing, with Philip waving his arms as though conducting the chorus.

Rumours of a plot against the Queen resulted in tighter-than-usual security. Police reinforcements were drafted into Canberra prior to her arrival and she was given a guard of three policewomen armed with .25 automatics. A watch was kept on pro-Irish organizations in Sydney, Melbourne and Adelaide, and in Sydney four men were detained at Kingsford Smith Airport but released again after they had been questioned and their baggage searched. Uniformed police were posted every few yards during royal walk-abouts, and marksmen stationed on rooftops. Such precautions seemed well warranted when two men were spotted on the roof of a government office block as the Queen and Prince Philip arrived for an official reception at the Sheraton-Wentworth Hotel in Sydney. However, it turned out that they had been drinking, and drink had given them the idea of trying to drench the royal couple with a fire hose. Fortunately for the Queen, the wind was not in the right direction for the drunken jape to succeed and most of the water was blown away. Indeed, the two men themselves were well soaked when the police got to them, and they later sent the Queen a letter apologizing for 'an act of spontaneous stupidity which we both deeply regret'.

Almost the only other untoward act of any consequence, also in Sydney, was when a forty-three-year-old feminist osteopath, viewing the monarchy as 'conservative and backward', sought to make it more liberal and contemporary by exposing her breasts to the Queen. Plain-clothes detectives formed a ring round her in an attempt to prevent such a demonstration, but she eluded them, climbed on to a wall and flaunted herself for all to see as the Queen walked by.

Among the pleasantest of the many duties the Queen performed during her nearly two weeks in Australia was the presentation of the Star of Courage, the country's second highest award for bravery, to an eleven-year-old Queensland boy, Alfred Collins, who had saved his father from an attack by a wild boar, grabbing a fallen branch and using it to drive the creature off after it had charged his father, ripping his leg with its tusks. 'Well done,' the Queen commended him. 'You are very brave.'

Royal embarrassment was feared in Adelaide when the Queen was guest of honour at a production of *Boojum*, a play based on the life of Lewis Carroll, during the course of which an actor playing the role of a caterpillar was required to perform what can only be described as a strip-tease. But if the actor concerned was, as he confessed, 'slightly embarrassed' at performing such antic in front of the Queen, she herself apparently was not. She not only laughed at what took place on stage but sought out the actor afterwards to congratulate him on his 'artful performance'.

More water was aimed at the Queen, though this time by the elements, on the day she attended a garden party in an Adelaide suburb. With a heavy swell running, a dummy run with the royal barge was essayed before the Queen went ashore from *Britannia*. Five attempts to land proving unsuccessful, the crew of the barge returned to the royal yacht, lying about a mile offshore, to report that the trip was too risky. Nevertheless, the Queen insisted 'having a stab'. With some difficulty, she and Prince Philip managed to get aboard the barge, though hardly had they done so that the sea slammed it against the yacht's side so violently that it sustained minor damage. With the couple clutching tightly to the cockpit rail, the barge headed again for the shore. But try as its crew might, it proved impossible to hold the barge steady enough for its royal passengers to climb onto the jetty. Members of the reception committee looked on anxiously as an extra-large wave crashed over the barge, wetting the Queen. She gave a despairing shrug, and Philip, experienced sailor that he is, shook his head. So it was back to the yacht and an eventual landing nine miles away. By the time she finally arrived at the garden party the Queen was three hours late. 'Now I know how the early settlers must have felt trying to get ashore in open boats,' she commented.

Little more than a week after her return from Australia the Queen was off to the United States again. But this was no state or official visit. As in 1984, when she went there after touring Canada, this was very much a private occasion. Again her destination was the 'blue grass' horse-lands of Kentucky and again she was pursuing the so far elusive dream of coming up with a Derby winner.

Following her previous visit, a number of royal mares had been sent across the Atlantic to be mated with stallions selected by the Queen. Now she was going partly to see the result of those pairings, among them the bay filly resulting from matching the Kentucky-bred stallion Alydar to the royal mare Christchurch, and partly to select further stallions for future breeding. As on her previous visit, the Queen was the guest of William Farish and his wife Sarah on their stud farm near Lexington, and again she was accompanied by her racing manager, Lord Porchester. 'She is seeing her American-bred foals for the first time,' Lord Porchester was quoted as saying. 'It's like opening your Christmas presents. Like every owner, she dreams of a Derby winner. It's the aim of all breeders. The odds are stacked against someone breeding their own winner rather than simply buying a contender, but we still hope.'

Royal tours and state visits are planned with all the thoroughness of a military operation, a lengthy and often complicated procedure. Even so, planning the Queen's 1986 visit to China, set in motion once the agreement to return Hong Kong to China had been signed and sealed, was to prove more complex than most. Originally the Chinese had suggested September as affording the most clement weather, but that is the month the Queen habitually spends at Balmoral. October would suit her better, she said. The possibility of rain did not deter her. So long as the water didn't come above her ankles she wouldn't worry, Buckingham Palace informed the Chinese. As it happened, the October weather turned out good.

The Chinese had also suggested that she might like to go for as long as three weeks. For her part, the Queen felt that seven days would suffice. She also made it clear that she preferred not to be whisked around in cars with darkened glass, as China's leaders are; she wanted the Chinese people to see her.

Over all this the Chinese gracefully gave way. In other ways too they did everything possible to ensure that the visit should be a success. One of the state guest houses on the outskirts of the city was refurbished for the Queen's stay in Peking, decked out afresh with Ming vases and calligraphic wall hangings. At Kunming, which she would also visit, another guest house was similarly refurbished with furniture specially made by local craftsmen. At Xian a new road was built to facilitate her visit to the archaeological site there. Another new road was built at Shanghai to speed her drive from the airport. The idea of a royal walkabout, strange though it must have seemed to China's Communist leaders, was conceded and the normal stringent control of the media was relaxed to permit full British Press and television coverage of the visit (though, as things turned out, not sufficiently so to please everyone). The Chinese are even said to have imported a consignment of Malvern water, knowing the Queen's fondness for it.

In China itself there was some small degree of advance publicity. Photographs of the Queen were published and snippets of film shown on television, though how many of the country's vast population got to see either is a matter for conjecture. The British Embassy sought to help out by displaying a chart on which the Queen's ancestry was traced back to Saxon times, roughly equivalent to China's own T'ang dynasty. Even so there was a degree of confusion, some Chinese who knew of the visit apparently thinking that it was Mrs Thatcher who was expected. Curiously for a country which has had its own empresses in the past, the concept of a female monarch also seemed to present difficulty, with the Queen referred to as 'the England country female King' (though 'King', in some quarters, was later upgraded to 'Emperor').

On the Queen's side there was a small, almost last-minute hitch. With Margaret Macdonald now of an age when she could no longer travel about the world with the Queen, her role of dresser had been taken over by Peggy Hoath. She had been with the Queen on her earlier 1986 visits to Nepal, New Zealand and Australia and was looking forward to going to China. Then she fell and fractured both wrists. Elizabeth Andrew, the assistant dresser who had let out an understandable 'Bloody hell, Ma'am. What's he doing here?' the morning she walked into the royal bedroom to find the Queen trying to cope with an intruder, was quickly deputed to take her place in masterminding the new fashion collection the Queen would take with her to China.

Included in the royal wardrobe on this occasion, as on several previous state visits and Commonwealth tours, was a magnificent gown specially created to be worn at the state banquet. Designed for the Queen by Ian Thomas, it was a full-length version of the traditional Chinese *cheongsam* in pink silk crêpe, with a modest split up the side and lavishly embroidered with a pattern of peonies, China's national flower.

Prince Philip was not with the Queen for the sixteen-hour flight to China. He was already out east, visiting Japan, from where he flew to join his wife in Peking (or Beijing, as it is known in China), so that they were together in the Square of Heavenly Peace, the largest public square in the world, for the official welcome ceremony.

Initially, it looked as though the Queen's desire to 'meet the people' was to be disregarded by her Chinese hosts, the square having been efficiently cleared of ordinary Chinese to make way for invited guests, a guard of honour composed of troops all of exactly the same height and an array of children almost as well drilled as the guards. There was red carpet for the Queen to walk on, a twenty-one-gun salute and a flutter of Union flags. (Not too much should be made of the fact that some of the flags were flown upside down, something which has been known to happen occasionally even in Britain.) Li Xiannian, the country's 77-years-old President, welcomed the Queen with a warm, if rather lengthy, handshake and was later seen to hold her briefly by the arm. The march-past by the guard of honour was performed in a style even the Brigade of Guards might have envied and the assembled children went into a song-and-dance act with an enjoyable exuberance that brought smiles to the Queen's face. There were more singing, dancing children outside the entrance to the walled-off compound of the state guest house in which the Queen would be staying, but her request for the car to slow down so that she could see them better was either not understood or disregarded. Either way, she was whisked past them so quickly that she hardly saw them or they her.

The Queen took tea with President Li in the Palace of the People, chatting with him through an interpreter. One of the presidential questions the interpreter had to translate was 'What do you think of the interpreter's English?' and it was doubtless with relief that she found herself translating back to the President that the Queen thought it 'Very good.' The Queen was taken on a tour of the Forbidden City, the ancient home of the Ming emperors. Chinese sightseers followed her in, to applaud softly and politely. Some of the British photographers present were a shade less diplomatic in their approach, and the result was the first of a number of small brushes between them and China's perhaps over-zealous security men.

On the British side, Press and television coverage of the visit was on a mammoth scale, enormously expensive. The BBC and ITN are said to have laid out close to £1 million between them in their efforts to outdo each other. Certainly ITN went to the trouble and expense of airlifting and assembling a satellite station on the Great Wall of China in order that the few minutes the Queen would spend there could be shown live in Britain.

Highlight of the Queen's stay in Peking was a ten-course state dinner in the Great Hall of the People, for which she wore the specially designed peony-embroidered *cheongsam*. Together with her diamond tiara, a ruby and diamond necklace and matching ear-rings, she looked every inch the 'England country female Emperor' of Chinese translation. President Li was reinforced for the occasion by Zhao Ziyang, Premier of the State Council.

The speech of welcome and the Queen's reply were delivered not at the table, as at state banquets in the west, but from an isolated position of honour on a raised platform, with the Queen able to follow the presidential speech from a printed translation contained in her programme. Relations between the United Kingdom and the People's Republic were closer now than they had ever been, said the President, and this owed much to the harmonious settlement concerning Hong Kong. He hoped very much, he added, that the Queen's visit would soon be followed by a visit from the Prince and Princess of Wales.

The meal was in the Chinese style. Table decorations included exotic birds skilfully fashioned from cabbage and live goldfish swimming under bridges of watermelon, the latter seeming to fascinate the Queen so much that one wonders if she may be tempted to introduce something similar at Buckingham Palace. The menu included chicken soup with jasmine blossoms, beef and duck cubes, mandarin fish, shark's fin and sea cucumber (sometimes more graphically referred to as 'sea slug'). Both the Queen and Prince Philip ate with chopsticks, which they wield these days with experienced expertise. There was wine to drink along with *mao-tai*, a somewhat fiery liqueur which the Queen carefully, and perhaps wisely, put to one side after an experimental sip.

Next day came the Queen's meetings with China's two paramount leaders, Deng Xiaoping and Hu Yaobang, who received her separately at their villas in an exclusive compound not far from the Forbidden City. Hu Yaobang is general secretary of the Central Communist Committee, but it is the diminutive octogenarian Deng Xiaoping who, as Chairman of the Central Advisory Committee, is generally acknowledged to wield the main power in China. He welcomed the Queen with 'greetings from an old man'. A heavy smoker with the Chinese habit of expectorating at intervals into a spittoon, he – like the Queen – had evidently done his homework. Out of deference to her, he refrained from either smoking or spitting during their meeting and the lunch which followed. Conversation, of course, was through an interpreter. Deng inquired after the health of Princess Margaret, due to visit China the following year. 'Very well, thank you,' the Queen told him. Was it true, Deng wanted to know, that you could see Britain from the top of the Eiffel Tower in Paris, and laughed when the interpreter translated the Queen's reply: 'It would be rather difficult. It's quite a long way.'

For the Queen's visit to the Great Wall of China it had been planned that she should take a gentle stroll along it of perhaps some 200 yards. But tour organizers had not allowed for the energy and enthusiasm of someone fresh from indulging in long hikes over the rugged terrain of the Scottish Highlands. Despite an uphill climb of one in three at this point of the Great Wall, the Queen trudged determinedly on and on at a pace which tested the stamina of some of her entourage. Her Private Secretary, Sir William Heseltine, produced a handkerchief to mop his brow, and the Queen saw him. 'I don't think Bill Heseltine will ever be the same again,' she observed, smiling.

She paused herself to click away with her camera. Then, like any ordinary tourist, she wanted someone to take her picture. 'So I can prove I was here,' she said. Prince Philip being busy at that moment inspecting one of the towers constructed at intervals along the Wall, her personal detective, Superintendent James Beaton GC,★ duly obliged. With Prince Philip's return a few minutes later, she

---

★ He was given the George Cross by the Queen for his gallantry during the 1974 attempt to kidnap Princess Anne.

suggested yet more pictures. Somewhat puzzled by her enthusiasm, her husband pointed out that they had already posed together for Press photographs. 'These will be different,' the Queen said, brightly. So husband and wife stood together on the Great Wall while members of their entourage clicked busily away. That done, it was time to think about getting back. 'It's going to be much worse going down than coming up,' said the Queen, making use of the handrail to check her descent.

While in Peking there was also a visit to the tombs of the Ming emperors and a somewhat livelier visit to a state kindergarten for the children of China's élite. 'A Warm Welcome To England's Female King' read a banner in Chinese which greeted the Queen on her arrival at the kindergarten, and a well-rehearsed children's performance staged for her benefit brought broad smiles of genuine warmth to her face. Prince Philip, who arrived in time for the finale after an engagement elsewhere, looked similarly delighted, perhaps because China's one-child-per-family policy accords with his own views on population control.

Coincident with the Queen's arrival in Shanghai, China's biggest and most bustling city, came the announcement that British industry, which had hitherto lagged far behind the Americans and West Germans in trade with China, had achieved a major break-through. While this was doubtless, in a sense, a form of Chinese thank-you for the agreement to hand back Hong Kong and though the negotiations involved stretched back well before the Queen's visit, it was equally doubtless her presence in China which created the atmosphere in which contracts were finally signed and sealed. As on other state visits, the royal yacht served as a floating exhibition and seminar centre for a delegation of British industrialists, this time headed by Sir James Cleminson, Chairman of the British Overseas Trade Board and Sir Eric Sharp, Chairman of the Sino-British Trade Council as well as Cable and Wireless. Two days of final negotiation aboard *Britannia*, moored at Shanghai while the Queen was in Peking, resulted in fourteen multi-million pound contracts, among them deals for the construction of a new steel complex, the first stage of Shanghai's new metro system, a telephone system linking twenty-seven towns in the Yangtze province and two other large telecommunications projects.

Shanghai, like Peking, welcomed the Queen with a well-rehearsed children's ballet featuring drums and trumpets, Chinese lanterns, fluttering fans and twirling parasols. Unlike those in Peking, the ordinary Chinese of Shanghai seemed to know what was going on, and an estimated 3 million of them flooded onto the streets to watch the Queen drive by. Over-zealous Chinese security men herded British photographers so far from the Queen on her arrival that her Press Secretary, Michael Shea, was moved to protest. 'They haven't had a decent picture yet,' he barked at the Chinese, followed by 'Don't lay your hands on me' as the security men moved to usher him away. There was to be a further and more heated brush between Press Secretary and a senior security man during a royal walkabout later.

The walkabout was hardly in the style to which the Queen has become accustomed. Security men set about clearing the area of people. However, like people everywhere, many filtered back, curious to see what there was to be seen. Not that the Queen got to meet any of them. Nor could she do much more than glance quickly at the shop windows to right and left as she was whisked briskly through a succession of narrow, winding streets before crossing the zigzag bridge to the Teahouse of the Heart of the Lake, where she took tea and was entertained by a musician who amused her with a virtuoso rendering of 'In An English Country Garden' played on what looked rather like an old-fashioned penny whistle. Later, however, on a visit to the Bund, Shanghai's waterfront, she did get to pop into one of the local curio shops.

Britannia, having fulfilled its temporary adaptation as a business centre, now reverted to its customary role of floating palace, with the Queen as hostess of a banquet for President Li and his wife. In response to a directive from his wife, the Chinese President obediently straightened his glasses as the two of them posed for photographs with the Queen and Prince Philip. The Queen added her own instruction. 'And smile,' she said. Dinner over, all four of them went up on deck to watch *Britannia*'s contingent of Royal Marines perform the traditional ceremony of Beating Retreat. Late into the evening though it now was, upwards of a million curious Chinese still crowded the waterfront.

Not many visitors to China – indeed, not many Chinese – get to see sights as diverse and breathtaking as the Forbidden City, the Great Wall and the tomb of the Emperor Chin Shi

Huang. The Queen saw all three and much else besides.

The tomb of Chin Shi Huang is perhaps the greatest archae-ological discovery of the century, revealed early in the 1970s when two peasants digging a well unearthed the first of the now world-famous terracotta soldiers. By the time of the Queen's 1986 visit painstaking excavation had resulted in the unearthing and restoration of some 6,000 of the lifesize figures which Chin Shi Huang had fashioned to be buried with him, with several thousand more still awaiting excavation. 'Fascinating . . . breath-taking,' the Queen murmured as she was accorded the privilege of being conducted down red-carpeted steps into the excavation site so that she could inspect the terracotta figures at close quarters. Further to mark her visit she was later presented with a model of one of the dead Emperor's terracotta army, while Prince Philip was given a similar model of one of the terracotta horses also found on the site.

It was while the royal couple were in Xian, where the Emperor's tomb is located, that Prince Philip had one of the attacks of 'dontopedology' to which he is occasionally subject. You won't find the word in a medical dictionary. Prince Philip invented it, years ago, as a joke against himself, defining it as 'the ability to open your mouth and put your foot in it'.

On this occasion he and the Queen were talking with a group of Scottish students in the process of learning Chinese at Xian's North Western University. Prince Philip asked how long they had been there. 'Six weeks,' one of the students told him. 'If you stay much longer, you'll go home with slitty eyes,' Philip joked. Or so it was said (and it sounds very much like his idea of a joke).

Worse was to follow. The student asked what Prince Philip had thought of the Forbidden City.

'Ghastly,' Prince Philip was reported to have said.

The Queen intervened hastily. 'It was fascinating,' she corrected her husband. 'I could have spent a lot of time there.'

'The Forbidden City, oh yes,' Prince Philip agreed. 'But Beijing was ghastly.'

All this emerged as British reporters besieged the student after-wards to ascertain what had been said. The result was to give Britain's national newspapers one of their royal field days, complete with joky headlines and satirical cartoons. Some newspapers, overlooking the fact that their own reporters had filed tongue-in-cheek reports of the royal visit hardly calculated to delight the Chinese, accused Prince Philip of having 'upset' China's leaders by his remarks, while in Hong Kong, where the population is naturally apprehensive about its approaching take-over by China, the leading English-language newspaper, the *South China Morning Post*, lectured him on his 'thoughtless outspokenness'. Tackled on the subject by British reporters, the Queen's Press Secretary made the best of a bad job, maintaining that Prince Philip had been 'in no way disparaging of the Chinese people, their welcome or of the tour'. While the British Press was revelling in big headlines, such newspapers as there are in China published nothing of all this, and Chinese officialdom limited itself to the diplomatic comment that the royal tour was going along 'very smooth – a success'.

Until now the Queen had displayed every outward sign that she was enjoying her visit to China, but the following day, whether from concern over her husband's remarks or because the strain of the tour was beginning to tell, she looked less than happy during a visit to a Buddhist temple some 7,000 feet up in the mountains near Kunming. The reason for her impromptu climb up the 152 steps of the lighthouse at Ardnamurchan Point in the Western Isles some two months previous became apparent as she toiled up the 118 steps leading to the temple. There was a pause for some refreshing jasmine tea before climbing down again, and later came lunch in an island pagoda at Dian Chi Lake. But it was only as the Queen watched a dancing display by young people of various tribes at the Institute of Ethnic Minorities that she relaxed and brightened, smiling happily again as she posed for pictures with some of the girl dancers. It was Prince Philip who suggested those particular pictures. 'I've got to do something right,' he quipped.

Final stopping-place of the tour was Canton, perhaps China's most westernized city, where no fewer than three Rolls Royces were at royal disposal. For the Queen there was a visit to the Children's Palace, an elite educational establishment for some of China's most talented youngsters, where the pupils put on a display of singing, dancing and acting which ended with the singing of 'Auld Lang Syne'. It was not the first time the Queen had heard that traditional Scottish song during her tour of China. It had been sung too at the Institute of Ethnic Minorities. For Prince Philip there was a visit to a farm commune where, anxious to please, he posed for

209

photographs with three generations of a local family. To speed the royal couple on their way as *Britannia* set sail for Hong Kong, an exuberant dragon dance was staged on the Canton quayside.

Her visit to China had been most exhilarating, the Queen said in a farewell message to President Li, and had set the seal on a warm Sino-British friendship.

However, the success of the tour did little to ease the fears felt in Hong Kong over the colony's uncertain future as part of the People's Republic. Nor was every one of the colony's 5½ million inhabitants entirely reassured by a speech from the Queen in which she said that Britain's agreement with China would ensure the preservation of Hong Kong's 'institutions, traditions and way of life'. It was only the second time in her reign that the Queen had been to Hong Kong and would perhaps be her last visit before the colony reverts to China in 1997. Whatever their doubts about the future, the citizens of Hong Kong, touched by the latter fact, gave her a magnificent welcome, turning out in their thousands. A visit to the races saw stands and course crammed with a record crowd of 62,000. The whole visit was highly emotional – and it was perhaps the emotion of the moment which resulted in an unexpected departure from protocol.

While the Queen is happy enough to sign official visitors' books, she has always made it a firm rule never to give autographs. The reason is obvious. She would be besieged on all sides if she did. Even Australian fast bowler Dennis Lillee, taking advantage of the 1977 Centenary Test in Melbourne to seek the Queen's autograph, did not get it. But in Hong Kong, visiting a family re-housed in one of the colony's new towerblocks, surprisingly she acceded to an interpreted request from the family's eight-year-old son and signed an elegant 'Elizabeth R 1986' above a photograph of herself in the boy's souvenir programme.

On the last night of her visit the Queen was treated to what was perhaps the most spectacular display of fireworks even she has ever seen, as thousand upon thousand of multi-headed, multi-coloured shells – some 70,000 in all – burst high in the night sky, at a cost of £160,000. If this was the last time it would see its Queen, Hong Kong was determined to say farewell to her – and to a century and a half of British rule – in style.

16 POSTSCRIPT

Extensive though the Queen's travels have been, and will continue to be for at least the immediate future, they constitute only a proportion of the royal travel total. Others of the family also do their share, and Prince Philip rather more than his share. In addition to accompanying the Queen on nearly all her state visits and Commonwealth tours, sometimes even standing in for her when she has been either indisposed (as in Canada in 1959) or obliged to return to London (as from Australia in 1974), he travels far and wide on his own account.

If neither Prince Charles nor Princess Anne can yet hope to match their mother, and certainly not their father, in miles logged, they too have travelled widely. Though one can perhaps hardly count those childhood visits to Tobruk, Malta and Gibraltar when Charles was only five and Anne not yet four, both served early apprenticeships as royal travellers.

Charles was eighteen and still at school when he made an unaccompanied (at least by his parents) three-day visit to Mexico. He has travelled abroad, often extensively, almost every year since. In 1986, for instance, he and the Princess of Wales visited Austria, Canada and Japan. It was in fact their second visit to Canada; they had been there together three years previously. They have also been (as this book nears conclusion) twice to Australia, to New Zealand, the United States, Italy, Spain and Saudi Arabia, creating something of a royal precedent on their first joint visit to Australia by taking their small son, William, with them.

Like his father, Prince Charles also makes numerous overseas trips on his own. Since his marriage he has, for instance, been to Brunei (representing the Queen at that country's independence celebrations), several times to Germany to visit various British regiments there and to several Commonwealth countries in Africa. Indeed, in recent years he has exceeded his mother in the number of trips he has made per year, if not in actual mileage travelled.

Of all royal travels, Princess Anne's tours in connection with her presidency of the Save the Children Fund have surely been both the most adventurous and the most hazardous. Suitably if informally clad in a sleeveless shirt and khaki skirt (or jeans), a bush hat on her head, she has trekked through some of the world's harshest areas to see for herself how the money raised through charity is expended in the field. To get there she has flown into improvised landing strips, ridden on the backs of a camel and an elephant, even foot-slogged where no form of transport was available. Disregarding possible danger, she visited refugee camps in the war zone between Somalia and Ethiopia and even went to war-torn Beirut to see children wounded in the fighting there.

In 1983 she was on the Afghanistan-Pakistan border to visit refugee camps there. She has slept in mud huts, and in Gambia lent a hand on the ropes when her car had to be ferried across a river to reach a leper colony she wished to visit. In 1985 she went to Mozambique, despite the fighting there, and then on to visit refugee camps in the Sudan. Asked in the course of a television interview if she was ever frightened, she said, 'I seldom think about it. If it's there all the time, you become unconscious of it. It's part of life.'

The Queen Mother too has done her share of royal travelling, as have Princess Margaret and the Queen's cousins, the Dukes of Gloucester and Kent and Princess Alexandra. Indeed, the Queen Mother in 1958 became the first of the Royal Family to fly round the world, visiting Montreal, Vancouver, Honolulu and Fiji on her way to tour Australia and New Zealand and calling at the Cocos Islands, Mauritius, Uganda and Malta on the way back. Now well into her eighties, it is inevitable that the Queen Mother's overseas travels should have diminished with the years, but it is surely remarkable that even since her sixtieth birthday she should have been six times to Canada, five times to West Germany (to visit various regiments), twice to France and once each to the West Indies, Australia, New Zealand, Fiji, Denmark, Norway, Italy, Iran and Cyprus.

There is, of course, no yardstick by which it is possible to gauge accurately the benefits arising from the overseas travels of the Queen and other members of the Royal Family. Such benefits take several different and intangible forms. They help to maintain and reinforce the far-flung influence of the monarchy (which is also Britain's own influence). Lacking the Queen's frequent visits, Australia and Canada might both have become republics by now. By the same token, she is now the only surviving link between those and other Commonwealth countries and the United Kingdom.

The Queen's visits to the countries of the Commonwealth, either as Queen or as Head of the Commonwealth, and her 'healing presence' at the Commonwealth Conferences of recent years, have done much to maintain the existence of that somewhat nebulous organization. Without her, the chains of Commonwealth, weakened as they have become by strains within its framework, might well have snapped by now. There are those, of course, who think that that would be no great disaster. It is not a view the Queen shares.

Her foreign visits have been used at different times by various British governments to help repair damaged international fences or reinforce long-standing relationships. Visits to the United States in particular have served to underline and strengthen the 'special relationship' existing between that country and Britain. British industry has benefited too, though to what extent it is impossible to quantify. The many agreements announced during the Queen's 1986 visit to China were a case in point. Of course, the Queen did not go to China with a clutch of contracts in her handbag, but her visit – and the use of the royal yacht as a floating business centre – did much towards creating the atmosphere in which business agreements could be successfully concluded.

So royal travels have their point and purpose. They are, most of them, a long way removed from being mere holidays. As Prince Philip said once in Canada, 'We do not come here for the benefit of our health.' They involve a lot of hard work, long hours and a degree of strain which has increased in recent years as protest groups have more and more taken advantage of royal visits to make them a focal point for demonstrations and as terrorist activity around the world has made the need for stringent security ever more necessary. Royal tours today are not like they were when the

Queen went so blithely around the world in 1953–4, and her continued insistence on being seen by the public wherever she goes, on going walkabout whenever possible, speaks volumes for both her courage and strength of character.

Over thirty years ago, soon after the Queen first succeeded to the throne and even before she had made her first Commonwealth tour as Elizabeth II, a parliamentary Select Committee pointed out that the 'increasing facilities for air travel' would surely lead to more frequent visits to Commonwealth countries (as indeed has been the case) and 'a considerable extension of the demands made on Her Majesty'. If this was intended as cautioning the Queen not to overdo things, as would seem to have been the case, it was a warning note to which she has paid no heed. Nor has her health suffered, as was feared at that time. On the contrary, she has seemed to thrive on a travel programme such as no previous monarch has ever known.

Though the Queen is now into her sixties, there is no sign yet of any slackening of pace. She has four grown-up children available to follow in her worldwide footsteps but prefers their travels to be in addition to, rather than instead of, her own. It is not in her nature to relinquish lightly what she conceives to be part and parcel of her duty as Queen and Head of the Commonwealth. Nor perhaps is there any reason why she yet should. Given good health, the Queen may be expected to continue her travels, if on a gradually diminishing scale, for several years to come, by which time she will surely have established a royal travel record which future monarchs, probably ascending the throne at a later age than did the Queen herself, will find it difficult, if not impossible, to surpass.

ACKNOWLEDGEMENTS AND BIBLIOGRAPHY

This book has been written from a record of royal tours and state visits compiled by us over a period of some thirty years and from material garnered from a wide variety of sources over the same period. The interpretation of events is therefore our own, and it should not be regarded as an 'official' or 'authorized' account of the Queen's travels. However, our thanks are due to those who have helped with information or answers to questions during the final writing stage, among them the Press Office at Buckingham Palace and Major John Griffin (Clarence House) for kindly supplying us with an up-to-date list of travels undertaken by the Queen and other members of the Royal Family; to those members of the staff of the Commonwealth Secretariat who answered queries concerning the Commonwealth and the Heads of Government Commonwealth Conferences; to Ann House, Librarian of the Canadian High Commission in London, and Margot Montgomery, Director of the Information and Reference Branch of the Library of Parliament in Ottawa, for details of the Canadian constitution; to Kuang Weilen of the Embassy of the People's Republic of China for clarifying points connected with the Queen's 1986 visit to that country; and to the staff of the Reference Department of Bromley Library.

In writing this book we have necessarily drawn to an extent on some of our earlier books, in particular *Monarch: The Life and Times of Elizabeth II*, *Consort: The Life & Times of Prince Philip* and *Monarchy and The Royal Family*. Other books, articles and documents consulted include:

The Queen, Anne Barrie (*Canadian Home Journal*, Sept. 1957)
Philip: An Informal Biography, Basil Boothroyd (Longman, 1971)
Her Majesty, Helen Cathcart (W. H. Allen, 1962)
The Queen Herself, Helen Cathcart (W. H. Allen, 1982)

Palace Diary, Stanley Clark (Harrap, 1958)

HRH Prince Philip, John Dean (Robert Hale, 1954)

Queen and Commonwealth, W. F. Deedes (*Daily Telegraph*, 24.9.84)

The Reality Of Monarchy, Andrew Duncan (Wm Heinemann Ltd, 1970)

King George V, John Gore (John Murray, 1941)

The World's Most Travelled Queen, Frank Harvey (*Weekend Magazine*, Canada, Vol. 7, no. 41, 1957)

The Essential Philip, Paula James (*Woman*, 12.6.1971)

Majesty, Robert Lacey (Hutchinson & Co Ltd, 1977)

Prince Philip, Peter Lane (Robert Hale, 1980)

Here Comes the Queen, Stephen Lynas (*Daily Mail*, 12.2.83)

Her Majesty the Queen, Hugh Montgomery-Massingberd (Wm. Collins & Sons/Willow Books Ltd, 1985)

The Queen, Ann Morrow (Wm. Morrow & Co Inc., 1983)

Does Britain Really Need a Queen? Malcolm Muggeridge (*Saturday Evening Post*, USA, 1957)

The Queen's World Tour, L. A. Nickolls (Macdonald & Co)

The Happy Wanderer, Charlotte and Denis Plimmer (*Daily Mail*, 20.10.60)

The Queen and Quebec, Mordecai Richler (*Sunday Times Magazine*, Oct. 1964)

The Australians and Their Queen, Denis Warner (*Daily Telegraph*, 29.3.77)

The Royal Family, R. M. White (David McKay & Co. Inc., 1969)

King George VI and Queen Elizabeth, Christopher Warwick (Sidgwick & Jackson, 1985)

King George VI, Sir John Wheeler-Bennett (Macmillan, 1958)

The Queen Gets Her Share Of White Elephants, Gilda Winton (*Star Weekly Magazine*, Canada, 28.9.57)

Elizabeth and Philip, Louis Wulff (Sampson Low, Marston & Co)

Prince Philip By His Friends, various (*Weekend*, 10/14.9.58)

Better Be Careful, Anon. (*Time*, USA, 23.12.57)

Queen Elizabeth's Fabulous Wardrobe (*Cosmopolitan*, USA, Sept. 1961)

Queen Travels In Style (*Star*, USA, 15.2.83)

Programme of the Queen's Commonwealth Tour, 1953/4

Programme of The Royal Visit to the United States, 1957

Programme of the Queen's Tour of Canada, 1959

Programme of the Royal Visit to Malta, 1967

The Royal Yacht Britannia (Central Office of Information, 1958 and 1975)

When Queen Elizabeth Flies By Comet 4 (BOAC, 1960)

Notes on the Commonwealth (Commonwealth Secretariat, 1985)

Highlights of the Constitutional Amendment Bill 1978 (Prime Minister's Office, Ottawa)

The Canadian Constitution 1981 (Canadian Unity Information Office)

INDEX

SUPPLEMENTARY INDEX

223

★ The places listed are those mentioned in the book only and are far from constituting a full list of Prince Philip's worldwide travels.